Merle Longwood
Jan. 1979

D1029085

LOVE AND SEX

A Modern Jewish Perspective

BOOKS BY ROBERT GORDIS

The Biblical Text in the Making

The Wisdom of Ecclesiastes

Koheleth: The Man and His World

The Song of Songs and Lamentations

The Book of God and Man
A Study of Job

Poets, Prophets and Sages
Essays in Biblical Interpretation

The Book of Esther

The Word and the Book
Studies in Biblical Language and Literature

The Book of Job
Commentary, New Translation and Special Studies

The Jew Faces a New World

Conservative Judaism

Judaism for the Modern Age

The Root and the Branch
Judaism and the Free Society

Judaism in a Christian World

Leave a Little to God

Sex and the Family in Jewish Tradition

A Faith for Moderns

EDITED BY ROBERT GORDIS

Max L. Margolis
Scholar and Teacher

Jewish Life in America
(with Theodore Friedman)

Faith and Reason
(with Ruth Waxman)

Art in Judaism
(with Moshe Davidowitz)

LOVE & SEX

A Modern Jewish Perspective

ROBERT GORDIS

Farrar Straus Giroux

New York

For Fannie—
in love

Copyright © 1978 by Robert Gordis
All rights reserved
Published simultaneously in Canada
by McGraw-Hill Ryerson Ltd., Toronto
Printed in the United States of America
Designed by Karen Watt
First edition, 1978

Library of Congress Cataloging in Publication Data
Gordis, Robert. Love & sex.
Bibliography: p.   Includes index.
1. Sex and Judaism. 2. Sexual ethics. 3. Marriage, Mixed. I. Title.
BM720.S4G67   1978   296.3′87′8341   77–20192

"Aria from the Psychiatrist," Copyright 1955 by
B & R Music Publishing Company, Inc. Used by
permission

Preface

Ours is an age of crisis teetering on the brink of catastrophe. This is the situation confronting us in virtually every aspect of life. It is true of the economic order, suffering simultaneously from mass unemployment and high inflation. It surfaces in racial hostility and group violence on every continent. The growing threat of an energy famine places our entire techno-logical civilization in jeopardy. Our cities are devastated by crime, overcrowding, filth, and noise, and the countryside is not far behind. Underlying all these manifestations of a world in chaos is the widespread corruption in government and poli-tics, commerce and industry, education and culture.

Yet all these ills could be borne by modern men and women, and ultimately be overcome through the exercise of their in-nate intelligence, courage, and energy, if they possessed a *locus standi,* a firm identity, and a strong sense of interper-sonal relationships that would serve them as an anchor in a turbulent sea. Human beings can face almost any external problem if all is well in their domestic affairs, if they are rea-sonably happy in their family ties and are secure in the behav-ior patterns that bind men and women, parents and children together in a warm bond of love and kinship.

The fact is, however, that it is precisely here that the

changes have been most far-reaching and, so far at least, most disturbing. Far from serving as a bulwark of stability in a world of kaleidoscopic change, the area of sex, love, and marriage has undergone a radical transformation in our times. No doubt the subject of love and sex is frequently treated with lurid sensationalism. Yet it is no exaggeration to speak of the sexual revolution in our day that is affecting ever-larger segments of Western society in general and of the American people in particular.

These trends have generally been evaluated from two opposed perspectives. Defenders of the official code that is derived from traditional religion and morality have deplored the breakdown of accepted behavioral patterns. Underscoring the chaos and disorientation in the lives of young people and older adults today, advocates of the *status quo ante* have lamented the widespread surrender of the ethical ideals of the Judeo-Christian tradition. Many of them regard the changes as the harbinger of the collapse of Western civilization as a whole. On the other side of the barricades, the advocates of the "new morality" have seen in it the herald of a happier age, in which future generations of liberated human beings will find a greater measure of freedom and self-fulfillment than ever before. Very often, both the opponents and the protagonists of the new order buttress their positions by citing the same phenomena—the extension of women's rights and liberties, the increase in divorce, birth control, and abortion, and the spread of extra- and premarital relations.

In this connection, one is reminded of the well-worn tale of the naïve rabbi to whom two congregants came to settle a dispute. After the plaintiff had presented his story, the rabbi nodded sagely and said, "You're absolutely right." "Wait, rabbi," said the defendant, "hear my side!" When he had completed his tale, the rabbi said to him, "You're positively right." The rabbi's wife, who had been eavesdropping on the proceedings, said, "How can they both be right?" To this he responded, "You, too, my dear, are right."

If we approach present-day sexual attitudes and practices objectively, it becomes clear, I believe, that both positions are right and wrong, that is to say, each is partial and inadequate. The advocates of both the old standards and the new values generally fail to explore the sources and the motivations of the present-day morality, and hence do not offer a balanced evaluation of its characteristics and goals. Little wonder, therefore, that neither school is able to offer adequate guidelines for our generation.

A viable system of behavioral standards in sex, love, and marriage for modern men and women still remains a *desideratum*. A rational sex ethic will need to reckon realistically with the individual drives of human nature on the one hand and with the collective needs of society on the other. It will need to consider the objective socio-economic conditions of our time, while relating them to the religio-cultural background of the past. In view of the constants of human nature, it will undoubtedly derive many elements from traditional morality, but it will also take newly articulated goals and desires into account. It will draw upon all the experience of earlier generations, but will not turn its back on the intellectual and moral insights available to contemporary society.

Among the resources frequently invoked in this connection is the body of ideas, ideals, and practices that are subsumed under the general term the "Judeo-Christian tradition." It is true that the validity of the concept has been much debated in recent years. Nevertheless, it is clear that in the area of love, sex, and marriage, at least, the two components of the Judeo-Christian tradition diverge most widely. It has not been generally noted that the classical Christian doctrine on sex and love, as embodied pre-eminently in the New Testament, patristic literature, and the great Protestant theologians, stands in sharp contrast to the sex ethic of traditional Judaism, as expressed primarily in the classic sources of the Bible and the Talmud.

It is true that, in the Middle Ages, Jewish attitudes moved

closer to Christian doctrine. Jews who came into almost daily contact with their Christian neighbors were inevitably influenced by their standards and values. The difficult conditions that ravaged medieval life in general, hunger, disease, and war, strengthened the ascetic tendencies that were present in Christianity from its inception. The same perils obviously threatened the survival of medieval Jewry as well, but they were aggravated by special problems, such as the perpetual threat of spoliation, expulsion, and massacre that loomed over every community and individual. As a result, many of the life-affirming attitudes of the biblical and talmudic periods lost ground during the Middle Ages. It should be kept in mind that the medieval period lasted for the bulk of world Jewry, who were concentrated in Eastern Europe, well into the twentieth century. Nevertheless, the insights of the authentic Jewish tradition in its most creative eras have remained available for our use and application today.

We are faced by a new paradox. On the one hand, some Jewish religious spokesmen insist upon incorporating into their interpretation of Judaism approaches which derive directly or indirectly from Christianity, even when their views contradict the clear teaching of the Bible and the Talmud. At the same time, many Christian theologians and ethicists, both in the Catholic and the Protestant communions, are engaged in reinterpreting their religious tradition so as to make it more responsive to contemporary needs and desires. In the process, they are led to emphasize the Hebraic component in Christianity and thus draw ever closer to the insights and attitudes of classical Judaism.

I, therefore, believe that modern people of every religious background and of none will find value and interest in exploring the content and thrust of the historic Jewish experience and teaching in the areas of sex and love. They may discover that Judaism is in position to make a significant contribution toward meeting the confusions and agonies of modern men and women as reflected in the stark realities of the contemporary scene.

While I venture to hope that this book is based on solid scholarship and reflects a firsthand knowledge of the sources, it is not an academic treatise offering a historical survey of the sexual ethics of the Jewish tradition or of the past behavior patterns of Jews. The work has a twofold purpose. The first is to present a fair-minded and objective survey of the new morality, its goals, its achievements, and its weaknesses. The second is to bring to bear on the subject the most vital and significant elements of the Jewish tradition, the wisdom and insight of which transcend any ethnic or sectarian boundaries. The claim is not being made that the answers to all the problems in this area are to be found in the Jewish tradition, only that there is a substantial measure of light and direction within it for all people.

For many years, the theme of this book has been one of my prime areas of interest. Research in the classic literature on the subject has gone hand in hand with observation of the lives of men and women on the contemporary scene and a sympathetic concern for their well-being. The conjunction of both these aspects has produced the present work. I hope that readers will agree that each aspect sheds light upon the other.

I am deeply grateful for the enthusiastic interest of the leadership of the Women's League for Conservative Judaism in the book and their friendship for the author. Women's League has co-sponsored the publication of the volume and provided me with a research assistant, my student, Mrs. Miriam Klein Shapiro, who proved exceedingly helpful to me. She has proofread the manuscript and has prepared the index, which, it is hoped, will enhance considerably the usefulness of this work. My sincere thanks are also extended to my devoted friend and secretary, Mrs. Trudy Kramberg, who labored at the decipherment of my handwritten text and retyped the manuscript time and again with exemplary devotion and efficiency.

Like all my earlier books, this volume could not have come to fruition without the love and understanding that my dear wife, Fannie, has lavished upon me. The years of our marriage,

Contents

Love is stronger than death,

   passion is unyielding as the grave;

its flames are flames of fire,

   a flame of God.

Song of Songs 8:6

Morals—
Past and Present

1

THE CONTEMPORARY CRISIS

An Age of Transition

According to an ancient tradition, when Adam and Eve were living in the Garden of Eden, he turned to her and said, "You know, my dear, we are living in an age of crisis." That feeling has persisted among all their descendants, every age feeling that the old verities are slipping and the foundations of the world crumbling. Only in retrospect has the past seemed safe, stable, and secure. Almost always, the older generation has believed that the changes were for the worse. The Romans had a phrase for this human tendency. Men were *laudatores temporis acti,* "praisers of the times gone by." The biblical Sage, Koheleth, warned his readers against this weakness: "Do not say, 'What has happened, for the early days were better than these?' for not wisely have you asked the question." (Eccles. 7:10)

Yet it is undeniable that ours is an age of multiple revolution, triple in character—scientific, socio-economic, and moral. As a result of scientific and technological progress, our generation has reached a level of plenty and of peril previously undreamed of in man's wildest fantasies or most horrible nightmares. In turn, the greater material abundance of the mid-twentieth century has produced a revolution of rising expectations. Submerged groups and individuals are now unwilling to remain on a marginal or submarginal level of subsistence. On the other hand, the horrible achievements in nuclear destruction and secret improvements in the field of germ and bacteriological warfare have bred a sense of desperation in the hearts of men and women. This is especially true of youth, who face a future not merely uncertain but potentially catastrophic. The plenty and the peril have united to produce a widespread demand for instant gratification.

The accepted ethical values of the past are being subjected to fundamental challenges, both positive and negative. The new scientific discoveries and technological instruments at the disposal of modern man, coupled with the worldwide revolt against racism and economic oppression, have led to the rejection of many of the traditional standards. Formerly, even when these were breached in performance, they continued to be honored in profession. Now there is no longer a willingness to wait for the slow process of change by legal and peaceful means, or for the use of persuasion and consensus. Brute force, cunning, and deception are highly esteemed as the only effective harbingers of a new day. The rapidly rising crime rate has spread from the cities, first to the suburbs, and then to the towns and villages. Nor is it by any means limited to the highly industrialized nations or to capitalist countries. The "white man's burden" in Africa and Asia has been eliminated, and in most cases white colonialism has been replaced by black dictatorship carrying banners marked "people's democracy," "socialism," and "liberation."

Such traditional virtues as speaking the truth, a sense of honor and fair play, the practice of compassion toward the weak, are increasingly being consigned to the dustbin as bourgeois prejudices. Corruption has become widespread in government and politics, in commerce and industry, in education and the media, in science and the arts. A healthy society is held together by an invisible sense of unity, in spite of the existence of divergent individual and group interests. This concern of the commonweal has been drastically eroded in our time. If we are looking for a symbol of the decay of standards of conduct in our age, we can find it by listening to what is called sports news. Today, any relationship between sports and sportsmanship is purely coincidental. Sports has become an amalgam of greed, big business, and mayhem. Fair play, decent manners, and regard for the truth are as extinct as the dodo.

The surging tide of rising expectations, sharpened by the demand for instant gratification, and fed by the cynicism aroused by the constant revelations of widespread wrongdoing both on the domestic and the international scene, has served to undermine moral standards where they matter most of all—in the personal relations and actions of the individual. There is no gainsaying the fact that the scientific and socio-economic revolutions have brought major advantages to practically every man, woman, and child in our day. But at least equally important for human welfare is the transformation wrought by the current revolution in personal morals and standards of conduct.

In the words of one observer,

> Put no trust in a friend,
>   place no confidence in a companion.
> Guard your lips from your wife,
>   who lies in your bosom;
> A son treats the father with contempt,
> A daughter rebels against her mother,
> A daughter-in-law against her mother-in-law;
> A man's worst enemies are the kinsmen
>   in his own house.

In the words of another: "Your daughters act like prostitutes and your daughters-in-law commit adultery. But I shall not punish your daughters when they play the harlot or your daughters-in-law when they commit adultery, for the men consort with prostitutes and feast with harlots."

To be sure, these observations are not drawn from newspapers of today, but from the Prophets Micah and Hosea, who lived twenty-seven centuries ago.[1] Now, the actions of men and women have always fallen far short of their professed standards. But today something new has been added—the standards themselves are being questioned and denied. The gap has been closing, not because people's actions have been raised to the level of their ideals, but because their ideals are being lowered to conform to their actions.

The problems are manifold and complex. Yet, if progress can be registered even in one area, it is important not only for itself but because it can strengthen confidence in our ability to solve others. This is especially true of attitudes and conduct involving love, sex, and marriage. For even if other problems are still acute, individual men and women can find a substantial measure of happiness and well-being if their private lives are satisfactory. On the other hand, even if we succeed in achieving national prosperity and international peace, serenity and joy may still be lacking in the lives of those who have failed in the art of building personal relationships. Moreover, as every conventional moralist teaches, success in the marketplace is no guarantee of happiness.

Even in an age that tries men's souls—or wrings them dry —there is no need to surrender to cynicism or despair. As André Gide reminded a youthful audience, "Never lose heart. Remember that life goes upward—in spirals." There is one fundamental mark of moral progress in our time over the past —for the first time in history the human race refuses to accept poverty, war, and disease as acts of God or as inevitable concomitants of the human condition. To be sure, in the manifold conflicts of our age, the Communist world blames the democracies and vice versa, and domestically each political party attacks its rival as responsible for the ills of the age—but they are no longer regarded as incurable.

The very word "crisis" offers a measure of hope. The term, derived from the Greek, means "judgment, a choice between alternatives." In Chinese, we are told, the idea of crisis is expressed by an ideogram meaning both "danger" and "opportunity." We may, therefore, define an age of crisis as a time for judging among various options and from the danger plucking a new opportunity. It cannot be denied that the far-flung revolution in personal morality, still growing in intensity, has brought disarray and disaster to many human lives. But it also offers the opportunity to correct the ills of the old order and to extend opportunities for human happiness in a vastly enlarged universe.

To advance this basic enterprise is the goal of this book. To achieve this purpose we need first to recall the traditional or official code of morality in the Western world as preached by religion and enforced by law. We shall then describe the principal features of the sexual revolution, as well as its consequences for both good and ill.

The approaches of the two great religious traditions of the West, Christianity and Judaism, to sex and morals prove on examination to be quite different and, in some respects, diametrically opposed to each other. This unexpected conclusion has a significant bearing on the sexual revolution in the present and a viable code of personal conduct in the future.

The frontier areas both on the contemporary scene and in Judaism are considered on the basis of a detailed analysis of the sexual patterns and standards of the past and the present. We propose the principles for a viable code for human relations in the future.

The Old Order

From earliest times, the basic social unit has been the patriarchal family, with the father as its dominant figure. A few anthropologists believe that a different social order once existed, a matriarchate, in which the mother was queen and ruler, of which some vestiges may be found.[2] Whatever the truth of this theory, the recorded past of the human race shows the family as patriarchal, whether in Mesopotamian inscriptions, in

Egyptian texts, or in Greek epics. Basically, Western civilization has known only the patriarchal family, finding its warrant
in the Bible, which has been variously interpreted, to be sure,
in Judaism and Christianity during the past twenty centuries.

Fundamentally, the father enjoyed total legal and economic
power over his wife and children. He had a right to the product of their labor and had a claim upon their support and
respect in old age. He could marry off his children as he chose,
or sell them into slavery. According to Ugaritic texts, when he
was drunk and unable to take care of himself, his son was
expected to escort and guide him.

Of course, powers are inseparable from obligations. A husband was required to provide his wife with food, clothes, and
her conjugal rights (Ex. 21:10). The biblical passage which treats
sexual relations as a woman's right is perhaps the earliest instance of the recognition of female sexuality. In rabbinic law,
the husband was also expected to ransom her from captivity.[3]
The Torah commanded the father to express his love for God
by teaching the Divine word diligently to his children (Deut.
6:7). The rabbis broadened the list of paternal obligations to
include circumcising the son, redeeming him from captivity,
teaching him the Torah, marrying him off, teaching him a
trade, and teaching him to swim.[4]

In theory, the husband and father was monarch of all he
surveyed in the family domain. In practice, this absolute
power was tempered by several factors. At every stage in the
life of a people or a tradition, the law always lags behind life,
since by the time a practice becomes officially enshrined in the
legal system, society generally has moved beyond it, even in
the most static of eras. Thus, at any particular point in time,
a realistic picture of the true situation will reflect the tension
between the law and life, between the official written code
and the norms of customary practice. Nowhere is this truer
than in the area of the family. Here, above all, relationships are
not determined by purely legal considerations but are affected
by deep personal ties of love and concern existing between
husband and wife, and between parents and children.

For this reason, a true view of the family in biblical times cannot be derived exclusively from the legal provisions in the various biblical codes alone. The picture of the husband and father exercising unlimited power needs to be rounded out by a consideration of the Bible's treatment of the non-legal aspects of human relations. There is the narrative in Genesis (29:20) of Jacob's working for Rachel for fourteen years after being cheated by his father-in-law and finding the period "as a few days because of his love for her." In a rough and lawless age, a Levite found that his concubine had left him and returned to her father's house. Four months later, he went after her halfway across the land, "to speak to her heart and bring her back." (Jud. 19:3) Most poignant of all is a central incident in the life of the Prophet Hosea. When he learns that his wife has been unfaithful to him, he drives her out of his home. But his love is stronger than his anger, so that he, too, goes after her, "speaks to her heart," and restores her to his home, betrothing her anew in an eternal covenant of righteousness and justice, love and trust (2:16–22). At times, the personal dimension emerges in a casual phrase, as in the description of Ezekiel's wife as "the delight of your eyes." (24:16) Above all, the Bible has preserved the great anthology of love and marriage, which is the Song of Songs. Here in the irrefutable accents of beauty, the one-to-one relationship of man and woman finds passionate expression.

In spite of the language and even some provisions in the law codes, women were not chattels but vital, active personalities, able to exert tremendous influence over their husbands. The Talmud recognizes that "a woman carries her weapons of defense in her own person."[5]

One has only to read the Book of Genesis to discover that all three patriarchs were largely governed by their wives. Sarah, who was childless, offered Abraham her slave girl Hagar, who bore him a son, Ishmael. Later, when she gave birth to Isaac, she found her servant's behavior insolent and insupportable. Sarah demanded that Hagar and her son be driven from Abraham's home. Abraham demurred, but Sarah prevailed (21:9–13). When the second of the patriarchs, Isaac, grew old, he wished to bestow his paternal blessing upon his first-born, Esau. His wife, Rebecca, felt otherwise, and it was her will that determined the outcome. She virtually forced an unwilling Jacob to disguise himself as his elder brother and to take the blessing that his blind old father had intended for Esau (27). Of the three patriarchs, Jacob was the shrewdest and most practical-minded, but he, too, proved no match for his wives, who, unbeknown to him, determined his schedule of conjugal activity (30:14–24).

But there is another side to the coin that must not be lost sight of. At times, wives prevailed over their husbands in family decisions, but not as of right, as equal partners. Sarah's passionate anger and jealousy of her son's position, Rebecca's stratagem, and the private arrangement between Rachel and Leah succeeded in subverting the desires of their respective husbands. To be sure, in these confrontations the Torah supports the wives in their objectives. Yet these were exceptional instances. As a general rule, a husband's will was law.

Vis-à-vis the children, particularly young ones, the authority of parents is more nearly equal. In the Decalogue, the Fifth Commandment reads, "You shall honor your father and your mother." The Holiness Code, which is of central importance in biblical law and ethics, begins with the injunction, "You shall each reverence your mother and your father." Taking note of the reversed order in which the parents are mentioned in the two passages, the rabbis deduce that there is an equal obligation of honor and reverence for both father and mother. They go further. Because, they declare, a child is normally closer to its mother, the Torah places the father first in the commandment to honor one's parents. Because a child is more likely to be overawed by its father, the mother is mentioned first with regard to the duty of reverence.[6]

These guidelines for the relationship between husband and wife, parents and children, remained fundamental for millennia. Enunciated in biblical times, they were elaborated upon in the Mishnah during the Greco-Roman era, when an agricultural-urban society of relative simplicity prevailed. The norms underwent little change during the Middle Ages. In fact, these standards of behavior persisted during the earlier phases of the Industrial Revolution. When the home served as a factory, and even when it did not, the family was an economic unit. Here the role of the father and his effectiveness as breadwinner were clearly evident to the entire family, a situation which strengthened his authority and cemented family unity.

The revolutionary transformations of society in our era of high scientific and technological development have undermined many aspects of this code in practice. However, in theory and in law the façade of the patriarchal family remains intact. It is not insignificant that a woman entering into marriage generally adopts her husband's family name, which, in turn, is handed on to their children. Married women with pretensions to "society" are willing, indeed insistent, that their given names not be used and that they be referred to as Mrs. John Doe rather than as Jane or Mary Doe.

Most aspects of the patriarchal character of the family go back to early antiquity. Not so the principle of monogamy in marriage. In biblical and talmudic times, polygamous marriage was permissible. Sarah gave her husband, Abraham, her slave girl Hagar as a concubine, or sub-wife. The patriarch Jacob had two wives, Leah and Rachel, and two concubines, Bilhah and Zilpah. Centuries later, after the settlement of the Israelites in the Promised Land, Elkanah, who was to be the father of the Prophet Samuel, had two wives, Peninah and Hannah. King David had a plurality of wives, even before he ascended the throne. Solomon had a thousand wives, a fact that may cast some doubt on his reputation for wisdom.

Nevertheless, polygamy was exceptional and rare. The first human pair, Adam and Eve, offer the prototype of a monogamous relationship, underscored by the biblical observation, "Therefore a man deserts his father and mother and cleaves to his wife." (Gen. 2:24) Abraham purchases the Doubled Cave as a burial place for Sarah and himself.[23] Tradition adds that the same site was used by Adam and Eve, Isaac and Rebecca, Jacob and Leah. There are references to the wives of the Prophets Hosea, Isaiah, and Ezekiel, all of which give the clear impression of monogamy.[7] The monogamous family is described in a short but beautiful idyll in the Book of Psalms:

Blessed is every one who fears the Lord, who walks
                                        in his ways!
You shall eat the fruit of the labor of your hands;
You shall be happy, and it shall be well with you.

Your wife will be like a fruitful vine within your house;
Your children will be like olive shoots around your table.
Lo, thus shall the man be blessed who fears the Lord.

The Lord bless you from Zion!
May you see the prosperity of Jerusalem all the days
                                        of your life!
May you see your children's children! Peace be upon Israel!
                                        (Ps. 128)

While the evidence for monogamy is partial, it is clear that polygamy could not be widespread, for biological and economic reasons, let alone psychological considerations. The ratio of males and females in the population is basically equal. In a society where nearly everyone marries, there is, therefore, no available surplus of women for polygamy. Militaristic societies meet the "problem" by engaging in raids and campaigns against their neighbors. The ancient Hebrews generally did not have the capacity for successfully carrying on such adventures. Moreover, polygamy is economically expensive. Maintaining more than one household requires substantial means, not available to most men. Finally, polygamy is psychologically trying both for the women involved and, it may be added, for their husbands as well. The Hebrew word for a co-wife is *tsarah*, literally, "enemy, rival." The opening verses of the Book of Samuel permit us to eavesdrop on the strains and tensions between two wives in a single household.

Moreover, as women asserted their personalities in ever-increasing measure, they would be less and less likely to accept a polygamous status. Some two thousand sages are mentioned in the pages of the Talmud and not one instance of polygamy is recorded. In the rabbinic period, special provisions in the marriage contract would frequently be inserted to prevent the husband from marrying a second wife.

In strictly legal terms, it was not until the tenth century that Rabbi Gershom of Mayence, "the Light of the Exile," convened a synod of the leading rabbis of France, Germany, and Italy, who, under penalty of excommunication *(ḥerem)*, forbade polygamy in the Jewish community. From the foregoing considerations, it is clear that the edict of Rabbi Gershom simply put the official stamp of legality on a situation that had been virtually universal for centuries. The interdict did not apply to Islamic countries, where polygamy was practiced by the general population. However, with the extinction of the Jewish communities in Arab lands in the twentieth century, the prohibition of polygamy in Judaism has become both practically and legally universal.

The traditional family possessed one more significant and far-reaching characteristic—for the vast majority of men and women, marriage was a lifelong, indissoluble bond. This held true for all Christians, whether Catholic, Protestant, or Greek Orthodox. With regard to Jews, the stability of the family, its closely knit character, and its permanence were universally recognized and widely admired. Whether or not the wedding ceremony contained the phrase "unto death do us part," marriage was, for the vast majority of Christians and Jews, an eternal covenant.

Whatever changes the marriage institution may undergo in the future, it is clear that in an age like our own, marked by an active and even aggressive campaign for women's rights, the reintroduction of polygamy is ruled out. The real challenge to the monogamous marriage comes from other directions—the rapidly escalating growth in the rate of divorce and extramarital liaisons, not only in the United States but throughout the world.

Some time ago, an Arab prince coming to the United States with several of his wives was questioned about polygamy. He replied that the Western world also practiced polygamy— through divorce, which meant "successive" as against "simultaneous" polygamy. The riposte was true, but only to a point. Tragic as the high incidence of divorce is, it differs from polygamy in one highly significant respect—it treats the sexes equally; the woman has the same right as the man to more than one mate. Moreover, the frequency with which divorce is followed by remarriage constitutes a tribute, however oblique, to the institution of monogamy as the basic structure of marriage in the Western world.

The legal institution of marriage rests, of course, upon ethical foundations, which may be described as chastity before marriage and fidelity within the marriage bond. The tremendous power of the sexual impulse has obviously beaten against this wall of prohibition throughout time with more than a little success. Always young people face the temptation of sexual intimacy, whether or not they contemplate marriage later on. This temptation is not easily resisted, and as we shall see later, Jewish religious law and practice had to reckon with it in the past. Extramarital relations have also been a widespread phenomenon everywhere. The same sexual drive created what has been called woman's oldest profession, from which no society has ever been free and against which law and religion have waged an unremitting battle through the centuries, though largely in vain.

The traditional code of chastity before marriage and fidelity within the marriage bond has been battered and beaten, but it is not yet broken. In the last quarter of the twentieth century, it still remains true that the traditional moral code commands the allegiance of most of our contemporaries. In practice, as well as in theory, the marriage ceremony, generally religious but sometimes civil, is still the socially preferred mode of establishing an intimate man-woman relationship. Most men and women marry, beget children, adjust to one another with greater or lesser success, and, the entertainment media to the contrary notwithstanding, achieve a fair degree of happiness in life.

Yet, while these standards still hold for most men and women, these people no longer constitute the overwhelming majority. For an increasing minority, traditional moral standards no longer are binding. What is even more significant, the percentage of adherents to traditional standards declines as we proceed from older to younger age groups. This erosion of the accepted code constitutes the principal element in the current sexual revolution. To understand its origins, evaluate its nature, and hopefully help direct its course is the basic purpose of this volume.

The New Life Styles

Before we turn to the far-reaching changes that are taking place in contemporary life, a caveat is in order. It should not be inferred that the old order was totally ideal or that the new developments are all reprehensible. Any fair-minded student of human society will recognize that, not infrequently, the traditional moral code sanctioned and perpetuated personal relations disfigured by oppression, hypocrisy, and suffering, even when it did not create them. The evidence is written large in literature and in the arts, as well as in history. In a male-dominated society, untold numbers of women lived lives of quiet desperation. A woman's basic and indeed only legitimate role was bringing children into the world in rapid succession, many of whom died young and all of whom made their mothers prematurely old. Household labors constituted an unending drudgery all their waking hours, while limited education and sexual prejudice excluded them from any participation in wider cultural activities or social interests. Probably the more docile women adjusted best to their inferior position, but the more intelligent and potentially creative ones suffered keenly from a sense of injustice, often spending their lives seething in helpless rebellion against their inferior lot. Rare indeed have been the women who were able to make their mark in society on a basis of equality or near-equality.

Among the few women in talmudic times who enjoyed an excellent education was Beruriah, the daughter of one great scholar, Rabbi Hananiah ben Teradyon, and wife of another, Rabbi Meir. Rabbinic literature, like every other culture, contains both favorable and unfavorable views of women's character and capacity. One famous derogatory statement declares, "Women are light-minded."[8] The great medieval commentator Rashi declares that Beruriah, as might have been expected, scoffed at the saying. Her husband, Rabbi Meir, decided to test her virtue by having one of his students seduce her. In her remorse, she committed suicide and Rabbi Meir fled to Babylonia. The story is totally out of keeping with the character both of Rabbi Meir and Beruriah and the entire spirit of Jewish tradition. The legend may have arisen in order to demonstrate that independent-minded women who rebel against the established order come to no good end.

Beruriah may well be the first feminist in history. In any event, she deserves to be the patron saint of the Jewish women's-liberation movement. One day, the Talmud relates, Rabbi Jose, the Galilean, asked her, "Which road leads to Lydda?" Beruriah retorted, "Foolish Galilean, haven't the Sages taught, 'Do not engage overmuch in conversation with a woman'?[9] What you should have asked is 'Which—to Lydda?' "[10] The bitter irony of this interchange has been generally overlooked. She is sarcastically upbraiding the disciple for using more words than absolutely necessary! It is clear that long before Nora in Ibsen's drama *A Doll's House,* there were individual women who resented their second-class position in society.

It was not until the modern period that this resentment was

transformed into an active mass rejection of the role, expressing itself in the demand for personal freedom and the right of women to make decisions for themselves and for their children on a par with their husbands. The air of liberty often proves an intoxicating drug for those long confined to close quarters. The essence of freedom is the power to choose—and the options may be right or wrong or, as is more often the case, merely better or worse. It should therefore come as no surprise that the consequences of the sexual revolution are variously shaded, with white and black only at the extreme ends of the predominant gray.

Basic to all aspects of the new morality is a *strong emphasis upon individual freedom and the fulfillment of personal desires.* As a result, the accepted moral code has been drastically modified or renounced by increasing numbers of people. It is important to recognize that these transformations are propelled by powerful social and cultural forces, many of which are inevitable and irreversible.

Perhaps the most obvious change in the pervasive climate has taken place in the area of communication. It is sometimes forgotten that speech is a basic aspect of life. Speech is not merely talk; it is action. There is far more plain speaking today on sexual behavior in general and on aberrant patterns of conduct in particular than ever before.

A Jewish teacher once said, "Not everything that one thinks should be said; not everything that one says should be written; not everything that is written should be printed." However, it may be added that what is thought, said, printed, and repeated offers a significant clue to what is being practiced. Such reticence is hardly characteristic of our day. Some time ago, the staid *New York Times* published a news item in its columns emanating from San Francisco. An advertisement appeared in a local newspaper, offering a Cadillac car of the current year for sale at $100. A reader responding to the advertisement inquired whether there was an error in the announced price or if the car was of an older vintage or whether it had been involved in a major accident. The woman who responded assured the caller that the car was new and in perfect condition, and explained, "My husband died recently and in his will asked that his new Cadillac be sold and the entire proceeds be given to his mistress."

Unrestrained discussion of sexual themes is characteristic not only of elite culture, embodied in books and the theater, but of the mass media—the press, movies, television, and radio —as well. Publication of pornography, soft- and hard-core, in books and magazines, has become an important industry. The so-called four-letter words are encountered freely today, not only in films and in print, but even in that bastion of morality, the family television screen. The spate of sex scandals involving members of Congress and other government officials has made words like "sexual favors," "prostitute," "mistress" household terms throughout the country.

I would not dream of arguing in favor of prurient curiosity or of spying on the private lives of men and women. Nonetheless, there is one aspect of the revelations of the 1976 sex scandals on which no one seems to have commented. Virtually all the officials who discussed the case of Wayne L. Hays, who had put his mistress on the government payroll, began with a statement that was universally accepted as axiomatic: "What a public official does in his private life is his own personal affair. But when he uses government funds to further his own desires, only then does it become an issue of public concern." To be sure, the line is not easy to draw, but no one seems even to have considered one question—if a man is free to disregard his marriage vow, not in one isolated and temporary episode, but over a long period of time, what are the implications for his honoring the solemn oath he takes in assuming public office?

Perhaps the most significant change has been the most unspectacular and unsensational. The traditional family as the basic unit of society has been so radically transformed that it has all but disappeared.

In this connection, the history of the term "family" is instructive. As recently as the first decades of the twentieth century, "family" referred to three generations or more, consisting of grandparents, parents, and children, often flanked by aunts, uncles, and cousins who lived in proximity and had frequent contact with one another. The grandparents have long since been separated from the family and "live alone," either independently or in old-age homes. Aunts, uncles, and cousins have become virtual strangers to one another. A new term has been coined, the "nuclear family," applied to a father, a mother, and their young children.

This is not yet the end of the process. With the rising tide of divorce and separation, there are millions of "one-parent" families. Either the father or the mother has the burden of earning a living and, at the same time, coping with the dual role of parent as homebuilder and model. Generally, it is the mother who is left with the task of raising the children. The proportion of female heads of families is rising rapidly. In 1960, the percentage of female heads of families was 8.7 for whites and 22.4 for blacks. In 1965, the percentages were 9 and 23.7 respectively; in 1974, 9.9 and 31.8.[11] These "parents without partners" may derive a wry consolation from noticing that even the two-parent families are proving increasingly ineffective in inculcating values and norms of behavior in their young.

Today, the rebellion of children begins in their teens, if not earlier, with regard to the hours they keep, their habits of study, their companions, and their personal behavior. Rarely are the parents willing or able to stem the tide of ever-greater permissiveness characteristic of the modern temper.

A major factor in the breakdown of paternal authority is the fact that the family is no longer the scene of economic activity. The father's occupation is completely sundered from his wife and children, whose only interest in it lies in the money he derives from it and makes available to them. Hence the American father at home has long been a semicomic figure, as in the older, well-known comic strip "Bringing Up Father." At best, he is tolerated rather than venerated. He has far less impact upon the molding of the character and behavior patterns of the children than has their mother.

Foreign observers have described "momism" as an American phenomenon, reaching its commercial climax on Mother's Day. "Momism" is a compensatory mechanism for the collapse of paternal authority in the modern home. But with more and more mothers fully employed or involved in voluntary activities outside the home, even this source of parental influence is becoming eroded.

A new trend has made considerable headway of late, particularly in the suburbs—but not only there. Young men and women, in college and out, are tending to leave the family home even before marriage and take an apartment for themselves. It is obvious that this step must lead to a drastic reduction of contacts with parents and, consequently, to a radical loss in parental guidance and authority.

After marriage it is taken for granted that the couple will be virtually free from parental "interference." I recall a couple who came in for a premarital conference. The young bride-to-be said, in the most matter-of-fact tone, "Of course, we want to live as far away as possible from Stan's parents and mine." This attitude she regarded as self-evident and perfectly natural. After the children attain maturity, parents or grandparents are likely to play little or no role in the lives of their children.

A very high proportion of adult Americans today are children of immigrants from Central, Southern, and Eastern Europe. As these new settlers crowded into the ghettos of the cities, bringing their foreign habits and ideals with them, it was taken for granted that their children, born in America under radically different conditions, would break with the life pattern of their parents. It was, however, anticipated that the next generation of children, born like their parents on American soil, would share a basic community of outlook with their fathers and mothers. This reasonable expectation has proved to be totally mistaken. Paradoxical as it seems, it has become clear that the immigrant generation and their American children, for all the differences between them, had far more in common than do the first and second generations of American-born. Nowhere is this fact more evident than in the changing attitudes and practices with regard to personal morality before, during, and after marriage.

Every age group reflects the powerful impact of the sexual revolution on human behavior. The new life styles generally originate with the young, in whom the sexual drive is strongest. The rapid increase in illegitimate births and abortions among the unmarried offers objective proof for the widespread impression that intercourse without marriage is tending to become the norm.

The new behavior patterns, as well as the unabashed frankness of speech now in vogue, are illustrated in a situation-comedy series televised nationally in prime time. The series bears the significant title *One Day at a Time.* Two young sisters, ages about sixteen and eighteen, are living with their mother, who is a divorcee. In one particular episode, the mother is away in Las Vegas and the sisters are engaged in conversation. The younger one is heartbroken because she cannot get to a dance to meet a young man with whom she is smitten. This reminds the older sister of an experience she had undergone when she was younger: "I had gone to the dance and found that I was the only virgin in Indianapolis." The younger one responds, "Well, I wouldn't do it, not until I was married—or was living with someone." In the face of this exhibition of traditional virtue, the older sister offers sage counsel: "Sure, do only what you think is right."

The objective truth of the plot and the characters is unimportant. What is significant is the light that the television program sheds on the image that the American people has of itself and of the standards it is willing to accept.

The sexual revolution has also modified the behavior patterns of the most conservative group in the population—the *older people.* Particularly during the last decade, more and more senior citizens (though still a minority) are disregarding the traditional standards of sexual conduct by which they were reared and which they themselves inculcated in their children. In growing numbers, older men and women set up life together without benefit of clergy. The practice has been so far accepted as to appear even on TV programs, where it is frequently treated as a comic situation in which the behavior of the oldsters scandalizes their middle-aged children.

The explanation, adequate or not, offered in defense of the practice is that social-security payments would be reduced if the couple were to marry legally. There are other alleged advantages. Such an arrangement avoids problems of wills, inheritance, and conflicts with children. Another factor is that the relationship operates so long as both are well. When the attraction fades or one partner takes ill, the other is free to walk out on the arrangement. There is, in other words, a minimum of involvement and the absence of responsibility— the two bugaboos of our age!

In my own counseling experience, I encountered a highly respected professional man of strongly traditional background, a widower. He met a charming and intelligent widow whose husband, a former judge, had been killed by the Nazis. She was receiving substantial reparation payments from abroad because of the government position that he had once occupied in Germany. These payments would be lost if she were to remarry. If the new marriage proved unsuccessful, she would be left without means. Being traditionally oriented, they were trying to find a way of having a religious ceremony without a civil registration—an arrangement next to impossible. How they solved their problem, I cannot say. There was at least a chance that with the tacit acquiesence of their children, who were religiously observant, they would nevertheless set up house together as man and wife.

The *middle-aged,* from the thirties to the fifties, have also been affected by the sexual revolution. The most obvious and widespread effect has been the dramatic rise in divorces among couples married in the neighborhood of twenty years, whose children are grown and have generally left home. Psychologists have no trouble explaining the phenomenon. In many instances, the divorce is a reassertion in middle age of youthful goals and dreams which have not been fulfilled in real life. Breaking the bonds of marriage is a last-ditch effort to "begin again," with presumably a more congenial and exciting partner, one more likely to gratify the fantasies still persisting from the past.

In other cases, couples who married when they were young find that they have grown away from one another. One partner may have matured more than the other, developed new interests, or achieved a higher level of success. It cannot be denied that biological urges and socio-economic promptings such as these play a decisive role in the upsurge of middle-aged divorce in our times.

However, these explanations are not altogether satisfactory. The factors we have mentioned are not new; they inhere in the human condition and have always been present. What is significant is that desires which tended to remain dormant in the past are no longer suppressed or sublimated. Obviously, the determining factor that is new is the emergence of the imperious desire for self-gratification, or, more euphemistically, for self-fulfillment, which proves more potent than the marriage bond.

Divorces and remarriages in middle age, though they are on the rise, are theoretically, at least, in conformity with traditional norms of behavior. But there has also been a vast expansion in this age group of extra-legal relationships in which existing marriages are not severed. These liaisons, marked by greater or lesser permanence, are usually carried on in borrowed apartments or in motels. They were, and generally still are, clandestine. But something new has been added during recent decades. Today, several patterns of quasi-public relations outside the marriage bond are widely known, often described, and not rarely practiced. Even in the area of private relations, ours is the age of public relations, and so the use of euphemisms is universal. These practices, and others to be noted later, are called "alternate life styles." These include such practices as wife-swapping parties, *ménages à trois et à quatre*, and so-called group marriage, practiced by two or more couples living together in a single household.

A distinguished scientist who has pioneered sex research among prostitutes told a select audience of scholars that at times he underwent acute embarrassment. His interviews in the brothels might be interrupted by visits, not only by male friends and acquaintances, but also by their wives; their motives were not quite scientific.

There have, of course, been periods in history when eras of sexual license were succeeded by ages of great restraint. The eighteenth-century Augustan age in England was succeeded by the Victorian nineteenth century. It is, therefore, not impossible that the present sexual revolution may be swept away in the wake of an oncoming counterrevolution. It is, however, highly doubtful that it can—or indeed should—be totally obliterated.

At all events, the tide is still running strongly in the opposite direction. Indeed, it is fanning out from the United States to Europe, from the democratic West to the Communist East, even from the industrialized nations to the developing countries in Asia and Africa.

Moreover, the difference in twentieth-century mores from the pattern of earlier periods is not merely quantitative, although the number of violations of accepted standards has certainly increased in extent. The significant change is qualitative. In the past, the majority of those who violated the moral standards recognized that they were in the wrong; they did not attack the validity of the code they had broken. Today, the code is not merely being disobeyed in practice, it is being disavowed in theory. What characterizes our age is not the violation of standards but the denial of standards. In the words of Methodist Bishop Gerald Kennedy of Los Angeles, "The atmosphere is wide open. There is more promiscuity, and it is taken as a matter of course now by people. In my day they did it, but they knew it was wrong."[12]

What are the factors that have created the sexual revolution and continue to sustain its momentum? The first group, primarily socio-economic in character, has frequently been noted. But there is another set of historical factors that have fashioned much of the value system of the modern world. These attitudes have been highly influential in the emergence of the new morality, though they preceded the modern age of technology by centuries. In addition, there is a third factor, whose relevance to our subject has not even been suspected —the traditional Christian outlook on love, sex, and marriage. On the contrary, it has generally been regarded as the antithesis and sworn enemy of the sexual revolution. Actually, by a curious inversion, it has had a powerful influence on contemporary attitudes and patterns of behavior. We now turn to an examination of all three.

2

THE NEW MORALITY
Its Origins and Character

Its Cultural Antecedents

When the history of the twentieth century is written, it is certain that the sexual revolution will bulk large as one of the most important developments of the age. In greater or lesser degree, the new life styles impinge directly on the lives of every man, woman, and child in the modern world. Unless all signs fail, they will continue to do so in ever-increasing measure.

Viewed against the background of history, the new morality constitutes a major end product of the far-flung process that began in the Middle Ages and culminated in the emergence of modern man. Movements can almost never be pinpointed with specific dates. A date as good as any for the beginning of the modern era is the year 1453, when Constantinople fell to the Turks and refugee scholars brought about the revival of learning to the West. The Renaissance, which began in the fourteenth century, continued into the fifteenth and sixteenth. Following the pioneering voyages of discovery of Columbus and Magellan at the turn of the fifteenth century, the whole earth was opened up to exploration and exploitation by the West. The same period saw the rise of the religious Reformation, the roots of which were earlier. The momentum increased in the seventeenth century with the emergence of the

Industrial Revolution, which found its cultural expression in the naturalistic philosophy of Spinoza and the mechanistic physics of Newton. The eighteenth century saw the shifting of power from a feudal society to a new, aggressive class, the bourgeoisie, consisting of entrepreneurs and merchants. In its wake came the Age of Reason, exemplified in the Enlightenment and the Emancipation, and culminating in the French Revolution. The Enlightenment launched a vigorous challenge to accepted ideas in all areas of life, government, law, education, the status of women, criminology, and, above all, religion. The Emancipation broke down the long-established social-political order and rigid class structure.

All these varied and even contradictory movements had far-reaching consequences. In the first instance, they broadened immeasurably the intellectual horizons of Western civilization. In the second, they proclaimed the virtues of free self-expression and untrammeled self-development for the individual, giving new currency and meaning to the classical Greek epigram "Man is the measure of all things."

The nineteenth century witnessed the triumph of modern nationalism in Greece, Italy, and Germany, the short-lived reign of European imperialism in Asia and Africa, and the sharpening of class lines throughout the industrialized world. In the cultural area, it was marked by scientific and philosophic revolutions in the wake of the evolutionary theory of Darwin and the rise of movements for social and economic change based on Marx.

All these trends continued into the twentieth century. In addition, a radical transformation took place in man's understanding of his own nature through the seminal work of Freud and his disciples, opponents, and successors. Simultaneously, the dimensions of the physical universe in the microcosm of the atom and the macrocosm of outer space were extended beyond the wildest dreams of earlier ages, through the researches and theories of Einstein and his co-workers in the realm of physics and astronomy.

Political democracy, born in the last decades of the eighteenth century, reached its apogee of power and prestige in the nineteenth century. It was now challenged and increasingly defeated by totalitarianism in all its forms, Communist, Fascist, and Nazi. Incredibly, the dictatorships of the left, in spite of their long record of violence and suppression of freedom, succeeded in establishing themselves as the allies and spokesmen of the newly independent states in Asia and Africa, the so-called third world. Actually this was less strange than it seems. While the authoritarian rulers of these new states loudly professed their adherence to "socialism," "democracy," and "freedom," they were merely echoing the teachings of their former imperialist masters. As they proceeded to use force to destroy every vestige of liberty within their borders, they added only the simple equation that "white equals racist" to the storehouse of propaganda slogans.

The process of cataclysmic change is by no means at an end, nor can the shape of things to come be discerned. A full description or analysis of these varied movements and tendencies is obviously not within the scope of the present volume, but three generalizations pertinent to our theme may be hazarded.

First, these phenomena are by no means monolithic in content or univocal in direction. Every one of them contains currents and crosscurrents modifying and even negating one another.

Second, no sweeping simplistic judgments, whether of approval or disapproval, can be pronounced upon them. Some of these manifestations are positive in nature. Many, if not most, are a mixed bag of good and ill, like most elements in the human condition.

Third, and perhaps most important, one dominant trait seems to characterize the history of the past five centuries. There is a constant effort to break bonds, to remove restraints, to discard any limits on human thought and action, without regard to any perils or costs the enterprise entails. There is an insatiable thirst for the new and the untrodden for the sake of achieving "freedom," which is regarded as the key to self-fulfillment.

It is no wonder, therefore, that the modern era has, by and large, been marked by a steady attrition in the influence of traditional religion in the Western world; this is so for two basic reasons. The first element of religion to suffer a decline was its world-view, the body of ideas it promulgated on life and death, man and the universe. Religious faith is based on fundamental principles, many, if not most, of which cannot be verified scientifically in a laboratory or demonstrated mathematically on a blackboard. The extraordinary achievements of technology, the child of science and mathematics, have therefore persuaded many modern men and women that what these all-powerful genii could not prove had no reality. To be sure, even mathematical propositions, like the theorems of Euclidean geometry, can be "demonstrated" only after a series of axioms and postulates are assumed to be true. In all, scientific and scholarly activity rests upon assumptions, principles that commend themselves as reasonable or true but are not susceptible to "proof." But this basic consideration is generally overlooked.

The second element in religion is its way of life, the standards of behavior it seeks to inculcate. During its history, organized religion has called for adherence to specific codes of conduct in which restraints play a basic role. The importance of these prohibitions may be illustrated symbolically by Jewish religious law. Traditionally, there are 613 Commandments, of which 248 are positive injunctions and 365 negative precepts. Such a pattern of discipline, restricting free activity, is repugnant to the modern temper in its relentless movement toward total liberation.

Be this as it may, there is one fundamental article of faith in biblical religion upon which all else depends, an insight maintained, even when modified, both by rabbinic Judaism and by Christianity—the conviction that man lives in a law-abiding universe, created by a just and righteous God, and, therefore, governed by the principle of moral retribution. In its simplest form, the law of moral consequence declares that right-doing leads to well-being, and wrongdoing leads to disaster, in the life of both the individual and the group, be it a family, a nation, or a civilization. The theme is stressed in the Torah, underscored by the Prophets, echoed by the Psalmists, and emphasized by the Wisdom writers times without number.[1]

Perhaps the most familiar statement of the doctrine is to be found in the second paragraph of the *Shema,* where the use of the plural in the Hebrew makes it clear that it is applied to the nation as a whole.

> And if you will obey my commandments which I command you this day, to love the Lord your God, and to serve Him with all your heart and with all your soul, He will give rain for your land in its season, both the early and the later rain, that you may gather in your grain, your wine and your oil. And He will give grass in your fields for your cattle and you shall eat and be full. Take heed lest your heart be deceived, and you turn aside and serve other gods and worship them, and the anger of the Lord be kindled against you, and He shut up the heavens, so that there be no rain, and the land yield no fruit, and you perish quickly off the good land which the Lord gives you. (Deut. 11:13–17)

Perhaps the clearest presentation of the law of consequence in terms of the individual is to be found in Isaiah:

> Tell the righteous that it shall be well with them
>   for they shall eat the fruit of their deeds.
> Woe to the wicked! It shall be ill with him,
>   for what his hands have done shall be done to him.
> (3:10, 11)

It was, of course, obvious to the ancients, as it is to us, that the law of consequence, if it is valid at all, does not operate in clear, simple, and unmistakable form. On the contrary, life seems to be engaged in a massive conspiracy to contravene the law of justice.[2] The painful contradiction between faith and experience felt by untold numbers of sensitive men and women creates the greatest stumbling block to faith—the problem of evil. Biblical and post-biblical religion wrestled with this challenge and in the process profound ideas of permanent value emerged for the life of the individual and society. The greatest book in the Bible, if not in world literature, the Book of Job, is dedicated to the agonizing question "Why do the wicked prosper and the righteous suffer?"

Always there were those who doubted or denied this basic article of faith. All too often these critics were unaware of the resources of insight for dealing with the problem to be found in the tradition and its literature.[3] Be this as it may, the number of doubters and deniers has increased tremendously in modern times. The process began long before the twentieth century.

The problem has become agonizingly personal for the generation of the Holocaust. More than any of its predecessors, our generation has seen evil, naked and triumphant. It has also witnessed and suffered through two world wars, a Korean war, the horror of Vietnam, and a score of other conflicts involving nations, races, and religions. For easily understandable reasons, many people blame God rather than man for the Holocaust, the greatest horror in history. The massive problem of evil, superimposed on the achievements of science and technology, which by their very nature operate without postulating any Divine *fons et origo* in the world, has convinced many others to dispense with faith in their personal lives. They follow in the footsteps of Laplace, the famous French astronomer. When he published his *magnum opus,* the Emperor Napoleon remarked to him, "I see, Monsieur Laplace, that you make no reference to the Deity." "Sire," replied the astronomer, "God is a hypothesis I can do without." Whether they deny God or challenge Him, countless human beings in our day have lost faith that the moral quality of their actions will determine their destiny for good or ill.

These two motivations for the breakdown of faith—the scientific world-view and the existence of evil—are fed by a revulsion toward the past. They are reinforced by a third factor deriving from a foreboding with regard to the future. Looming over the human race is the sword of nuclear annihilation, which is never totally absent from the conscious thought or the unconscious awareness of our generation, particularly the youth. The cornucopia of plenty that modern science and technology have delivered on mankind's doorstep is far less powerful in its impact than the Pandora's box of perils tied up with it.

In sum, the weakening of faith in a just God and a law-abiding universe, the sense of desperation in the face of an uncertain tomorrow, and the new, enlarged opportunities for instant personal gratification available today—these factors have undermined the authority of religious teaching, particularly in the area of personal morality. The dominant theme of our age is the ancient cry, "Let us eat and drink, for tomorrow we die." (Isa. 22:13)

The far-flung decline of religious loyalty has naturally led to a critical approach to the specific do's and don't's preached by traditional religion. There is little disposition today, except perhaps in small isolated pockets of ultratraditional believers, to accept without question or hesitation the imperatives and prohibitions promulgated by religion. Even among the vast majority of religious believers, there is a strong desire for the rational justification of religious commands.

It is the thesis of this book that many positive and negative commandments rest upon long and varied experience and reflect a sound understanding of human nature transcending the moods and fashions of the passing hour. But mere asseveration or exhortation, however sincere and passionate, will not suffice. If the values and insights to be found in the traditional approach to love, sex, and marriage are to win the allegiance of modern men and women, especially the young, they need to be understood, interpreted, and applied with due regard to the complexities of a new and untried world.

Before this task is undertaken, we need to reckon with the full spectrum of causes that have produced the sexual revolution. One set of factors has been discussed in this section. Two others must now engage our attention.

The Socio-Economic Background

As we have seen, the complex of ideas and values that made the sexual revolution a possibility emerged from five centuries of Western civilization. What made them a reality was a radically changed set of socio-economic conditions.

First and foremost was the new economic role of women in the labor market. To be sure, women had always been engaged in manual labor, with time out for childbearing, which came with unfailing regularity virtually every year. For centuries they had been the beasts of burden everywhere, in the Far East, the Middle East, Africa, and pre-Columbian North and South America. Their male counterparts engaged in hunting, fishing, sometimes in trade, preferably doing nothing or making war. The women worked in the gardens, the fields, and the orchards, planting, tending, and reaping the harvest, and preparing the fruits, vegetables, and grain for use. They tended the flocks, cared for the domestic fowl and livestock, and thus supplied the milk, the wool, and the meat for the family.

From earliest times, women had been in labor—in both senses of the term—but they were not in the labor market. The economic gains produced by their toil did not accrue to them in fact, nor were they even recognized as theirs in theory. The crucial point was that a woman's work in the home and around it was not paid for in coin of the realm. It did not constitute gainful employment.

In the eighteenth and nineteenth centuries, certain limited areas were open to women outside the home. These included domestic service, at the very bottom of the economic ladder, and schoolteaching and nursing on a somewhat higher rung. But married women, who constituted the majority, were virtually restricted to household duties, the raising of children, and religious worship.

Not until the twentieth century did women begin entering into the labor market on a mass scale. At the beginning, they encountered substantial resistance, but the process could not be halted. Increasingly, women found employment in factories, in offices as clerks and stenographers, and in retail establishments as salespeople.

A major transformation occurred as a result of the First World War and successive conflicts. The mass mobilization of men depleted the male labor supply and women entered into new areas of commerce and industry. After each cataclysm, the tide receded, but never completely. The economic positions won by women were by and large retained and proved a springboard for the next great step upward in their penetration of the labor market.

The changes registered in the economic sphere began slowly, but the tempo has been increasing rapidly. In 1960, women constituted 31.2 percent of the labor force; in 1965, 33.6 percent; in 1974, 37.9 percent.[4] Within a few decades, the percentage of women will approach that of men in employment.

Several factors played a part in this phenomenon. The rising tide of inflation made additional income welcome in most homes. Other non-economic motives also played an important role. Once the husband had gone off to work and the children had been sent to school, outside employment became all the more feasible, especially as the availability of labor-saving devices and prepared foods reduced the time and energy needed for home duties.

For a minority of women, but a highly significant one, there was a desire to find creative work and thus fulfill the potential of their talent and ability. The opportunity for new and wider human contacts in a more interesting and exciting environment outside the home also had an irresistible appeal.

The same motive had long played a part in the high percentage of women active in communal work and public service on a voluntary basis. Often the women's organizations ranked higher in achievement than men's agencies in the same field. Yet the women's groups were usually relegated to an auxiliary role. Since Jews constituted a highly urbanized group, somewhat higher than the general population on the economic scale, the phenomenon was clearly visible in the Jewish community. In religion, philanthropy, social service, and Zionism, women often demonstrated that they were not equal to men —they were clearly superior.

Above all, women craved and, for the first time, saw the opportunity of satisfying their desire for personal independence and a sense of dignity. In a society where material means are by and large regarded as the test of personal worth, a salary attached to a job has been a status symbol, much sought after, beyond its intrinsic value.

The expansion of women's economic role was largely an automatic process, unconscious and undirected. The conscious and aggressive movement for the legal and political recognition of women's rights did not gain momentum until the middle of the twentieth century. To be sure, voices had been raised much earlier. In the nineteenth century, Mary Wollstonecraft Godwin, in her *Vindication of the Rights of Women,* and John Stuart Mill, in *The Subjection of Women,* had challenged the morality involved in subjecting one half of the human race to the domination of the other. In the first half of the twentieth century, the battle for women's rights shifted to the political arena, until women's suffrage became a reality.

The perimeters of the struggle for equality continued to expand, affecting every area of life, economic, cultural, and political. It reached its apogee in the movement for the adoption of the Women's Equal Rights Amendment to the Constitution, which prohibits discrimination on the basis of sex anywhere in the national life. The amendment has not had easy sledding. Its foes have included many women reared in the old tradition who oppose it on various grounds.

Nonetheless, it is clear that it represents the wave of the future. One hundred years of American experience in race relations since the Civil War has demonstrated that the doctrine of separate but equal is specious and unworkable. No matter on what side one stands, it is clear that discrimination is organically related to segregation, so that a breakdown of the first must inevitably lead to the disappearance of the second. Moreover, in the decade and a half since the historic decision of the United States Supreme Court in outlawing school segregation, Americans have learned that the process of major social reconstruction is marked by tension and conflict.

The massive economic and political transformation in the role of women has had a powerful impact upon the personal relationship between both sexes and the moral postulates that support it. For the first time in recorded history, women as a class have options besides marriage open to them. The new economic independence achieved by women makes them less and less willing to submit to conditions in marriage that they find unpalatable or worse. The Talmud quotes an Aramaic folk-saying, "A woman would rather live an unhappily married life than dwell in singleness as a widow."[5] While a true description of conditions in its time, the saying hardly applies today. Insults or injuries, whether real or fancied, that would have been borne in silence and submission in the past arouse active resistance today. The employment market gives women the opportunity to live alone and like it, or, at least, to live alone—and manage.

Undoubtedly, most women today, like most men, find that marriage offers the most satisfactory means of coping with the loneliness and *anomie* that are besetting ills of modern society. But the unmarried woman is less and less confined in her movements. While in the past unaccompanied women rarely appeared in public, today they participate freely in cultural and political activities. Their social life runs the gamut from the opera to the singles bar, with few inhibitions or restraints.

As a result, the double standard, according to which women were expected to uphold morality and men were free to flout it, is rapidly disappearing. In another connection, we have already quoted the prophet Hosea, who, twenty-seven centuries ago, had objected to this idea of different norms of behavior for the two sexes. What is happening today is not that men have adopted the more rigorous standards traditional for women but that women are tending to accept the freer norms of behavior condoned for men.

Another dominant trait in contemporary society is mobility. Increasingly, workers on every level, professional, technical, and academic, find it necessary to move with their families every few years. This characteristic holds true particularly of middle-level executives and administrators, but is not limited to them. As a result, more and more modern families cannot strike roots in any community and rarely develop a sense of belonging. They may not feel bound by prevailing community standards, which, however much resented at times, nonetheless exert a positive influence in maintaining basic patterns of behavior.

In the Middle Ages, the average peasant never traveled more than ten miles from his home during his entire lifetime. Even after the Industrial Revolution, most people tended to live in one area all their lives. This is almost never the case today. A constantly diminishing number of grown children live in the same community as their parents. Most grandparents are little more than benevolent strangers to their grandchildren, unable to exercise any of the traditional functions of the older generation, not only because of changing standards, but also because of distance.

The mobility is not merely geographical but also social and economic. Less and less Americans are content to remain on the same economic level as their parents. Undoubtedly, economic stratification is much less rigid in the United States than in other lands. The widespread pressure by poor Americans, white and black alike, for quality education is rarely an expression of a desire for transmitting to their children the cultural background associated with a liberal education. Basically, the quality education they have in mind is better vocational training, whether in technical trades, professions, or business. The goal is a better job and higher pay, objectives which are, of course, by no means reprehensible in themselves.

In the face of constant and accelerating change, a husband-and-wife relationship does not remain unaffected. As the couple grow older, they may conceivably grow apart, developing new interests and contacts, and thus undermining the stability of their marriage relationship. The city of Washington, it has been said, is full of brilliant men married to women whom they met when they were young. Observing the operations of government, one may doubt the truth of the adjective in the first phrase. Nevertheless, the capital city may serve as a symbol of the dislocations brought about by the frenetic social and geographic mobility in our day.

Sexual behavior has also been powerfully influenced by another type of mobility in its most literal sense. The automobile and the motel have become normal ingredients of the American way of life, and with the Americanization of the world, the pattern is rapidly becoming universal. The mobility of the car and the privacy of the motel make possible intimate relations between youngsters and between adults with a minimum of interference or supervision. The motel also has the sorry distinction of frequently serving as the locale for what is perhaps the ultimate degradation in human relations, wife-swapping parties for "respectable" families in middle-class communities.

Finally, several major deterrents to free sexual relations have lost their power. The fear of venereal disease has been reduced because more potent drugs are available. Mechanical and chemical improvements have taken place in the various technical devices for contraception, which are now more widely used. To be sure, the hazards are far from eliminated.

As we shall have occasion to note later, society is confronted by an unanticipated growth of venereal disease in sufficient size to warrant the description "epidemic" by public-health officials. The rise in illegitimate births and the increase in the abortion rate, which will soon engage our attention, demonstrate that contraceptive devices are not the total answer. Nevertheless, it is possible today for young people and their elders as well to embark upon sexual adventures with considerably less fear of untoward physical and social consequences.

The most significant challenge to the traditional marriage pattern remains to be mentioned—the inundating tide of divorce and its all-but-universal acceptance as a normal feature of modern life. The growing ration of divorce to marriage in the United States is now 1 to 3 and is still rising. The incidence of divorce is, in large degree, the consequence of the vast economic and social changes in the status of modern women. At the same time, the easy availability of divorce causes these factors to be increasingly operative in modern society.

These new social and economic conditions have created a new outlook. We have seen that the new morality represents the end product of basic tendencies in the evolution of a humanistic, secular culture during the past five hundred years.

In a deeper sense, however, the new morality is not a new morality at all. Ours is a civilization that is variously described as Christian or post-Christian. Whatever designation is adopted, it remains steeped in attitudes and impulses derived from classical Christianity that continue to operate below the conscious level, even for those who have surrendered the structure of Christian belief. With this natural bias built into the Western system of values, it is no wonder that the close relationship between the Christian outlook on sex, love, and marriage on the one hand and the new morality on the other has been overlooked. It has always seemed self-evident that the two were totally opposed to each other. Paradoxical though it seems, we hope to demonstrate that the sexual revolution is an inversion of the traditional Christian conception.

3

CHRISTIANITY AND SEX

The Teaching of Classical Christianity

At first blush, nothing could seem more preposterous than to suggest any affinity between Christianity and the new morality. The advocates of traditional behavior patterns sound dire warnings against the license and irresponsibility of contemporary mores. Simultaneously, spokesmen for the sexual revolution heap scorn upon the benighted preachers of an outworn sex code. Virtually the only subject on which the two camps would agree is that they are at opposite poles from one another.

If our fragmented and directionless generation may be said to have any unifying conception of the good life, it is the glorification of sex as the ultimate and most desirable form of human pleasure. Love as a marketable commodity makes the wheels of industry and commerce go round. Vast energies in our economic order are devoted to the production and distribution of products and services that promise a greater sexual attractiveness and more gratification for both sexes and at every age level. Not only cosmetics, drugs, and clothes, but food, health services, automobiles, vacation resorts, and employment agencies all utilize sex appeal as the staple of their advertising campaigns. The love-hate relations of men and women have always been basic themes in literature and

music. But today the music, publishing, and art industries—
the term "industry" is highly instructive—have all learned to
exploit this interest with a skill and concentration unheard of
in the past. Most manifestations of our culture, books and
magazines, television and radio, the theater and the cinema,
have sex as their principal subject matter and the most effective lure for the consumer.

One of the principal reasons why old age is regarded today
as a major disaster, if not a capital crime, is the loss of physical
attractiveness that comes with advancing years, marked by
sagging muscles, wrinkled faces, added weight, and the decline in sexual prowess. There is no way of estimating how
many middle-aged men and women venture into dalliance
and end in misery, guilt, and broken marriages because, at the
time of the female climacteric or the male menopause, they
were driven by the desire to demonstrate that their sexual
potency and attractiveness were still functioning. In the contemporary scale of values, sex occupies the highest position,
challenging even the primacy of money as the highest good.

In classical Christianity, on the other hand, the attitude toward sex is decidedly negative. The basis for this outlook is to
be sought in the complicated early history of the new faith.
Originally, Christians constituted one small Jewish sect among
many that arose in Palestine during the troubled decades between 150 B.C.E. and 150 C.E. At this time, the Jewish community was still living largely in its own homeland, but it was no
longer free, being oppressed, exploited, and humiliated by the
power of Rome that held sway over their country and the
entire Near East during most of this era. Though Jews were
groaning under the yoke of the foreign tyrants and their native apologists and defenders, they clung fervently to their
faith in the righteousness and power of God. In their extremity
they looked forward passionately to the Messiah, the heaven-
sent redeemer who, in God's time, would lift the yoke from
His people and usher in universal justice, brotherhood, and
peace.

Only the Sadducees, the party of the rich classes, were satisfied with the status quo. The vast majority of the Jewish population followed the religious guidance of the Pharisees. Their leaders, the rabbis, were strong in their yearning for the Messiah, but they taught their followers to refrain from seeking to hasten the time of his advent, and to remain content to await the will of God.

However, various elements in the people, particularly those who felt themselves most bitterly oppressed, like the farmers in Galilee, found this waiting for redemption intolerable. As the Roman tyranny grew steadily more rapacious and arrogant, these groups became increasingly certain that God's redemption was at hand and could not be long delayed. To be sure, the objective, external conditions offered little hope that the Jews could, unaided, throw off the Roman yoke. That meant only that an intervention from on high was imminent, a supernatural cataclysm that would overturn the "kingdom of arrogance" and usher in the Kingdom of God. These sects differed vigorously on many questions, such as the identity of the Messiah and the steps to be taken to prepare for his coming. But they shared a powerful faith in imminent eschatology, the conviction that the End could be expected at any moment. By and large, the revulsion that these sects felt at the world about them, disfigured by cruelty, corruption, and falsehood, impelled them to adopt an ascetic attitude. Turning their backs on the world seemed to them the appropriate posture to adopt during the brief period remaining between the sorry present and the glorious future. By renouncing the goods and the goals of a sinful world, they would attain to a state of purity and thus be worthily prepared for the Messianic Age.

The Dead Sea Scrolls, discovered during the last three decades, have brought to light the literature and the life of some of these sects and added greatly to our knowledge—and our sense of ignorance—of the intense and passionate faith of these apocalyptists, "revealers of secret tidings of redemption." Members of the Qumran community were probably identical with or similar to the Essenes, who are known from the writings of Philo, Josephus, and various Greek and Roman authors. It would seem that some groups, like the Zealots, combined their mystical faith with military prowess and sought to throw off the Roman yoke by force of arms. Most of these groups, however, opposed violence and adopted a peaceful, if not passive, way of life while they awaited the coming of the redeemer.

The earliest Christians constituted one of these apocalyptic Jewish sects. They arose in Galilee and looked upon a young carpenter from Nazareth, called Joshua (Jesus in the Greek), as their Messiah, who proclaimed that "the kingdom of God is at hand." The sources for the life of the Christian Savior are fragmentary and incomplete on the one hand, and complex and contradictory on the other. By and large, they reflect the inner struggles and outer fortunes of the early Christian Church and the contending factions within it. Scholars, therefore, differ in their interpretation of the available material and in their reconstruction of the history of early Christianity.

What seems clear beyond reasonable doubt, however, is that the ascetic strain, common to all the apocalyptic sects of the period, characterized the Judeo-Christians as well. The expectation of the imminent advent of the kingdom of God reenforced their hostility to the present world order, which they regarded—and not without reason—as evil and corrupt. The sayings of Jesus transmitted in the Gospels, while subject to varying interpretations, express what we have called "the ethics of self-abnegation."[1]

In the Sermon on the Mount, and elsewhere, Jesus makes extreme demands upon human nature. This is entirely understandable in view of his conviction that the existing social and political order was on the verge of destruction and that the Kingdom of God was on the threshold of realization. In this context, turning the other cheek to the enemy or non-resistance to evil was a plausible ideal for an interim ethic. The classic utterance of Jesus "Render unto Caesar the things that are Caesar's and unto God the things that are God's" has been subjected to a vast amount of interpretation. No matter how it is understood, it was clearly not a call for armed resistance to Rome.

So, too, there is no concern with economic problems, since they, too, would become obsolete in the new heavenly order. The young man who claims to have observed all the major injunctions of the Decalogue and asks how he may inherit the Kingdom of Heaven is advised, "Sell all thou hast and give to the poor."[2] Such mundane tasks as burying one's father, bidding farewell to one's family before leaving, or plowing one's field, were to be surrendered in order to "be fit for the Kingdom of God."(Luke 9:59–62)

Such ascetic tendencies would obviously come to the fore in the area of sexual experience. Adultery had been forbidden long before in the Decalogue, but the new dispensation added, "I say to you that everyone who looks at a woman lustfully has already committed adultery with her in his heart." (Mat. 5:28) The Law of Moses had made provision for divorce, but this, Jesus explained, is only because of men's "hardness of heart." (Mark 10:5–9) Thus, according to the Gospel of Mark, Jesus forbids divorce and remarriage.[3] The parallel passage in Matthew goes further and extols celibacy over marriage as the ideal state for a human being, of which not all people are capable (Mat. 19:10–12).

These ascetic tendencies, characteristic of apocalyptic Judaism in Palestine, were carried further by Paul, the indefatigable missionary who laid the foundations of Christianity. Paul was born a Jew and regarded himself as "a Pharisee, son of a Pharisee." (Acts 23:16) But he was raised in the Greek city of Tarsus in Asia Minor and his outlook was molded by his Hellenistic environment. Both because he was a Roman citizen and because he was eager to win recognition for the new faith as a licit religion, Paul counsels submission to political tyranny, explaining that the powers that be are divinely ordained (Rom. 13:1–8). He exhorts slaves to obey their masters (I Pet.

2:13–20) and wives to be submissive to their husbands (I Pet. 3:1).

From the Greek culture surrounding him, Paul derived his concept that there are two elements in a human being perpetually at war with one another—the body and the soul. While the soul is immaterial, perfect, and eternal, the body is gross, corruptible, and the source of sin. It therefore follows that the highest goal of human existence lies in transcending the physical and in living purely on the spiritual level. Hence the ideal state is that of celibacy. Paul himself was unmarried and wished all could emulate his example. Since, however, most people cannot attain to this exalted level, marriage is created, basically as a concession to the weaknesses of human nature. Moreover, marriage is necessary for the procreation of the race and can be justified in the eyes of God on this basis and only for this purpose.

Paul's fullest discussion of the subject represents the classic New Testament teaching on sex, marriage, and divorce. The salient sections read as follows:

> It is well for a man not to touch a woman. But because of the temptation to immorality, each man should have his own wife and each woman her own husband. The husband should give his wife her conjugal rights, and likewise the wife to her husband. . . .
>
> Do not refuse one another, except perhaps by agreement for a season, that you may devote yourselves to prayer; but then come together again, lest Satan tempt you through lack of self-control. I say this by way of concession, not of command. I wish that all were as I myself am. But each has his own special gift from God, one of one kind and one of another.
>
> To the unmarried and the widows I say that it is well for them to remain single as I do. But if they cannot exercise self-control, they should marry. For it is better to marry than to be aflame with passion.
>
> To the married I give charge, not I but the Lord, that the wife should not separate from her husband (but if she does, let her remain single or else be reconciled to her husband) and that the husband should not divorce his wife. . . .

I think that in view of the impending distress it is well for a person to remain as he is. Are you bound to a wife? Do not seek to be free. Are you free from a wife? Do not seek marriage. But if you marry, you do not sin, and if a girl marries she does not sin. Yet those who marry will have worldly troubles, and I would spare you that. . . .

If anyone thinks that he is not behaving properly toward his betrothed, if his passions are strong, and it has to be, let him do as he wishes; let them marry—it is no sin. But whoever is firmly established in his heart, being under no necessity but having his desire under control, and has determined this in his heart, to keep her as his betrothed, he will do well. So that he who marries his betrothed does well; and he who refrains from marriage will do better.

A wife is bound to her husband as long as he lives. If the husband dies, she is free to be married to whom she wishes, only in the Lord. But in my judgment she is happier if she remains as she is. And I think that I have the Spirit of God.[4]

Paul's outlook on sex and marriage has remained central to the Christian faith. It was Paul who was the architect of the Christian drama of salvation, in which the Fall of Man represents the primal sin that has left its taint upon all future generations, to be removed only by acceptance of the belief in the Savior. The cosmic proportions of the sin of Adam and Eve are, therefore, fundamental to traditional Christianity.

In normative Judaism, the sin of Adam and Eve bears no transcendent theological significance.[5] The disobedience of the first human pair led to their punishment, the specific nature of which is spelled out in the biblical text.

The Lord God said to the serpent, "Because you have done this, cursed are you above all cattle, and above all wild animals; upon your belly you shall go, and dust you shall eat all the days of your life. I will put enmity between you and the woman, and between your seed and her seed; he shall bruise your head, and you shall bruise his heel."

To the woman He said, "I will greatly multiply your pain in childbearing; in pain you shall bring forth children, yet your desire shall be for your husband, and he shall rule over you."

And to Adam he said, "Because you have listened to the

voice of your wife, and have eaten of the tree of which I
commanded you, 'You shall not eat of it,' cursed is the
ground because of you; in toil you shall eat of it all the days
of your life; thorns and thistles it shall bring forth to you; and
you shall eat the plants of the field. In the sweat of your face
you shall eat bread till you return to the ground, for out of
it you were taken; you are dust; and to dust you shall return.
(Gen. 3:14–19)

Aside from the specific penalties, there are deeper consequences clearly indicated in the biblical narrative. By disobey-
ing God's command, Adam and Eve estranged themselves
from God and deprived themselves of the boon of personal
immortality that would have been theirs had they not been
expelled from the Garden of Eden.[6]

Christian theologians, on the other hand, were confronted
by a major question—what was the nature of the heinous sin
committed by Adam and Eve that could provoke a penalty as
severe as eternal damnation upon all their descendants? In the
writings of the Church Fathers and the medieval Christian
theologians, there is virtually unanimous consensus that the
basic sin was concupiscence. The term is defined in the dictio-
nary as (1) "ardent, sensuous longing," (2) "sexual desire; lust."
Some Christian thinkers are at pains to point out that the term
encompasses not merely the sexual drive but illicit desires in
general. However, the sexual impulse has always played a
central role in the concept.[7]

The doctrine was given its extreme form by Augustine,
whose outlook was influenced by his background in Manichae-
ism, which regarded man as the creation of the devil and
human procreation as evil. Augustine found in the Fall of
Adam the basis for his overwhelming feeling of extreme
human depravity, for his sense of absolute dependence upon
God's free grace, which was his sole anchor, and for his conception of sexual relations as sinful. "The act of generation
. . . is sin itself and determines the transmission *ipso facto* of
the sin to the new creature." The objections of Pelagius to
Augustine's views were ruled out by the Church as heretical.

Medieval scholars, such as Thomas Aquinas, John Duns Scotus, and Pierre Abélard, tempered the rigor of Augustine's views in varying degree. The Council of Trent (1545–63) declared the view of Aquinas authoritative, according to which Adam's Fall deprived man only of his original righteousness or his superadded grace. Nonetheless, the hereditary effect of Adam's sin persisted for his descendants.

The Reformers, however, notably Martin Luther and John Calvin, reasserted several elements of Augustine's position which Catholic scholasticism had modified. They stressed the innate depravity of human nature and declared that sexual desire per se partook of the nature of sin. Thus, both Protestant theology, which maintained the extreme form of the doctrine, and the Roman Catholic Church, which had modified its position, agreed in regarding man's nature as inherently corrupted by Adam's sin. They differed only with regard to the degree and the nature of the injury wrought. With few exceptions, they all viewed sexual desire or concupiscence as evil.

In essence, classical Christianity looks upon sex as basically negative, marriage as a concession to the lower aspects of human nature, and divorce as forbidden. To be sure, some modern Christian thinkers have sought to reinterpret these doctrines or to limit their applicability. Thus, celibacy has been surrendered in Protestantism and a vigorous battle for relaxing this requirement is going on in the Catholic Church. As for the Christian laity, millions have quietly abandoned the New Testament teaching on love, sex, and marriage.

However, it would be a major error to dismiss classical Christian teaching in this area as purely antiquarian, inoperative, and irrelevant to modern life. Actually, these doctrines continue to wield a powerful influence on the lives of modern men and women on both the conscious and the unconscious level. The full extent of their impact, as we shall see below, has not been fully recognized. From the classical Christian attitude on sex and marriage flow several momentous consequences, even in our day.

Celibacy is regarded in the Catholic Church as the highest

ideal and is, therefore, obligatory for the priest, the monk, and the nun. In 1952, Pope Pius XII "severely censured those who, despite the Church's warnings and in contrast to her opinion, give marriage a preference in principle above virginity."[8] Pope Paul has repeatedly stated that marriage will remain forbidden to the clergy.

Marriage is an estate which can be countenanced only because it is essential to the perpetuation of the human race and therefore it may be conceived of as a sacrament. It is, however, also a concession to man's lower nature, and hence it must bear the stigma of a punishment.

This ambivalent attitude toward marriage has its parallel in the contradictory standpoint on divorce long enshrined in the civil law of many states and countries. From the logical point of view, if marriage is a concession to the physical impulses, release from this condition through divorce should have been facilitated, as marking a return to a higher state of grace. That is emphatically not the case. Since marriage is also a sacrament, it cannot be dissolved, except for reasons of adultery.

Civil law has also felt the impact of this attitude. When divorce was permitted, it was conceived of as a punishment for the party guilty of adultery, the only ground for divorce in New York State until recently. In South Carolina, no divorce was civilly possible. The Roman Catholic Church fought a strenuous battle to prevent the introduction of civil divorce in Italy, but lost. Divorce is still totally forbidden in Catholic canon law, although annulment occasionally offers a way of terminating a marriage. Various Protestant churches have relaxed the New Testament interdict on divorce, but virtually all continue to regard divorce as a punishment for a crime. Some communions forbid, at least in theory, the remarriage of the "guilty" party.

Since sexual relations are permissible only when they may lead to the begetting of children, official Catholic doctrine regards the practice of birth control through chemical or mechanical means as sinful and forbidden. Only abstinence, or reliance upon the rhythm method (when conception is less likely to take place) is permissible.

It is obvious that attitudes such as these, aside from their inherent contradictions, are bound to come into conflict with the many problems, opportunities, and temptations confronting men and women, particularly in modern society. As a result, Protestantism, which never officially surrendered the New Testament attitudes, accepted their attenuation in practice. Celibacy was abandoned as the ideal state and divorce was tacitly recognized as permissible on various grounds. The pressures for family limitation became increasingly imperious, and Protestantism did not oppose the planned-parenthood movement. Indeed, church leaders found it not only legitimate but morally incumbent under various circumstances.

The Roman Catholic Church, on the other hand, has continued to reaffirm vigorously the New Testament standpoint. Yet the inexorable march of events has weakened this point of view even among Catholics. All birth-control clinics report large numbers of otherwise devoted Catholics who utilize their services. A nationwide study in 1965 based on interviews with 5,600 married women of all faiths indicated that a large proportion of the Roman Catholic wives regularly attend church. For those who went to Mass every week, avoidance of contraception fell from 78 percent in 1955 to 69 percent in 1960, and to 56 percent in 1965, a pattern matching the rate of decline for Catholic women as a whole.[9]

At the Second Vatican Council, a commission was appointed by Pope John XXIII to restudy the traditional Catholic teaching on birth control. Pope Paul VI enlarged the commission, which was authoritatively reported to have favored authorizing the use of anovulants—the so-called birth-control pills. Many members of the commission were prepared to go further and to permit the use of mechanical contraceptives as well. Nevertheless, Pope Paul, on October 28, 1966, restated the traditional prohibition for Catholics and declared that he "must defer any modification still for some time."[10]

Resistance to the official Catholic standpoint on sex and marriage is on the increase, even among those who remain active
communicants and regard themselves as loyal believers. Some
observers believe that the Pope's stand on birth control may
undermine loyalty to the Church all along the line. In spite of
the disciplined structure characteristic of the Catholic hierarchy, priests and nuns have been calling for change with regard
to the principle of celibacy for the clergy. Large numbers have
not waited for an official modification of this ancient doctrine
and are leaving the priesthood and the monastic orders. These
new attitudes undoubtedly play a role in the reduced numbers
of young men studying for the priesthood and young women
entering into the novitiate. The struggle between age-old
Catholic tradition and the imperious demands of the day gives
every promise of being long and drawn out, with the end not
yet in sight.

In the fall of 1976, an unprecedented laymen's Conference
on Catholic Action was held in Detroit. The declaration of
principles drawn up at the close of the conference called for
new directions in Church doctrine and practice in many areas,
with considerable attention devoted to sexual ethics and family morality.

As for the large number of our contemporaries, particularly
among the young, who no longer attend church regularly and
whose relationship to organized religion is limited to baptism,
the marriage ceremony, funeral rites, and occasional holiday
observances—and sometimes not even these—the teaching of
the classical Christian tradition on sex is felt to be completely
irrelevant and plays no part in their life style, at least on the
conscious level. This can hardly be a cause of self-congratula-
tion or complacency. The present situation means that a very
high proportion of the men and women of our generation are
deprived of one of the major sources of ethical guidance in
their personal lives. They are cast adrift on tempestuous seas,
with no rudder except their instinctual drives, which are all
too powerful, and no compass except the authority of a state
that is often much too weak.

The New Morality—
an Inversion of the Christian Ethic

Our presentation of the classical Christian outlook on sex would seem to demonstrate only that the sex ethic of traditional Christianity and the new morality are totally opposed to one another. How can one possibly speak of Christian roots for the new morality? In responding to this legitimate question, we are not compelled merely to fall back upon the familiar French proverb, *les extrêmes se touchent,* "extremes meet." As we have seen, Paul, as well as other seminal teachers of Christian doctrine, regarded sex as an unfortunate aspect of human nature at best and a major threat to salvation at worst. Every human being is a perpetual battleground between *sarx,* "the body" or "the flesh," and *psyche,* "the spirit" or "the soul." This conflict is mirrored in two types of love, for which Greek has distinct terms, *eros,* "physical or carnal love," and *agape,* "spiritual love."

The traditional Christian outlook on sex as evil has created the concept that the less love is involved in sex, the higher it becomes. *Agape* is holy, but *eros* is low; love is pure, but sex is unclean.

The dichotomy introduced by Christian theology was secularized in the Middle Ages in the concept of "romantic love." The ideal of knightly devotion was a love never physically consummated. The knight who gave his fealty to his lady, vowing to protect her and defend her interests, worshipped her only from afar. In medieval life and literature, the classic examples of romantic or ideal love are instances where the sexual component is either totally lacking or tragically frustrated. Romeo and Juliet are star-crossed lovers whose passion for each other is scarcely gratified, because death intervenes. The passion of Tristan and Isolde, intense as it is, is illicit and, therefore, cannot look forward to normal fulfillment. In the world of reality, Dante and Beatrice, who saw each other only a few times during their lifetime and never established any personal contact, symbolized the noblest type of love relationship. The love affair of Héloise and Abélard was doomed to tragedy because she was a nun and he was a monk, both pledged to celibacy.[11]

In the modern period, romantic love has been brought down from the aristocracy into the lives of the masses and vulgarized in the process. Our mass culture, with all the media at its command, glorifies "love" in words and song, in books and magazines, on the screen and the stage, on television and the radio. It is noteworthy that, by and large, the love that is glorified is still romantic love *par excellence,* unfulfilled or incomplete, the passion experienced either before marriage or outside it. It has been noted that while illicit or thwarted love is the theme of countless operas, only one, Beethoven's *Fidelio,* is concerned with marital love and devotion. Conventional wisdom or popular cynicism has it that whatever feelings may exist between a husband and a wife, the climax of their love is reached at the marriage ceremony, after which it will decline. Nevertheless, modern society, particularly in America, regards love as the essential, indeed, often as the all-sufficient basis for entering into marriage. The results are written in the mounting divorce statistics.

It becomes clear that the old sanctities of the traditional code and the contemporary sexual revolution agree on one fundamental. While it is impossible, for obvious reasons, to sever love and sex completely in practice, both value systems believe in keeping them as far apart as possible, at least in theory. Actually, the modern view is an inversion of the traditional standpoint. Traditional morality exalts love and declares that sex is, or should be, irrelevant and unrelated to love. The modern age glorifies sex and maintains that love is, or should be, irrelevant and unrelated to sex. The conventional moral code strives to minimize contaminating love with sex. The new morality tries to avoid complicating sex with love. What they share in common is the conviction that love and sex are not integrally bound up with each other and therefore do not

—or should not—involve each other. Both in theory and in practice, many modern men and women, and particularly the young, have accordingly drawn the conclusion that sexual experience is permissible even where there is no love. A recent television broadcast series dealing with prostitution reported that there are 100,000 episodes of prostitution in New York City each day. Whether the figure is realistic is subject to question. The reporter then proceeded to describe the average "client" as middle-class, middle-aged, and married. One man who was interviewed explained, "Sex is what you do with a woman you don't like. Love is for your wife, whom you wouldn't want to soil with sex."

The classical Christian outlook on love, sex, and marriage remains significant in the modern world, not only for the devout. The view of sex as inherently evil has persisted in our age of disbelief and continues to haunt many who no longer adhere to Christian doctrine. The conviction that sex is immoral, if not sinful, continues to survive in the world-view—and what is even more important, in the emotional makeup—of many non-believers. The theme of sex as guilt bulks large in the dramas of Eugene O'Neill. Frequently, heretics who have surrendered the basic dogmas of traditional Christianity on the conscious level continue to retain subconsciously the negative attitude toward sex inherited from Paul and his patristic successors.[12] As a result, many modern men and women who have lost the sense of sin continue to be oppressed by feelings of guilt. It is one of the great insights of modern psychoanalysis that psychological disturbances of varying intensity, running the full gamut from minor neurosis to major psychosis, are induced by contradictions in the human psyche between conscious attitudes and subconscious feelings.

It is no accident that our society exhibits a deep-seated schizophrenia—sentimental glorification of love on the one hand and widespread pornography, prostitution, and promiscuity on the other. All these unhealthy manifestations have arisen because the sex code preached by traditional religion and embodied in contemporary law all too often runs counter to the promptings of human nature. What has been driven out through the door comes in through the window, with one tragic difference: the visitor is no longer a respectable caller, amenable to law and order, but a surreptitious law breaker. Untold numbers of men and women who no longer accept the outlook of the traditional religion in which they were reared and often have broken violently with the morality based upon it remain subject to its compulsion, and never more strongly than when they flout its teachings in word or in deed.

It is clear that the new morality, at least in many of its aspects, is no temporary aberration likely to disappear like a passing fashion.

The ideological base for the new morality is much older than the twentieth century. It is grounded, as we have seen, in the entire historical development of Western man since the Middle Ages. Humanism, like any significant world-view, has many levels and variations, but its fundamental thesis is that the satisfaction of human needs and desires should be the goal of human endeavor.

Long exposure to the Christian concept of the dichotomy between love and sex has penetrated deeply into the consciousness—and the subconsciousness—of Western man, and simultaneously has produced a reaction against the code of behavior based upon it. Thus, modern men, women, and young people were prepared to welcome the new freedom of the sexual revolution.

The radical transformation of social, economic, and cultural conditions in the twentieth century made this freedom possible, not merely for the well-born and the rich, but for millions in the middle and lower classes.

The sexual revolution, for all its excesses and errors, is an expression of this humanistic impulse in the single most significant area of human experience. Perhaps the errors and excesses that have been charged against it—and we shall try to evaluate the movement fairly—have carried it beyond humanism to hedonism, the pursuit of pleasure as the ultimate goal. Hedonism has always possessed a power of attraction for some human beings. It has become almost irresistible today. In an age when society seems incapable of solving its massive problems and the future looks bleak, so that a sense of despair and hopelessness grips men—a feeling widely prevalent today —only the pursuit of personal pleasure seems to make sense.

The breakdown of the sense of the commonweal and the increasing polarization, violence, and hostility among races, classes, and nations evident everywhere—on the international arena, within the nation, and within each community—have affected the attitude toward the family as well. Basic to the marriage compact is the sense of shared responsibility and mutual involvement. The two partners undertake to care for each other in sickness and in health, in prosperity and in tribulation. They also undertake far-reaching responsibility for children, for bringing them into the world, raising and educating them, and guiding them toward careers and the building of their own families. In a time when responsibility and involvement are the last thing people want, marriage appears less and less attractive as an option.

Finally, in an age of speed, people demand instant gratification of their desires. If any justification is needed, Freud is interpreted, or misinterpreted, and cited to prove that the control or the suppression of the sexual impulse is fraught with psychological danger.

When all the factors, past and present, are taken into account, it is clear that the sexual revolution is one of the major phenomena of the century. The wringing of hands and the hurling of anathemas will not exorcise it from the human condition. Neither wholesale condemnation nor uncritical approbation will serve human needs. We would do well to adopt the attitude of a second-century Jewish Sage, Rabbi Meir. When his teacher, Elisha ben Abuyah, became a heretic and broke with the pattern of Jewish belief and practice, his colleagues ostracized him. But Rabbi Meir continued to visit his master and learn Torah from him. When Rabbi Meir's more conventional colleagues remonstrated with him on this score, he answered, "A pomegranate I found, its fruit I ate, its rind I cast off." It is in this spirit of open-mindedness that the new morality, as well as the older tradition, should be approached.

4

THE PURSUIT OF HAPPINESS
An Inalienable Right

The biblical thinker Ecclesiastes regarded the desire for happiness as the most powerful impulse in human nature. Since God has created man, it is He who has implanted this desire in the human breast. Koheleth accordingly comes to the apparently radical conclusion that satisfying this desire means obedience to the will of God. This is the basic message of his remarkably modern book, which charmed its way into the biblical canon, overriding any opposition stemming from the author's generally unconventional approach to life. To be sure, when Koheleth speaks of "eating and drinking," he is not counseling debauchery, as a reading of his entire book makes abundantly clear. The phrase is his mode of expressing the conviction that the enjoyment of life is a Divine imperative. He writes:

> There is no greater good for man than eating and drinking and giving himself joy in his labour. Indeed, I have seen that this is from the hand of God.
> Here is what I have discovered: it is meet and proper for a man to eat, drink and enjoy himself in return for the toil he undergoes under the sun in the scant years God has given him, for that is man's portion and not long will he remember the days of his life. Indeed, every man to whom

God has given wealth and possessions and granted the power to enjoy them, taking his share and rejoicing in his labour, that is the gift of God, for it is God who provides him with the joy in his heart.

Therefore I praise joy, for there is no other good for man under the sun but to eat, drink, and be joyful and have this accompany him in his toil, during the days of his life, which God has given beneath the sun.

> Go, then, eat your bread with joy
> And drink your wine with a glad heart,
> For God has already approved your actions.
> At all times let your clothes be white,
> And oil on your head not be lacking.
> Enjoy life with the woman whom you love,
> Through all the vain days of your life,
> Which God has given you under the sun,
> Throughout your brief days,
> For that is your reward in life
> For your toil under the sun.

Whatever you are able to do, do with all your might, for there is neither action nor thought nor knowledge nor wisdom in the grave towards which you are moving.

> Sweet is the light
> And it is good for the eyes
> To see the sun!
> For if a man live many years,
> Let him rejoice in them all,
> And remember that the days of darkness will be many,
> And that everything thereafter is nothingness.
> Rejoice, young man, in your youth,
> And let your heart cheer you in your youthful days.
> Follow the impulses of your heart
> And the desires of your eyes,
> And know that for all this,
> God will call you to account.[1]

Koheleth has been cited at some length because, more than any other biblical writer, he is concerned with the goals of life that the individual should set for himself. To be sure, Koheleth is highly unconventional in his life philosophy, but the conviction that happiness is a legitimate goal of human life, ordained and willed by God, who has created the blessings of the world, is not limited to him. It permeates all the pages of the Hebrew Bible. Thus, the Book of Psalms, which is the mirror of popular Jewish piety, amply reflects this outlook. No term is more characteristic of its approach to life than the Hebrew word *ashrei*, "happy." Though not limited to this book, it occurs twenty-four times in Psalms: "Happy is the man," "Happy is the people," "Happy are they whose life is blameless," "Happy is he who fears God."

This clothing of the hedonistic principle is to be met with in language that recalls Koheleth; the conventional Book of Proverbs counsels:

> Hear, my son, and be wise,
> And walk in the ways of your heart.
> (23:19)

Similarly, the Apocryphal Book of Ben Sira, whose general outlook is traditional, makes the enjoyment of life a duty:

> My son, if you have the means, treat yourself well,
> For there is no pleasure in the grave,
> And there is no postponement of death.[2]

Judaism was always characterized by an abundance of competing sects and parties who vigorously fought with one another on various elements of belief and practice. Yet virtually all these factions held fast to the basic conception that well-being in this world would reward those loyal to the particular teaching of the group. Thus the Dead Sea sectarians, bitterly opposed to the official religious establishment centered in Jerusalem during the two centuries before the destruction of the Temple, promised all who would walk in "the ways of truth" that their reward would be "health and abundant well-being with long life and fruition of seed, along with eternal blessings and ever-lasting joy in the life ever-lasting, and a crown of glory and a robe of honor amid life perpetual."[3]

Even more striking are the words of the Babylonian Sage, Samuel, of the third century, cited in the Talmud:

Seize hold and eat, seize hold and drink, for this world whence we depart is like a wedding feast.[4]

Samuel's great contemporary Rab expresses the same sentiment in typically religious language:

Every man must render an account before God of all the good things he beheld in life and did not enjoy.[5]

Not very different is the spirit of the utterance by Rabbi Simon ben Yohai, who said, "Beauty, strength, riches, honor, wisdom, old age, the hoary head, and children—all these are proper for the righteous and proper for the world."[6] The rabbis were, of course, keenly aware of the suffering that is part of the human estate. After enumerating the material deprivation that a scholar may have to undergo, they nevertheless declare, "If you experience all these hardships you are happy in this world and it is well with you in the world to come."[7]

However, deeply rooted as the desire for happiness is in the human psyche, it is rarely satisfied. Primarily for this reason, philosophers and religious teachers have often attempted to suppress the instinct or, better still, to stamp it out root and branch. The most consistent effort in this direction is to be found in Buddhism, which regards the desire for happiness both as an illusion and as the source of all evil. Accordingly, it teaches that the highest happiness is Nirvana, the total elimination of desire and of the misery that follows upon nonattainment.

Because the attainment of happiness is beset with frustration, this point of view has a strong appeal for all sensitive human beings. Moralists in the West, and not merely as in the East, have often taught a similar approach to life, urging the surrender of life's pleasures as unworthy and, in any case, unattainable.

As we have already seen, this ascetic approach is prominent

in classical Christianity and lies at the base of celibacy and monasticism. Nor is asceticism lacking in Judaism. It comes to the fore particularly in periods of chaos or oppression, when life's possibilities seem tragically limited and man's capacities for coping with these problems all but useless.

The dominant tradition in Judaism, however, did not follow in this direction, adopting instead an attitude of yea-saying to life and its potentialities. The conviction that the joys of the world are worth seeking and enjoying is laid down in the first chapter of Genesis, which declares that "God saw all that He had made, and behold it was very good." The full purpose of God in creating the world may be veiled from man, but it is clear that it is His will that His children enjoy its blessings during their sojourn upon it, "He created it [i.e., the world], not for chaos but for human habitation."(Isa. 45:18)

Moreover, Judaism finds it intolerable that a just God would willingly bring suffering upon the righteous. The English philosopher and essayist Francis Bacon declared, "Prosperity is the blessing of the Old Testament; adversity of the New." He meant this to be a criticism of the Hebrew Bible as against the Christian Scriptures. But Judaism has no quarrel with his judgment. Prosperity is a blessing in a world which God its Creator has pronounced to be very good.

Moreover, the Jewish tradition has been keenly aware of the dangers inherent in passively submitting to pain without necessity and yielding to suffering without protest. Whether the religions of the Far East were a prime cause for the poverty, squalor, and disease of the masses in India and China or, on the contrary, were the expression of the despair induced by these massive ills may be subject to argument. What is certain is that the Hebrew Prophets would have found these extremes of destitution and luxury morally intolerable and religiously an affront to the God of righteousness in whose name they spoke. The entire thrust of the prophetic tradition underscored the truth that "rebellion to tyrants means obedience to God." The rabbis taught that man is God's co-partner in the work of creation. The daily liturgy reminds the worshipper that he must serve his Maker by striving to perfect the world after the pattern of the Kingdom of God.

However, the Messianic Age has not yet dawned, and in an imperfect world man's reach is always greater than his grasp. In the words of Koheleth, "All the toil of man is for his mouth, yet his appetite is not satisfied."(Eccles. 6:7) Hence, the goal of Jewish ethics is to teach men to moderate their desires within acceptable limits. Not abstinence from life's pleasures, but their sensible enjoyment, is the proper course for human beings to adopt. The rabbis of the Mishnah urged contentment as representing true riches: "Who is rich, he who is content with his lot."[8] Maimonides makes "the golden mean," the avoidance of extremes of behavior, the cornerstone of his entire ethical system.[9] It is from the perspective of this article of faith—that life is to be enjoyed—that we propose to examine the new morality and its effect on human life in our times. In modern times, the Hasidic teacher Rabbi Michael put it in striking fashion, "I thank God that I never needed anything until I had it."

In sum, Jewish tradition is poles apart from that of the English Puritans of the seventeenth century, whom Macaulay may have slandered by his remark that they were opposed to the sport of bear-baiting, not because it caused pain to the bear, but because it gave pleasure to the spectators. Nor would it share the pessimism inherent in Alexander Woollcott's complaint, "All the things I really like to do are either immoral, illegal, or fattening."

The affirmative attitude in Jewish tradition toward life's pleasures is not limited to the Haggadah, the religious and ethical teaching embodied in the rabbinic literature. It entered into Jewish law and found expression in Jewish practice. One of the most remarkable features of normative Judaism, unique to the tradition, is its elaborate system of benedictions. Special blessings are ordained to be pronounced before the enjoyment of food or drink, on witnessing the power and majesty of nature, or of thunder and lightning, or on meeting human beings possessing outstanding wisdom or beauty. The system is climaxed by the blessing for the gift of life itself, repeated on every festival and at each joyous experience, the *sheheheyanu*, which praises God, "Who has kept us in life and preserved us and permitted us to reach this day."

Now the avowed purpose of the sexual revolution is to increase the happiness of men and women and to decrease their misery. In making human happiness its *summum bonum*, the new morality has adopted an ethical standard which per se is by no means inconsistent with religion. If it is really achieving this result, even if it involves changing accepted patterns of behavior, one cannot rationally object to the rise of alternate life styles. The history of culture offers untold instances where deeply ingrained attitudes and practices from the past become outmoded under changed conditions and fall into desuetude. Moral and legal codes are not immune to change; new conditions and new insights modify these as well. If these new patterns add to the sum total of human welfare, they cannot be dismissed out of hand as outrageous, blasphemous, or immoral.

Human nature is so constituted that men cannot adopt and sustain a given course of conduct unless they are convinced that their behavior is right. The Nazis had a rationale even for the unspeakable horrors that they perpetrated upon defenseless men, women, and children in the millions. The sexual revolution is obviously not to be compared to the bestiality of Nazism. But it, too, has its ethical rationale, with regard both to its practitioners and to those that are affected by it. Those who adopt the new morality for themselves would doubtless accept the touchstone for morality proposed by Ernest Hemingway: "I only know that what is moral is what you feel good after and what is immoral is what you feel bad after." I believe that this definition can hardly be improved upon—one has only to understand the meaning of the adverb "after." How much "after"? Five minutes after, two hours, a day, a week or a month, one year, or five, or ten? Apply this test to any given course of conduct, not to the moment after, but to a longer span of time, and the definition is quite satisfactory.

Far better known is the golden rule of the new morality as it impinges upon others—*everything is permitted so long as no one gets hurt.* The guiding principle of the new morality is the ideal of freedom, the right of men and women to enter into intimate interpersonal relationships on the basis of their mutual desires without any external constraint and to terminate them as well on the same basis. The liaison of two people drawn to each other by some form of attraction is morally justified, the new morality maintains, irrespective of any marriage bond into which either or both principals may have entered previously with another person. It is contended that intimate sexual relations between men and women outside of conventional marriage are at least as legitimate as the traditional pattern. In the view of many of its advocates, the new morality is superior in creating happy men and women. It has produced two characteristic life styles widespread in our day. The first is the extramarital liaison, in which at least one of the participants is married to another partner. It is to be met with principally in middle-aged and older people. The other, more frequent among young people, is that of two people living together with no intention of marriage. Each of these two patterns will be examined in greater detail later in this book, but a brief evaluation of both life patterns in the light of the two criteria for happiness cited above is in order.

Consider the sweet young girl of eighteen who "shacks up" with her boy friend. She may be ecstatically happy now and tomorrow and even the day after. She will still be sweet, but not quite so young, ten years later, or twenty. What will be her lot and her prospects when new sweet young things come into her boy friend's orbit and there is no legal, social, or ethical deterrent to his forsaking his former love? The power of sexual desire is undeniable, but not its permanence.

No one would seriously maintain that the dissolution of a

love affair is a pleasurable experience. At least one partner is bound to be hurt, and probably both, because feelings of guilt are a potent source of pain for all but the most callous of natures.

It is true that extramarital relations are as old as history. The appeal of these affairs was clearly understood by the biblical Wisdom writer, who quotes the seductress as saying to her victim, "Stolen water is sweet and bread eaten in secret is pleasant." To be sure, the Sage warns the young man, "He does not know that the dead are there, that her guests are in the depths of Sheol."(Prov. 9:17, 18) Nonetheless, the new morality has undoubtedly relaxed many inner inhibitions against the practice, while the new mobility has removed many external obstacles in its path. Obviously, comparative figures for the past and statistical data for the present on premarital and extramarital sex are unavailable. Yet most observers would agree that both categories have increased in extent and achieved a greater acceptance today under the aegis of the sexual revolution. Are these affairs an example of a relationship where no one gets hurt? To be sure, the involved pair generally seek to establish a many-faceted program of clandestine living, in order to keep the truth from the innocent party, but they rarely succeed. In addition, the deceptions they must practice and the restrictions on their freedom of movement and activity hardly contribute to their lasting joy, even aside from the guilt feelings they experience. In Ingmar Bergman's masterly film *Scenes from a Marriage,* a modern marriage is depicted with extraordinary sympathy and depth of insight. We see the cruelties and falsehoods that become second nature for the straying husband and the agony that results for the wronged partner. But we do not need the testimony of art; life offers its own impressive evidence at every turn.

In these situations, society is generally concerned with the innocent husband or wife. Sympathy is expressed for the suffering experienced by the innocent spouse, the collapse of self-esteem, the sense of betrayal and loneliness as the whole world collapses for the unsuspecting partner. The feeling of outrage may express itself in a wide variety of ways, running the gamut from mute suffering and voiceless agony to violent attacks and loud vituperation. The moralist may interpose with considerable justice that sympathy should be directed to no one else in a love triangle, and that the participants in an extramarital relationship deserve whatever misery their actions may bring upon their own heads.

But if we seek to assess the full effects of the new behavior patterns on the sum total of human happiness, we must register the fact that even for the erring partners the quality of the love experience in an extramarital relationship is gravely warped. For it is the essence of love at its fullest that it seeks to express itself in every aspect of life without restriction or limitation, in public as well as in private, in social intercourse as well as in intimate sexual activity. Lovers enjoy experiencing together the beauties of nature, the charm of music, the glory of art, the stimulus of the stage, not to speak of the untold number of mundane and minor experiences like walking or shopping together which enter into the program of a husband and wife living together. Manifestly, most of these experiences are impossible for participants in an affair which must be carried on with a greater or lesser degree of secrecy and maintained under the perpetual fear of discovery.

The types of relationships we have been describing have had important consequences, or at least are marked by significant concomitants in many other aspects of contemporary life. While these will be analyzed in greater detail in a later section, they are highly relevant to our present concern because they shed light on the fundamental question of the degree to which the sexual revolution has contributed to the enhancement of life in our times.

Undoubtedly, the most obvious phenomenon in the area of personal relationships, which, incidentally, is easily measured, is divorce. Judaism is realistic enough to understand that a bad marriage may be worse than a divorce. Hence, it regards divorce, not as a sin, but as a tragedy. For divorce is a tombstone on the grave of hopes that once lived in the hearts of two human beings who looked forward to finding happiness together. Obviously, the underlying causes of divorce, as well as its external symptoms, are as varied as human beings themselves. But human nature is fairly constant and yet divorces are skyrocketing. Obviously a new element has entered the picture. In modern divorces it is often not the inability of the partners to adjust to one another but their unwillingness to do so, because they demand instant gratification, a "fun relationship," a life without obligation or involvement.

Statistics make dreary reading unless we see the human beings behind the figures. The history of divorce, simply as an index of human unhappiness, is devastating. In 1867 there were 10,000 divorces in the United States; in 1916 the number had grown elevenfold to 112,000; in 1929 it had again almost doubled, to 201,000. The economic depression which followed produced a temporary drop, due largely to the cost of securing a divorce in the face of the archaic laws prevailing in the United States, but the upward trend of divorces was resumed shortly thereafter. In 1937, there were 250,000 divorces; in 1940, 300,000; in 1948, 415,000. More significantly, in the seventy-year period from 1870 to 1940, the American population increased threefold, marriages fourfold, and divorces twentyfold.

The process has continued with ever greater momentum. In 1960, there were twenty-six divorced persons under thirty-five for every one thousand married persons under thirty-five; in 1965, twenty-nine; in 1970, forty; in 1975, seventy-nine. In the United States at present, there is approximately one divorce for every three marriages. In Great Britain, one marriage out of four ends in divorce.[10]

An acute social historian summarizes the changes of a half century with wit as well as with accuracy in these words: "Most of the elderly *grandes dames* at the resorts have lived from a day when they had to leave the room when the subject of divorce was mentioned, to a day when a wedding invitation has only approximately a fifty-fifty chance of being issued by parents of the same name as the bride."[11]

The situation is even graver with youngsters. Fully 40 percent of American marriages involve teenagers, and of these teenage marriages, 50 percent end in divorce in five years.[12]

Of late, a new fashion of "divorce parties" has sprung up. One cannot help feeling that the gaiety of such occasions is highly artificial, a whistling in the dark, a beating of drums to drown out the pain and the bitterness in the hearts of the principals.

The husband and the wife may or may not be happy at the prospect of their freedom from one another—and in any event, they may well deserve their lot. But increasingly divorces occur where children, including very young children, are involved, whose innocence is beyond doubt. Few children of divorce can grow up without undergoing various traumatic experiences. The psychological hazards of life in a chaotic world are increased manyfold in the absence of the security, however limited, that two parents can supply. The antagonism between the father and the mother, even when their relationship is "polite" and "civilized," always creates a tug-of-war in the heart of the youngster.

Nor is it true that in a divorce both principals are treated equally, even if a fair financial settlement is agreed to by all parties concerned. When, as is usually the case, the mother wins the custody of the children, it is usually a hollow victory. It is upon her that most of the burdens of child-rearing fall. It is she who must sacrifice her leisure and her freedom of movement and association in order to be at home with her children on evenings, holidays, and weekends. When the father is given custody, the burden is shifted to him; it can never be equal for both.

Social-service agencies are, of course, aware of the problem and try to meet it as best they can. Increasingly, they have set up special programs for the "single mother." The problem has been described in these terms by a social worker at the Jewish Family Service in Philadelphia: "Suddenly removed from the security and status of wife and homemaker, usually either by desertion or divorce, such women come to the agency 'overwhelmed by feelings of isolation and loneliness, sexual frustration, hopelessness, anxiety, fear, inadequacy, guilt, failure and immobilizing anger.' "

The one-parent family, going one stage beyond the nuclear family, is one of the most striking social phenomena of our times. There are no broken homes in America any longer. One child in seven is now raised in a one-parent home. According to the U.S. Census Bureau, 8 million children under the age of eighteen are raised by a mother alone, and 800,000 by a father alone.[13] It is the result either of desertion, divorce, or illegitimacy, and its tragic consequences for the children involved have not been fully plumbed. The single parent who must earn a living to support the family or who is driven to seek occasional pleasure and relaxation away from the home is unable to supervise or protect the child against the dangers of modern living. The horror of children who had been left alone being burned in apartments is one sensational aspect of the problem. The spiraling number of cases of child abuse and child murder by the one parent is a lurid index of the bitterness and frustration induced by the need for bringing up a child single-handed. The failure of the public-school system with many children stems from the absence of motivation and supervision particularly common in homes of this character. The absence of religious training and moral guidance plays a part in the growing incidence of juvenile crime on the streets.

The problem of the one-parent family is compounded when, as is often the case, the mother is herself a child desperately needing to be cared for, instead of being saddled with the awesome responsibility of caring for another helpless human being.[14] Raising a child to be human is no easy task, even for two parents. When there is only one parent, who generally must work, it places an all-but-impossible burden upon him or her.

What is the lot that awaits the fortunate escapees from an unhappy marriage? After the first fine rapture induced by the new freedom subsides, it is discovered that paradise has not yet been regained. An enterprising reporter interviewed at random a dozen young women in New York City. The consensus among them was that "the swinging life was too superficial and the career-oriented life too lonely." A fear of divorce was one area upon which most of the twelve women agreed.

They also had several other things in common, including a loathing of singles bars as a place to meet men, a belief that New York men are wary of getting involved in "relationships," and contempt for the so-called one-night stands.[15]

More recently, it is being recognized that neither is the lot of the single or newly single male a happy one. The swinging life is not as exhilarating as it appears in the feature stories of the glossy magazines. Loneliness, artificial merriment, perpetual searching after new stimuli, these are hardly the ingredients of a happy life. The situation of the single male has been described in these words:

> Depression, addiction, venereal disease, chronic disability, psychiatric treatment, loneliness, insomnia, institutionalization, poverty, "discrimination," unemployment and nightmares—these are "the dirty sheets and unmade mornings" of the majority of swinging single males.[16]

This picture has been challenged as too extreme, but that it has a considerable measure of truth can hardly be denied.

After due allowance is made for the various difficulties encountered by married couples that impel them to divorce, it cannot be denied that the rapidly escalating tide of broken marriages is, in substantial measure, the consequence of the new morality, which may, therefore, be charged with increasing the burden of unhappiness to all concerned.

One of the principal rationales advanced in favor of non-marital unions is the availability of contraceptive devices. If young people, the argument runs, could live together before embarking upon a permanent relationship, they would be all the more mature for the experience. This philosophy undergirds the increasing attention being given on college campuses to guiding the sex activity of the students.[17] The purpose is to minimize the necessity for advertisements like the one that appeared in a college student newspaper: "MALES—My girlfriend needs an early marriage. For further info, call . . . and tell where to reach you and we will contact you." Moreover, there would be no risk of children coming into the world whose parents are not ready for them. The contention has proved abysmally mistaken. The wider dissemination of contraceptive devices has led to no decrease in the number of illegitimate births. On the contrary, illegitimacy is steadily on the rise. In 1950, illegitimate live births in the United States represented 3.9 percent of all births; in 1955, 4.5 percent; in 1960, 5.3 percent; in 1965, 7.7 percent; in 1970, 10.7 percent; in 1971, 11.3 percent; in 1972, 12.4 percent; in 1973, 13.3 percent.[18]

Nearly three out of every ten teenage American girls who have premarital intercourse become pregnant, with 35 percent of the pregnant girls marrying before their babies are born. Nearly one half of all unmarried women have had sexual intercourse by the age of nineteen. Of the births to teenage girls that have resulted from first pregnancies, 45 percent are illegitimate. Six out of every ten births among girls in this age group were conceived before marriage.[19] The British figures are even higher. It is claimed that six out of ten brides *of all ages* in Great Britain are pregnant.[20]

Recent surveys indicate that 80 percent of all illegitimate babies are now being retained by their mothers, who undertake to rear them, instead of giving them up for adoption. One reason for this dramatic change is that the stigma attached to illegitimate children has been considerably relaxed. Another is the fact that a woman today has a better prospect of supporting herself by gainful employment.

The rising tide of illegitimate births is matched by the spiraling numbers of abortions. Many married women utilize abortion as a way of preventing the increase in the size of their families, though mechanical and chemical methods of family limitation are available. To a much higher degree, abortion is resorted to by women who become pregnant outside the marriage bond. The moral climate that apparently makes abortion seem a more attractive option than contraception for many women will engage our attention later, as will the presumed status and rights of the foetus, which is a subject of passionate argument today. At times, too, abortion is resorted to when other means of birth control fail. What seems clear is that abortion frequently brings death and crippling to the poor married women and unmarried girls who fall into the hands of butchers and charlatans. Even when abortion is legal and proper medical and sanitary safeguards are taken, it remains a traumatic experience, leaving a heritage of guilt and sadness behind. Whether or not an abortion is legal or moral, neither or both, it is clearly a tragedy.

Another totally unexpected development has been the steady rise of prostitution. It has become a major industry in our cities, protected by vast economic interests and organized crime, against which citizens and public officials find themselves helpless. The motion picture and the television screen, the newspaper and the magazine, have made "hustler" and "pimp" household words today. Advocates of the new morality prophesied that the prevalence of free relations between the sexes would reduce the incidence of prostitution. That has emphatically not proved to be the case. Perhaps there has been an expansion of the market for sexuality, whether it be free or compensated.

A bold effort was recently made to combine the "best features" of prostitution and extramarital relationships, while avoiding any possibility of personal involvement. *The New York Times* published an advertisement occupying almost a full page for a book entitled *Contract Cohabitation, an Alternative to Marriage.*[21] "Contract cohabitation" is defined as:

An eating and living arrangement, based on a written or unwritten employment contract . . .
All contract terms are defined by the employer and accepted by the employee in advance . . . including salary, free hours, annual vacations, social and work activities outside the CC relationship . . .
A lifestyle that demands *both* partners be strong, independent, even selfish adults able to stand alone—without being lonely.

A few years ago, medical authorities were convinced that venereal disease, already controlled by prophylactic drugs, was on the road to elimination. This expectation, too, has been disappointed. The official U.S. Government figures in thousands for all venereal disease, outside of the military, are 513 in 1950, 362 in 1955, 384 in 1960, 440 in 1965, 693 in 1970, and 931 in 1973.[22]

It is not being suggested that all these tragic expressions of sexual mores in our time are to be imputed entirely to the new morality. Divorce, marital infidelity, illegitimacy, abortion, and venereal disease have been characteristic of the human condition for centuries. But the rapid rise in the incidence of these phenomena may, in substantial measure at least, fairly be laid at the door of the new morality and the attitudes it has fostered. At the very least, it has not improved upon the *status quo ante.*

The massive ills of our age are legion. Poverty, racial tensions, corruption, greed, violence, and crime at home, and the threat of war and nuclear destruction abroad—all tend to undermine the joy in life for young and old. That so large a percentage of our population hungers desperately for a modicom of serenity and peace in life is clear from the increasing use of hallucinatory drugs, marijuana, hard drugs, pep pills, and sedatives by millions of men, women, and young people. Drugs that seek to induce a temporary euphoria, and alcohol, which blots out the real world, are equally pernicious. These dangerous addictives hold in their grip millions of men and women who have not experienced divorce, illegitimate births, or abortions and yet are unhappy. But it is probable that sexual maladjustments play an important part in driving men and women to drug addiction and alcoholism, both of which are on the increase. Their proliferation in contemporary society indicates that the new patterns are not noticeably increasing the amount of personal happiness available to the age.

The happiness of individual men and women must undoubtedly be our prime concern, but there are also larger interests of society as a whole that cannot be ignored and that may well be threatened by the sexual revolution. Freud has taught us that sex is the libido, the life-force which, when sublimated, becomes a source of creativity and achievement in science, literature, music, and art. That civilization depends upon the sexual impulse is an insight nineteen centuries older than Freud. The rabbis of the Talmud had declared, "Were it not for the sexual impulse, no man would build a house or marry a woman or engage in an occupation."[23] If sex alone becomes the *summum bonum* and love is banished from human experience, or, if that proves impossible, if it is derided, denigrated, and suppressed, what effect does this have upon the creative capacities of men and women? Where can culture, the noblest product of the human spirit, derive its strength and impetus, if love is outlawed? If responsibility and involvement are eliminated, the relationship of men and women is reduced to that of animals in heat, for mutuality of concern is the essence of the human condition.

I believe that the problems raised by the new dispensation have not been exaggerated or overstated in our discussion. It is not merely that the present practices run counter to religious preachment or traditional morality. Some observers would argue that the new patterns of sex conduct have made people worse and more miserable. What is clear, at least, is that they have not made people better or happier.

After all allowances are made for the weaknesses of the traditional sex code in theory and in practice, and due regard is shown for the high motives that inspired many of the advocates of the new morality, one conclusion seems to us unassailable. An approach is needed to love, sex, and marriage that will draw upon the best of both systems and be better adapted to our present condition than either. In this enterprise of exploration the millennial experience of the Jewish people, embodied in its tradition and way of life, has significant resources to offer, not only to adherents of Judaism, but to all men and women everywhere.

Resources
in the Jewish Tradition

5

SOME GUIDING PRINCIPLES

A Glance Backward

It may be worthwhile to summarize our discussion thus far, in order to indicate the thrust and direction of our quest. We began with a survey of the traditional family, which has undergone many transformations from ancient through medieval to modern times, but which has remained basically male dominated to our day. We then proceeded to describe the new life styles emerging in the second half of the twentieth century. Basically, they are characterized by an insistence upon the total equality of men and women in every area of experience, upon the right to untrammeled freedom of action in interpersonal relationships, and upon the enthronement of pleasure, or, to use a popular Americanism, "fun" as the *summum bonum* of life. When these doctrines are applied to love and sex, the current code of behavior emerges.

An analysis was then offered of the factors that led to the rise of the sexual revolution. It was pointed out that it had deep roots in the cultural background of Western civilization and the rise of humanism. These new ideas could be put into practice only in modern times with the emergence of new socio-economic conditions in general and a new status for women in particular, resulting from both technological progress and the rationalization of industry. The new morality is clearly radical and iconoclastic as against the traditional sex code of the Christian world. Yet we have sought to demonstrate that, paradoxical as it may seem, the sexual revolution has its roots in classical Christianity, having accepted from it the dichotomy between love and sex, but inverting the hierarchy of values.

We then tried to evaluate the results of the new morality in contemporary society, the degree to which it has achieved its goal of enhancing human joy and well-being. Even without regard to traditional religious and moral standards, a survey of the current scene suggests that, in many respects, the new morality has actually increased the sum total of human misery. At the very least, it has not contributed significantly to the happiness of modern men and women.

It is clear that neither the old code nor the new pattern offers a definitive solution to the manifold problems in this area. Our commitment should be neither to the new because it is fashionable nor to the old because it is venerable, but to the good.

One of the most seductive temptations is the call of nostalgia. Nostalgia is a besetting weakness—and characteristically a major industry—of our age. It is being offered as a remedy for all our ills, but, like other nostrums, it has little real efficacy. In spite of the insistent voices dispensing the old-time religion, the old-time economics, and the old-time morality, they can serve but little for grappling with contemporary problems, many of which are without precedent in human experience in their intensity and scope. It is not true that the simpler days of yesteryear were better than the present. They seem better only because memory tends to blur the sharp outlines of past miseries. Mercifully, we who are alive today cannot experience and relive the agonies suffered by millions of men and women in the past, which they carried to their graves—loveless marriages, sick wives and mothers, at best overworked and oppressed, at worst tyrannized and physically maltreated. Who can estimate the buried treasures of talent and genius among women, generally unsuspected, nearly always crushed, never destined to find expression? To be sure, men were also victims of tyranny and oppression in all stages of history, but always there were some fortunate few who escaped and succeeded in fulfilling their gifts. In the case of women, almost everyone in every generation was a victim.

We easily forget that nearly all men and women in the past were crushed by the sheer mass of boredom, fatigue, illness, and premature death that was their lot. If we broaden Thoreau's statement to include the other half of the human race, he described the past far more truly than the present-day advocates of nostalgia when he declared, "The mass of men lead lives of quiet desperation." The truth is that the good old days were not good when they were not old. We could not return to the past even if we wished, and we would not wish it even if we could. There has been no mass stampede back to the Middle Ages by the glorifiers of medievalism in the Western world. Nor have the practitioners of Jewish nostalgia, who describe the halcyon days of the pre-Emancipation ghetto, rushed to return their citizenship papers.

There is another sobering observation that must be kept in mind, particularly in an area so prone to fantasy and dream images as sex; anticipated joys are rarely matched by their realities. No social or legal system can fully satisfy human beings and deal adequately with their hopes, their fears, their desires, their joys, and their frustrations. This holds true of past patterns as well as of present programs.

Finally, we must be on guard against throwing out the baby with the bath water by condemning the new morality lock, stock, and barrel because of its lack of success in achieving its objectives. On the contrary, we must approach our fellow human beings with insight and compassion. This is particularly true with regard to our young people, whose destiny it is to grow up and live in a world of terror and chaos, against the background of which they clutch at whatever joy and security they can find in intimacy with a loving companion. The aspirations, fears, and goals of the new morality deserve to be treated with respect. Its code of practice must be studied with genuine sympathy, in order to discover to what degree it can genuinely advance human happiness.

We must, therefore, approach this area above all others with genuine humility and diffidence, in the fine Hebrew phrase, *kesho' el v^{e}lo k^{e}meshibh,* "as one who raises questions rather than lays down answers." What is needed is a process of discrimination and selection.

The Nature of Judaism

If we are to make any significant progress, we need to tap new resources of experience and insight. In particular, Judaism has a significant contribution to make. It represents the oldest living tradition of the Western world; it is the distillation of millennia of experience, observation, and reflection, having survived and functioned under the greatest possible variety of conditions. The tradition begins with the semi-nomadism of the patriarchal and desert periods and progresses through the agricultural and early urban stages of civilization. It spans the ancient Oriental empires of Egypt, Babylonia, and Assyria, the Greco-Roman world, as well as the medieval and modern epochs. It has confronted and survived an ancient slave economy, medieval feudalism, and modern laissez-faire capitalism. It has continued to function in the democratic welfare state and has shown surprising vitality in the face of Communism. It gives every sign of continuing to live in whatever social, economic, and political systems the future may develop.

In order to utilize the Jewish tradition significantly, as a stimulus and not as a sedative, we require a true perception of the nature of Judaism. There are several important principles that must be kept in mind in this connection.

1. One of the most frequently encountered terms in the area of group relations and public policy is the "Judeo-Christian

tradition." The validity of the concept has often been challenged by theologians, particularly in Judaism, and a not inconsiderable literature has grown up on the subject. Nevertheless, I believe that the term possesses a substantial measure of validity. Not merely the proverbial visitor from Mars, but an adherent of Far Eastern religion, like Buddhism or Hinduism, who is observing Judaism and Christianity for the first time and noting the elements they have in common, as well as their differences, might well regard them as two branches of a single tree. Far more fruitful than affirming or denying the concept is delineating the contents and limits of the traditions of Judaism and Christianity.[1]

However, it is particularly in the field of personal morality, as well as in several others, that Jewish teaching diverges most fundamentally from that of Christianity. Thus, unlike Christianity, Judaism cannot be held responsible for the tragic bifurcation between love and sex to which so much of the current moral chaos must be attributed. This is true for two reasons. The major one is that, as we shall see, Judaism emphatically rejects the division between love and sex. The minor one is that it is Christianity, and not Judaism, "the despised faith," as Judah Halevi called it, that has been dominant in Western civilization. It is in the area of sexual ethics that the Jewish tradition has something distinctive and valuable to contribute to the world.

2. Moreover, no matter how much information we amass about Judaism, we do not understand its true nature unless we recognize that it has had a history. That is to say, it has not only survived but has continued to develop through the passing of time. Social, economic, and political changes in the environment and the consequent emergence of new problems, the influence of new cultural trends, and the birth of new insights and attitudes, all have their impact on every generation. The factors of the present interact with the tradition of the past and the product becomes the next stage in the history of the tradition, ready to undergo the same process of development

anew. Growth embodies two elements of continuity and change, and both have been present, though in varying degrees, in every period of Jewish history.

3. Judaism has a comprehensive world-view expressed in a system of beliefs, and it also possesses an all-embracing way of life embodied in a ritual system and an ethical code. Often misunderstood both within and without the Jewish community, it is Halakah, Jewish ritual and ethical law, that has fashioned the character of the Jewish people and guaranteed its survival. The nature of Jewish tradition may be encapsulated as follows: growth is the law of life and law is the life of Judaism.

Hence, Jewish tradition must be pictured, not as a rivulet, but as a mighty stream with many currents and crosscurrents, and even countercurrents, both large and small. Both the major as well as the minor influences must be evaluated properly if we are to find it a fountain of living waters rather than a mass of congealed ice.

4. It must also be recognized that not all stages of the Jewish historic experience are of equal significance. The greatest creative periods were the eras of the Bible and the Talmud, when the Jewish people enjoyed political independence or autonomy, and were in lively contact with the great Oriental and Greco-Roman civilizations. In the Middle Ages, when Jews lived under far more constricted conditions, their outlook was influenced by the narrower perspectives of medieval Christianity and by the tragic limitations and perils of their own ghetto existence. Hence, in the Middle Ages, there emerged a Jewish attitude toward sex and the family which was a mixture of the life-affirming biblical-talmudic attitude on the one hand and the medieval emphasis upon asceticism and the negation of the natural on the other.

5. In ascertaining the teaching of the Jewish tradition, it is, therefore, important to ask not merely where Jewish tradition *stands*, but in what direction it *moves*. What is the spirit, the thrust of Jewish tradition? If we are not content to know Juda-

ism superficially, but seek to understand it from within, it is important to recognize it not as a point but a line, not merely as an event, or even a series of events, but as a process.

Law and Society

Because of the centrality of law in Judaism, some general observations on the relationship of law to society are in order. In view of two limitations which are inherent in law itself, we cannot depend exclusively upon law and its power for the creation of the good society. In a healthy and functioning society, law represents a lower rung of a ladder of which ethics is the highest. The Hebrew term "Halakah," which we have translated above as "law," encompasses more than law. Etymologically, the word means "a way of going," and thus it includes legal enactments and also ethical norms—both of which are indispensable.

1. First, *there will always be a tension between legal statutes and ethical standards.* At any particular time, the law tends to embody, however imperfectly, the ethical standards of an earlier age, because it takes time for new ethical norms to win general acceptance and become translated into legislation and judicial decision. While this process is going on, the attitudes of society continue to advance beyond the limits of existing codified law, so that the task of bringing the law up to the level of ethics must begin again, or—more accurately—must continue in a never-ending process. In relatively stable periods, when change is minimal, the gap will be less extensive and the tension between the law and the life of society less marked. In an age of rapid changes, the strains will be greater. Always, however, the tension is vital to the well-being of society, because it is the cutting edge of progress.

In the area of sex and marriage, the Jewish tradition exhibits a vital principle of the highest importance—*the tension between a legal structure relatively permissive and a standard in society relatively restrictive, with the balance between the two making for a viable life style.*

A case in point is afforded by the traditional Jewish attitude toward divorce, which will be discussed in detail in Chapter 7. Suffice it to note here that in talmudic law divorce is very easy to obtain, the initiative being vested in the husband. Virtually any reason, including incompatibility or culinary incompetence, is admissible as a basis for divorce. It is now becoming clear, on the basis of recent research, that during various periods in Jewish history women could sue for a divorce, even the ground "I don't love him" being acceptable. Jewish law can, therefore, be fairly described as permissive or liberal with regard to divorce. On the other hand, in traditional Jewish society, great emphasis was placed upon the sanctity and permanence of marriage, the term for betrothal, *"kiddushin,"* being interpreted as "holiness." As a result, marriages were stable and divorces were rare in traditional Jewish communities. Thus the tension between a liberal law and a conservative social attitude helped to preserve the structure of the family, but made it possible to dissolve the relationship if the marriage proved genuinely intolerable.

One more illustration of this creative tension is to be found in the area of male supremacy, which is discussed in Chapter 13. It is undeniable that Jewish law, which originated and developed in a male-centered society, enshrined the doctrine of male supremacy in every area. On the other hand, Jewish society accorded women a status far higher than the specific provisions of the law codes would suggest. To evaluate fairly the condition of women in Judaism, both law and life must be fully taken into account. The man's powers were extensive, according to the letter of the law. But ethical admonition and social standards limited them in practice and accorded the woman high status as an honored and influential personality.

That is not all. If Jewish law, both codified and customary, is studied historically, one discovers a two-pronged policy at work, one extending women's rights, the other circumscribing men's prerogatives. Thus the basic thrust of Jewish law, from the biblical age through the talmudic eras and the medieval period to our day, was in the direction of enhancing the status of women in life and in law. Not every authority and every age were equally energetic and creative in enhancing the status of women, but each period made its contribution to the goal. It is not being suggested that women have achieved equality in Jewish law, any more than they have in modern society as a whole. The process must go forward, but the goal is clear.

2. Second, by its very nature, *the law is and can be concerned only with physical actions and the punishment of violations. It is too gross an instrument to be able to cope with such subtleties as attitudes and emotions.* Thus the law can prescribe a penalty for the person "who strikes his father and his mother" (Ex. 21:19), but it cannot punish the man who hates his parents.

To be sure, men's and women's states of mind and feeling, their entire inner world, ultimately determine their actions and affect the external world of reality. Hence, people are always tempted to use the law for policing thoughts and attitudes. The attempt continues to be made time and time again, but always it is doomed to failure. When society yields to this temptation and attempts to legislate and punish in this area, tyranny results. Such phenomena as laws of thought control, seditious acts, and loyalty oaths lead to witch hunts and concentration camps, but never achieve their objective.

Pornography—A Case in Point

A striking illustration of this truth lies in the history of legal attempts to deal with obscenity. Pornography for profit, cool, calculating, and cynical, is a major industry in American today. Yet all efforts by the courts and the legislatures to frame a definition of obscenity that will screen out the purveyors of filth without undermining freedom of thought and expression for the genuine artist and thinker have proved a failure. The honest artist and writer gets caught in the net of the law, but the smut merchant is able to escape its toils and becomes enriched in the process.

In 1933, in the famous case involving James Joyce's novel, *Ulysses,* Judge Wooley ruled that a work is constitutionally protected unless it is "utterly without redeeming social value," even if the work taken as a whole lacks serious literary, artistic, political, or scientific value. The purveyors of pornography lost no time in injecting some teaspoons of "social significance" into their potpourri of filth and thus satisfied the law while their profits kept mounting.

This basically unworkable definition of obscenity was replaced by a new decision. In 1973, the U.S. Supreme Court ruled that whatever violates the moral standards and attitudes of a given community is obscene within the meaning of the law. Obviously, this test is all but impossible to apply with any clarity and consistency, since standards are shifting rapidly from year to year and from month to month, almost from day to day. That is not all. Granted that a film or a play is pornographic if it violates the community attitudes. But what are the boundaries of the "community"? Is it Times Square or New York City or the metropolitan area or a state in the union or an entire region, like the North, the West, the South? Are we to assume that moral standards are on a par with the varying cuisines of different sections of the country or the world?

What the courts have seemed unable to achieve is now being attempted by local executive ordinance. Pornographic entertainment and massage parlors are being restricted to specially designated areas. The establishment of the so-called combat zone in Boston, and adult areas and red-light districts proposed for other metropolitan centers, may well be voided by the courts. Even if they are not, they are scarcely likely to achieve their stated objective of preventing the spread of pornography into residential areas. Moreover, even if they succeed and these areas are declared constitutional, the remedy would almost be worse than the disease. It would be tantamount to licensing houses of prostitution and recognizing hard-core pornography as a legitimate business enterprise.

Faced by the failure to control such activities, some public officials and other citizens have suggested decriminalizing sexual solicitation and other related activities on the ground that they are victimless crimes, since the principals participate in them willingly.

The Sense of Sin

In truth, there are no victimless crimes; fundamentally, the participants themselves are victims. We cannot grasp the nature of such offenses if we approach them through the concept of legal crime. What is indispensable is the reintroduction of the concept of sin. This venerable insight has been largely abandoned in the modern world because of its theological character. It is indispensable, however, for dealing with a vast variety of social ills. A sin is an offense whether or not the perpetrator is apprehended, or whether another human being is the victim. Religion declares that sin is an offense against God, whose creatures we are and in whom we live and move and have our being. If, in deference to the reigning mood of the day, we seek to secularize the concept, at least partially, sin may be described as an offense against the doer, who will be faced with the inexorable consequences of his act devolving upon himself. Martin Buber has defined sin as what cannot be done with the whole being. An act which violates the body of a man or a woman and pollutes the soul is, therefore, a sin, even if it cannot be prevented by the policeman's club or punished by a jail sentence. To borrow a fine rabbinic phrase, "Sin diminishes the Image [of God]," in which man is created.[2]

Until very recently, modern psychology had succeeded in expunging from its vocabulary not only the theological term "sin" but even the more neutral term "guilt." To be sure, there were many men and women who came for psychiatric help or psychological guidance who were still afflicted with guilt feelings, but the function of the practitioner was to expunge those unhappy vestiges of an outmoded upbringing. In other words, guilt had no objective reality; guilt feelings existed only subjectively. Sin was imaginary.

Sin was not the only concept of traditional religion that modern psychology and psychiatry exorcised. Human beings were generally the victims either of poor heredity, a subhuman environment, or both. Since free will did not exist, responsibility was an illusion. Anna Russell expressed the dominant philosophy, perhaps in somewhat exaggerated form, in her "Aria from the Psychiatrist."

> At three I had a feeling
>   of ambivalence toward my brothers
> And so it follows naturally
>   I poisoned all my lovers.
> But now I'm happy I have learned
>   the lesson this has taught,
> That everything I do that's wrong
>   is someone else's fault.

After a few decades of trial and error, a reaction is beginning to set in among scientists. Increasing numbers of psychiatrists are recognizing that, far from obliterating guilt from human consciousness, it is important to recognize its existence and utilize it as a valuable therapeutic agent.[3] Various schools of contemporary psychiatry now speak of ego strength, reality therapy, or the rational-emotive control of behavior. They emphasize the importance of creating an internal locus of control in the patient and of seeking to inculcate the idea of delayed gratification. While practitioners like David Ausubel, O. Mowrer, William Glasser, and William Mainord have not restored the term "sin" to the psychologist's lexicon, they have, to all intents and purposes, rehabilitated the concept. For the offenses with which they are concerned are acts not punishable by law, and to a large degree, they fall within the purview of love and sex.

To revert to our concern, the law cannot be expected to deal satisfactorily with the entire area of interpersonal relations when no overt physical crime against another human being has been committed. The gross pincers of legal statute and judicial decision cannot take hold in this vast and delicate area of personal emotions and relationships.

It is here that the Jewish tradition can be of inestimable value in forging instruments for dealing with this subtle and sensitive area of human experience.

Significant Categories in Jewish Law

Much can be gleaned from the Aggadah, the vast corpus of religious thought and ethical admonition to be found in the pages of the Talmud and the Midrash. But there are also highly significant categories of thought to be found in the voluminous pages of rabbinic Halakah. As we have noted, the term is generally rendered "law," but it basically means "a way of going." Thus, it includes ethics as well as law, particularly when it is concerned with establishing the rationale for a given enactment or when it deals with matters beyond the reach of law. Moralists have often quoted the wisdom and insight of the Aggadah as guides to conduct. We believe, however, that the conceptual world of the Halakah contains significant categories which, to our knowledge, have not hitherto been invoked for dealing with personal and family morality. These categories, utilized either literally or symbolically, can be of inestimable help in formulating a relevant approach to the love and sex problems of the modern age.

Thus the Halakah has a category of offenses which it stigmatizes as sinful but not as criminal, "free from human punishment but forbidden,"[4] and "unpunishable by human courts but punishable by the heavenly court."[5] The Halakah describes acts and attitudes which, being internalized, are not subject to external enforcement as "matters entrusted to the heart."[6]

There are also acts which per se are permitted, but are declared forbidden as a safeguard against violating a closely related action which is prohibited. This the principle calls *seyag*, "a fence." To cite a familiar instance, the Sabbath is not ushered in nor does it end at sundown; it begins some seventeen minutes before sundown on Friday evening and does not end until the stars are visible on Saturday night. This "margin of immunity" is added to the Sabbath at its inception and conclusion to prevent any infraction.

Ethics, Principles, and Applications

Because Judaism is a revealed faith, it maintains the existence of universal principles of conduct. Such are the Golden Rule, the Ten Commandments, and the great utterances of the Prophets, like Micah's formulation, "He has told you, O man, what is good and what the Lord your God requires of you, to do justice, to love mercy, and to walk humbly with your God."(6:8) On the other hand, Judaism, in its most creative periods, those of the Bible and the Talmud, never succumbed to the tendency encountered in other religions to formulate dogmas and abstract norms of conduct. The Torah, the Prophets, and the Sages took their point of departure from concrete life situations which were never lost sight of. In the Jewish tradition, dedication to high ideals went hand in hand with a sympathetic understanding of human nature and a realistic awareness of the facts of existence.

As a result, there was no need for Judaism to adopt the stance of "situation ethics" popular in many quarters today which maintains that there are no general rules to which we may turn for guidance and that standards of conduct should emerge out of each particular situation. On the contrary, Judaism has always maintained that there are fundamental standards and ideals that are normative, and that without them we have chaos, "each man doing what is right in his own eyes," the situation prevalent in the days of the biblical Judges (Jud. 17:6; 21:25) and during the recent American past, from which we have not yet emerged.

Nevertheless, the Halakah displayed both compassion and insight when it reckoned with the frailties of human nature and formulated principles that took these weaknesses into account. Thus, the rabbis declared, "One does not enact an ordinance that the community is unable to observe."[7] "Better that people should violate the law through unconscious error than through conscious defiance of its provisions."[8]

Another legal category frequently invoked consists of acts which fall into a gray area. These actions would have been better left undone, but once performed are not so serious as to deserve a penalty. Here the law frequently makes a distinction in time between "acts prohibited in advance but unpunishable *ex post facto.*"[9]

The Halakah was well aware that circumstances alter cases and therefore was prepared to modify general norms when the particularities of the situation made it necessary or desirable. A decision was often mitigated if it would have worked pecuniary hardship, "in cases of major economic loss."[10]

Always there was a lively perception of larger concerns, transcending the immediate interests and desires of the parties involved. Two such far-reaching principles invoked in rabbinic law are "a permitted deviation for the sake of peace in the community,"[11] and "for the sake of the welfare of society."[12] On the other hand, situations may arise where social utility and considerations of public policy suggest that what the letter of the law may permit, it is wiser to prohibit. In rabbinic terminology, "This is permitted by the law, but we do not decide cases accordingly."[13]

The most fundamental concept that not only played a very great role in the law but helped to mold the ethical education

of the people was the principle that "one should act beyond
the strict requirements of the law,"[14] doing more or less than
the law demands because of concern for equity and compassion. On the highest level of conduct are the acts of *Kiddush
Hashem*, "acts that hallow God's name," which include self-
sacrifice and even martyrdom for the glory of God and the
honor of Israel.

The canons we have cited here are utilized by the Sages in
the entire range of the Halakah, which includes what we today
would call civil law and criminal jurisprudence, as well as
ritual enactment. In relating these concepts to the area of
personal morality, we are, in a sense, breaking new ground.
However, we are not proposing the specific applications of
these norms to problems of sexual conduct. Basically, we are
seeking to relate the historical experience of the Jewish people
and the sympathy and the insight into human nature that
characterize its tradition to the issues of love, sex, and marriage. We shall have to utilize a great deal of Jewish teaching
on the subject. Admittedly, the ideas chosen will be selected
from the vast, variegated, and even contradictory material to
be found in our sources. Jewish tradition includes the entire
corpus of codified and customary law, regional and community custom, religious and ethical admonition, folk belief, and
folk practice from biblical days to our own. In spite of claims
to the contrary in some quarters, no code of practice can
embody it all. Even the most fundamentalist groups, who
loudly proclaim their adherence to the total tradition, unchanged and undefiled, must, of necessity, make a selection
from this vast reservoir, adopting some elements, stressing
some, soft-pedaling others, and ignoring still others. Nonetheless, the use of the resources of the past for meeting the problems of the present is not arbitrary and subjective. It is significant that there are fundamental attitudes in the tradition that
have crystallized in the Bible and the Mishnah, and have persisted to our own day.

When Judaism is approached in the light of the approaches

set forth in this chapter, we believe that not only those committed to Judaism but all men and women, young and old, can find value and interest in the experience and wisdom of the tradition. Its insights can help extricate men and women from the mass of misery in this, the most intimate and basic area of experience.

6

SEX IN JUDAISM

The Jewish attitude toward sex takes, as its point of departure, the fundamental principle that marriage and marriage alone is the proper framework for sexual experience. The marriage relationship between a man and a woman is not a concession to the lower instincts, but, on the contrary, the ideal human state, because it alone offers the opportunity for giving expression to all aspects of human nature. Speaking of his celibacy, Paul said, "I would that all men were as I." But when the sage Simeon ben Azzai did not marry, he felt constrained to apologize by saying, "My soul loves the Torah," explaining that he wished to dedicate himself wholeheartedly to study without worldly concerns.[1] The difference in attitude is highlighted by the emergence of monastic orders in Christianity, which have no counterpart in Judaism.

Ideally, every human being should live as a unit within a family, for the family is the ideal human group. The rabbis declare that he who has no wife is deprived of joy, of blessing, of all good, and lacks Torah, protection, and peace.[2] Strictly speaking, the Hebrew legal term for betrothal, which was virtually tantamount to marriage, *kiddushin*, means "separation from all others." It was, however, popularly interpreted, quite in the spirit of the tradition, as "the state of holiness."

From its inception, Judaism has always recognized two purposes in marriage, both spelled out in the opening pages of Scripture. The first is the fulfillment of the first commandment, "Be fruitful and multiply" (Gen. 1:28), which is as much a blessing as it is an imperative throughout the tradition. Children are uniformly regarded as a blessing. The Bible is replete with references to children as God's greatest boon. When the patriarch Abraham is assured, "Fear not, I am your shield; your reward will be very great," he responds, "What can You give me, if I die childless?" (Gen. 15:1,2) Rachel, Jacob's beautiful wife, knows that he loves her deeply, but she nevertheless cries out in pain, "Give me children, or otherwise I die." (Gen. 30:1) Psalm 128, already cited, paints an ideal picture of the family gathered around the table, with a consistent emphasis upon children as a good.

The commandment "Be fruitful and multiply" is defined by the Halakah with characteristic minuteness. The obligation is fulfilled as soon as two children are born, the only question being whether two boys are necessary, as the school of Shammai insists, or one boy and one girl, as Hillel avers.[3]

To be sure, families at that time were generally larger, often substantially so. The reason is to be found in several factors, personal and social. Since sexual intercourse was a constant in the lives of married couples, the absence of contraceptive devices naturally led to regular pregnancies and the birth of large numbers of children. The health of the mother and even the economic condition of the family were rarely, if ever, taken into account. In part, this was due to the subservient position of women in society at large. But in the Jewish community, another factor, operating on both the conscious and the unconscious levels, was the powerful desire for group survival. In the ancient and medieval eras—and the Middle Ages continued for the bulk of Eastern European and Oriental Jewry well into the twentieth century—disease and malnutrition carried off many infants and children. In addition, there was the persistent prospect of expulsion and massacre threatening the physical preservation of the Jewish group. Obviously, the problem of overpopulation which confronts us in the twentieth century was not remotely dreamed of. Nevertheless, the minimal limits of the biblical commandment, as laid down by the Halakah, are clear.

The procreation of children is a basic goal of marriage, but it is not the only one. It is noteworthy that, in the Bible, Eve is created for Adam before procreation is contemplated, while they are still in the Garden of Eden. The second function of marriage is that of companionship. Actually, it is the only motive assigned in the creation of a helpmate for Adam: "It is not good for man to dwell alone; I will make a helper fit for him." (Gen. 2:18)

The insight that companionship which includes sexual relations is a legitimate end in itself in marriage is not merely an implication of the biblical story but is explicitly spelled out in Jewish law. Moreover, the joy of sexual activity is a good in itself, distinct from procreation. The Halakah teaches that weak, old, and sterile persons should marry, even when there is no possibility of children.[4] Thus the rabbis could endorse wholeheartedly the sentiment of a modern sociologist: "Sex exists not only for the propagation of the race, but for the increase of individual human happiness."[5]

While a negative attitude toward sexual relations is sporadically encountered in Jewish literature, particularly under the impact of medieval asceticism and pietism, it is far from representing the normative view. Basically, sexual relations between husband and wife, while naturally private and intimate, are held to be a perfectly legitimate form of pleasure which justifies itself as such, even without the goal of procreation.

Indeed, Judaism holds fast to two complementary concepts in this area. First is the ideal of *tzeniyut*, which can be rendered imperfectly by a series of terms, "modesty," "propriety," "delicacy," "good taste." This ideal is expected to govern men and women in their dress, their speech, and their conduct, both publicly and within the privacy of their homes.[6] At the same time, Judaism regards it not merely as permissible but as mandatory for a man and his wife to derive pleasure from the sexual act, which has been ordained by God and, by that token, is holy. Thus Jewish tradition established the practice of the husband's reading the Song of Songs on the Sabbath eve,[7] and the Halakah spells out the woman's conjugal rights in marriage, which are explicitly indicated in the biblical text.[8] The talmudic injunction that scholars and their wives have conjugal relations on Sabbath eve is explained by Rashi on the ground that the Sabbath is "for pleasure, rest, and physical enjoyment." Nahmanides justifies the rule on mystical grounds, since a holy act should be performed on a holy day.[9]

While Catholicism considers various irregular forms of sexual play between man and wife as sinful and includes them in the confessional, Judaism holds that they are all permissible, although it favors the more normal form, lest the others become habitual and exclusive.[10]

Until our day, the accepted view was that sexual desire was basically a masculine trait, and a low one at that, and that decent women were "pure" because they were untainted by this weakness. This myth derived from the Christian attitude that sex is essentially evil. The Jewish tradition was free from this form of cant. It recognized female sexuality long before the advent of modern psychology. From the very beginning of the human adventure, sex is a basic component of the female psyche. When Adam and Eve were in the Garden of Eden, they were permitted to partake of the fruit of the Tree of Life, which confers immortality on those who eat it. The other miraculous tree in the Garden, the Tree of Knowledge, was, however, expressly forbidden to them. Elsewhere we have shown that the Tree of Knowledge represents sexual awareness and experience with its concomitant power of procreation.[11] If Adam and Eve had continued to have access to both the Tree of Life and the Tree of Knowledge, they would have become, as the Bible clearly indicates, "like God," possessing both immortality in their own persons and the power of procreation, which is the human counterpart of the Divine creative power. Since man is not and cannot be co-equal with God, the human pair were driven from the Garden, and thus deprived of the blessing of personal immortality and limited to the lesser, vicarious immortality available through children. The act of disobedience leads not only to expulsion but to other consequences. Adam was condemned to back-breaking toil in order to have food. Eve was punished with the pain of childbirth. Moreover, since she had taken the initiative and had clearly dominated Adam in having him eat of the fruit of the Tree of Knowledge, she would be henceforth under his power. In this connection, her sexuality is underscored: "Your desire will be for your husband, but he will rule over you." (Gen. 3:16) But the sin Adam and Eve have committed is disobedience, not sex.

The oldest biblical legislation ordains that the husband "shall not deprive his wife of the food, clothing and conjugal rights" that are her due.[12] After marriage, the husband was exempt from military service for a full year in order to fulfill the obligation of "bringing joy to his wife." (Deut. 24:5)

In the superb anthology of love which is the Song of Songs, the avowal of desire by the beloved is no less frank and passionate than that of the lover, who declares:

> How fair and how pleasant art thou,
> O love, for delights!

and she responds:

> I am my beloved's,
> And his desire is toward me.
>
> (7:7, 11)

It is noteworthy that the same term for "desire," *"teshukah,"* is used as in Genesis in the Garden of Eden.

The rabbis of the Talmud recognized the existence of female sexuality with its ebb and flow. The Talmud, therefore, declares that a woman has a right to reject sexual overtures from her husband; the husband is forbidden to pressure his wife to have sexual relations when she is not so disposed. If he disregards this injunction, he is warned that his children will not be worthy. On the other hand, the woman is encouraged to make overtures to her husband and promised fine offspring as a reward. However, brazen conduct, even between the couple, is not countenanced. The rabbis declare that the husband may approach his wife in words, but that she should do so by subtler, unspoken means.[13]

Since sex and love are indissolubly linked, the term *"ahabhah"* is used both for the physical and the spiritual aspects of love. Christian theologians have been wont to emphasize the fact—and take pride in it—that besides the word *"philia,"* "friendship, liking," there are two Greek terms for "love": *eros*, representing "carnal love," and *agape*, meaning "charity, spiritual love." The Hebrew outlook, on the contrary, finds it entirely proper to apply the same root, *ahabh*, to all aspects of love. The ideal relationship of man to God ("You shall love the Lord your God"), the love of one's fellow man ("You shall love your neighbor as yourself"), and the love of man and woman ("How fair and how pleasant you are, O love, with your delights!") are all expressed by the same Hebrew root.[14]

The Song of Songs in the Bible is a superb, lyrical anthology containing songs of love and nature, of courtship and marriage, which glorify the physical aspects of love and reveal its spiritual character. That the Song of Songs was admitted to the biblical canon is evidence of the persistence in Judaism of the basic concept that the natural is holy. In John Donne's words, "Love's mysteries in souls do grow, but yet the body is his book." If the two basic imperatives of religion are the love of God and the love of man, the Song of Songs, no less than the Book of Psalms, deserves its place in Scripture.[15]

It is true that the rabbis of the Talmud explained the Song of Songs as an allegory and that this interpretation was undoubtedly decisive in having it enter the biblical canon. Nonetheless, the Sages were well aware of its literal meaning.

Thus Rabbi Akiba, who described the Song of Songs as "the Holy of Holies," issued the warning, "He who gives his voice a flourish in reading the Song of Songs in the banquet halls and makes it a secular song has no share in the world to come."[16] For the same reason, some of the Sages expressed doubts regarding the canonicity of the Song.[17] That the Song deals with the love of man and woman is implicitly recognized in the statement of Rabbi Jonathan, "Solomon wrote the Song of Songs in his youth, then Proverbs, then Ecclesiastes. This is the way of the world. When a man is young he writes songs; when he gets older he writes proverbs; when he is old he says, 'All is vanity.' "[18]

This healthy-minded, affirmative attitude toward sex, which is recognized as an essential and legitimate element of human life, is rooted in a religious world-view. Since God created man with his entire complement of impulses, sex is a manifestation of the Divine. It is not to be glorified as an end in itself, as in paganism, or in the exaggerations of romantic love. Hence, the Bible and the Talmud are frank and outspoken in dealing with the sexual component of human experience. The pages of our classic literature are free from both obscenity and false modesty, from pornography and prudishness, which are essentially two sides of the same coin.

In the medieval mystical treatise *Iggeret Ha-kodesh,* attributed to Nahmanides, the classic Jewish attitude is clearly and vigorously expressed: "We who are the descendants of those who received the sacred Torah believe that God, blessed be He, created everything as His wisdom dictated, and He created nothing containing obscenity or ugliness (*genai' o kiyyur*). For if we were to say that intercourse *(ha-ḥibbur)* is obscene, it would follow that the sexual organs are obscene. . . . And how could God, blessed be He, create something containing a blemish or obscenity, or a defect; for we would then find that His deeds are not perfect, though Moses, the greatest of the prophets, proclaims and says, 'The Rock, whose work is perfect.' (Deut. 32:4) However, the fact is, as it is said, that 'God is pure-eyed so that He sees no evil.'[19] Before Him there is neither degradation nor obscenity; He created man and woman, fashioning all their organs and setting them in their proper function, with nothing obscene in them."[20]

In a right and perfect union, the love of a man and a woman is, and should be, inseparable from sexual experience. The emotion of love which is spiritual expresses itself in sexual acts which are physical, so as to create total human participation. The sex-love relationship is not complete unless it is accompanied by a feeling of permanence. It is not an act of deception or even honest hyperbole that impels lovers to swear that their love will endure forever. What is deep and all-inclusive will not be satisfied without the conviction that it will endure.

The love of a man and woman expresses itself not only in a physical desire for each other but also by a sense of concern for one another, a desire to make the partner happy at any cost, even a major sacrifice. To be sure, when the strength of the passion subsides, as it must in the rise and fall of human experience, the sexual manifestation of love will become less intense. But even when moderated, the responsibility between the partners toward each other and, above all, for any child that is born as a consequence of their relationship, remains constant. It is this on-going concern that is the touchstone of love, rather than a passing fancy.

The Talmud devotes one of the most extensive of its six sections *(Nashim,* "Women"), as well as many passages in other sections, to marriage law and personal morality, and the post-talmudic codes maintain the tradition. This detailed preoccupation in the Halakah with all aspects of sexual life, even the most intimate, testifies to the recognition that "this too is Torah and one must learn."[21]

Nevertheless, Judaism, which never succumbed to the modern myth of the perfectibility of humankind preached by Rousseau and his assorted followers, was too honest to fall victim to the neo-paganism which distorts Freud and misuses his ideas to justify the doctrine that sexual experience is the highest good.

Judaism has a realistic understanding of the power of sex,

both for good and for evil. Rabbinic sources generally refer to it as *yetzer ha-ra*, "the evil impulse," because they recognize how often the sexual impulse becomes a source of evil, leading men to violate the dictates of reason and the canons of morality, overriding their ideals and distorting the pattern of their lives.

Yet the mere translation of the term *"yetzer ha-ra"* as "the evil impulse" does not do justice to the breadth of understanding in Jewish tradition. Long before modern psychoanalysis, rabbinic Judaism was aware of the central role of sex in civilization: "Were it not for the sexual impulse [literally, the evil impulse], no man would build a house or marry a woman or engage in an occupation."[22] The role of sex in stimulating men to activity and thus furthering human progress is mirrored in another rabbinic epithet, "the leaven in the dough." Like the more common term, "evil impulse," this term is at times used simply as a designation for the sexual proclivities of men.[23] Leaven is ferment—it may bring decay, but it is also the source of growth.

In a charming and witty tale, the Talmud ridicules the fear of sex which characterized some ascetic groups during the period of the Second Temple. This fear was personified as the Evil Impulse, *yetzer ha-ra,* and the rabbis tell that the Men of the Great Synagogue were greatly exercised by the troubles brought into the world by him. In response to their importunities, the Evil Impulse was handed over to them and they proceeded to imprison him for thirty days. As a result, not an egg could be found in all the land. They could not kill him, lest they be destroyed, nor would Heaven agree to cut his power in half. Finally, they blinded one of his eyes and released him, thus reducing but not eliminating his hold upon men.[24]

The rabbis did not hesitate to interpret the great commandment "You shall love the Lord your God with all your heart" to mean "with your two impulses—the good impulse and the evil impulse."[25] Thus, sex becomes an instrument for the fulfillment of the love of God, a powerful force that can be channeled for good, in spite of its capacity for evil.

The attitude of traditional Judaism in its great creative periods may therefore be summarized as a denial that man's nature *eo ipso* is evil, whether as a result of Adam's sin, or because of any theoretical distinction between body and soul, or on any other ground.[26] God's judgment on Creation, "And God saw all that He had made, and behold it was very good," was unflinchingly taken by the rabbis to include even death itself.[27]

It therefore follows that man's nature, all of which is the handiwork of God, is good, either actually or potentially. Man's misuse of any of his instincts or faculties constitutes his own sin, *het*, missing the mark for which he should have aimed and which he could have reached.

Judaism has always remained realistically aware not only of man's proclivity to evil in general but of the power of the sexual impulse in particular. "Two impulses God created in His world, the impulse to idolatry *(avodah zarah)* and the impulse to immorality *(zenut)*. The impulse to idolatry has already been uprooted, but the impulse to immorality still remains. God said, 'Whoever can resist the second is considered as though he resisted both.' "[28] Nevertheless, Jewish tradition insists that the sexual impulse, like all other attributes of human nature, per se, is neutral in character and malleable to men's goals. It can be utilized as an instrument for building or for destroying the world.

It is true that traditional Judaism envisaged the proper sphere of the woman to be the home. A passage in Psalms originally sung in praise of a princess on her wedding day was interpreted homiletically by the rabbis to mean "All the glory of the princess is within her home." (45:14) Medieval folk wisdom expressed the same thought alliteratively in the German proverb that women's role was *Kinder, Kirche, und Küche*, "children, church, and kitchen." But this attitude stemmed not from a religious outlook but from the social and cultural conditions of an ancient and medieval society that was unabashedly male dominated. Now that the balance is in process of being redressed, it should be emphasized that there is nothing in the tradition, particularly as expounded by its greatest masters, that requires or implies that a woman must be confined to her home, be denied the opportunity for education, or be cut off from a career. Obviously, the wider horizons of modern life raise new problems and increase the range of temptations. Freedom has its hazards, but it cannot be relinquished merely to make life simpler.

The late Harry Emerson Fosdick underscored the potentialities and the perils of the new freedom by a brilliant interpretation of the passage in Isaiah that describes the setting up of a tent: "Lengthen your cords and strengthen your stakes." (54:2) He pointed out that in modern life we have lengthened our cords and enlarged the boundaries of experience for the generality of men and women. There is a corresponding need to strengthen the stakes so that the tent will not collapse under the added strain.

In a world increasingly felt to be cold and forbidding, there is a correspondingly greater need for the warmth and security of a family, in which husband and wife, parents and children, live in true harmony and mutual enrichment. The great word "love" has been so abused and vulgarized in our society that one is strongly tempted to abjure its use, but there is no substitute at hand. In its true meaning, love embodies mutual respect and concern. Both the husband and the wife must recognize the need that the other has to fulfill the needs of his own nature and to give expression to his interests and talents to achieve these ends. But each must relate his own desires to the concerns and needs of the other. A similar mutuality must also prevail in the relationship of parents and children, though with obvious differences. Parents will necessarily be involved in furthering the fullest physical, intellectual, and ethical development of their children. Because nature is committed to the preservation of life, it has made this parental attitude of love for children the norm, and aberrations like child neglect and child abuse are the exception even today. But the concern of children for their parents, while not being biologically rooted, is equally essential in a truly civilized society. In fact, the true measure of a humane civilization may be the attitude it takes toward those who are no longer needed biologically for procreation or economically for the production of goods and services.

The great Hasidic teacher Rabbi Levi of Berditchev said that he had learned the true meaning of love from a drunken peasant. One day the rabbi had occasion to come into a tavern owned by a Jew. In one corner two peasants were sitting, well advanced in their cups. Suddenly Ivan turned to Peter and said, "Tell me, Peter, what hurts me?" Peter replied, "How can I know what hurts you?" Whereupon Ivan retorted, "If you do not know what hurts me, how can you say you love me?" The ideal of companionship and equality in marriage is superbly expressed in the rabbinic dictum "He who loves his wife as himself and honors her more than himself, of him Scripture declares, 'You shall know that your tent is at peace.'" [29]

Frontier Issues
in Contemporary Society

7

THE INCIDENCE OF DIVORCE
AND THE INSTABILITY
OF MARRIAGE

The far-flung sexual revolution in our time confronts society as a whole with a host of problems, many of which have already been touched upon earlier in this volume. A well-worn aphorism has it that Jews are like all other people, only more so. It is therefore to be expected that they would be involved and bedeviled by the same conflicts and ambiguities as their neighbors, indeed, to an even higher degree. There is nothing arcane or sinister in this fact, if fact it be. As we have seen, most of the problems in this area are the results of the scientific and technical revolution of the nineteenth and twentieth centuries. In its wake have come the rationalization of industry and the growth of commercial and financial activity on a gigantic scale. These developments required and stimulated an irresistible drift toward urbanization, moving vast numbers of people from the country to the city. The process shows no sign of abating. Today metropolis is giving way to megalopolis, the great industrial-commercial complex in the northeastern United States extending almost unbroken from Boston to Washington. The new social and economic conditions in the urban environment have led to the emergence of new standards of interpersonal relations, marked by far greater freedom for women than ever before in history.

Now Jews were a highly urbanized group long before the modern era, for reasons rooted in their medieval status. In the Middle Ages, they were the only significant element of the population that was almost exclusively urban in character. Even today, when an increasing proportion of the general population is moving from a rural to a city environment, Jews still remain the single most urbanized element in the nation. They are, therefore, most exposed to the new winds of doctrine and patterns of practice that constitute the sexual revolution.

Judaism is an ancient and complex tradition that had its genesis and development under conditions radically different from our own. What can it contribute to illumine the issues confronting our age? Obviously, it cannot be expected to offer specific and detailed blueprints for the problems besetting men and women today, particularly in an area in which the deepest and most imperious human instincts and desires are involved. Nonetheless, its long contact with human nature, its insight into the human condition, and its special, if not unique, vision of life can help illumine the path modern men and women must tread. It can help in the emergence of a way of life that will fulfill their deepest aspirations.

The single most far-reaching change in the area of sexual behavior, which has affected more human lives than any other during the last half century, is unquestionably the incidence of divorce. Divorce is the acid test of marriage, the litmus paper revealing the stresses and strains that threaten the survival of the institution. With the proportion of divorces to marriages in the United States reaching the figure of one to three, it is clear that marriage as the basic pattern of male-female relationships is in jeopardy.

For nearly nineteen centuries, until the beginning of the twentieth, Western society saw the dissolution of a marriage as a sin against God and a crime against society. The attitude derived directly from the New Testament teaching attributed to Jesus and repeated several times in the Gospels. In one version, divorce is categorically forbidden:

> And he said to them, "Whoever divorces his wife and marries another, commits adultery against her; and if she divorces her husband and marries another, she commits adultery."[1]

In another formulation, also occurring twice, the same prohibition is set forth, with one exception. Divorce is allowed and perhaps even ordained in the case of "fornication," that is to say, adultery on the part of the wife:

> But I say to you that every one who divorces his wife, except on the ground of unchastity, makes her an adulteress; and whoever marries a divorced woman commits adultery.   (Mat. 5:32)

In this statement, Jesus's position is identical with that of the rabbinical school of Shammai, which also forbade divorce, except for reasons of adultery.[2]

In another passage, the prohibition of divorce is followed by a section in praise of celibacy:

> The disciples said to him, "If such is the case of a man with his wife, it is not expedient to marry." But he said to them, "Not all men can receive this precept, but only those to whom it is given. For there are eunuchs who have been so from birth, and there are eunuchs who have been made eunuchs by men, and there are eunuchs who have made themselves eunuchs for the sake of the kingdom of heaven. He who is able to receive this, let him receive it."
> (Mat. 19:10–12)

This addition occurs in none of the other Gospel passages and is completely at variance with the attitude of normative Judaism, with which Jesus generally agrees. The glorification of celibacy would seem to be an addition reflecting the later Paulinian standpoint, which is strongly negative in its attitude toward sexual activity, as we have noted earlier (I Cor. 7:1–7).

This attitude was not restricted to the pulpit but became embodied in canon law and secular jurisprudence. In Catholic countries like Spain, Ireland, Austria, and Italy, divorce was completely forbidden in the civil code. A marriage could be dissolved only by annulment, a long, cumbersome, and costly process available only to the affluent and the influential, and utilized by only a tiny proportion of the population. The Catholic Church has never retreated from its position that divorce is a mortal sin bringing in its wake the penalty of automatic excommunication decreed by the Third Council of Baltimore. In Italy, and in other Catholic countries where the Catholic prohibition of divorce prevailed, there were millions of men and women living "in sin," a phenomenon to which civil and ecclessiastical authorities closed their eyes.

Overriding the opposition of the Church, civil divorce was recently established in Italy. Though dealing with a symptom rather than with the cause, the new law has reduced the hypocrisy and dishonesty that are inherent in clandestine or illegal unions. It has also minimized the complications and tragedies which arise when children are born whose status would otherwise be under a cloud of illegitimacy. In Spain and Ireland, Catholic doctrine still remains civil law.

Even in Protestant countries, the New Testament outlook on divorce was highly significant. In religious ages it obviously molded the attitudes and behavior of Christians. It exerted a strong influence in preserving the stability of marriage which was conceived of as lasting "until death do us part," as the Episcopal wedding service expresses it. The Duke of Windsor's insistence upon marrying a divorcee was the direct cause of his sensational abdication of the British throne.

The impact of this opposition to divorce in civil law was also substantial, varying in different legal systems. In South Carolina, divorce was totally prohibited. In New York State, until 1967, the only ground for dissolving a marriage was adultery. Since a crime had been committed, divorce was the punishment imposed on the guilty party. If, therefore, both parties wished to terminate the marriage, this agreement was a conspiracy, an act of collusion punishable by law. Far from reducing the number of divorces, this approach simply converted law courts in New York State into hotbeds of perjury. Incidents of adultery were manufactured, with paid participants and witnesses, and all the officers of the law, judges and lawyers alike, shared in a tragicomic charade of deception and law breaking.

The pressures of modern life led to a radical revision of the New York divorce law, and a long list of grounds for divorce are now admissible. The other states of the union vary radically in their divorce provisions. Several, like Nevada, are unabashedly interested in the income generated by the divorce mills. They have made the dissolution of a marriage little more than a formality, except for the cost of the required period of residence.

Even in the Catholic Church, pressures have been mounting, especially among the laity (but not limited to them), for a modification of the present attitude. On October 21–23, 1976, a massive "Call to Action" conference was held in Detroit. The conference represented the culmination of a two-year consultation process which involved a half million Catholics under the direction of the American bishops. Among the eight documents which emerged from the conference was one on the family which requested the bishops to repeal the time-honored penalty of excommunication for divorced Catholics.[3]

A thoroughgoing revision of the age-old attitude of the Roman Catholic Church on the subject is not likely to take place in the foreseeable future, but a relaxation of attitude is by no means ruled out. Bishop Carrol Dozier of Memphis conducted several Mass services for thousands of Catholics in which he expressly gave communion to divorced Catholic couples numbered in the thousands. In their personal lives, American Catholics have rarely obeyed the teaching of the Church on divorce. It is estimated that there are four million divorced and remarried Catholics in the United States.

Figures on divorce in the Jewish community are not easy to come by. The general impression is that, in spite of the vaunted stability of the traditional Jewish family, the percentage of divorces is now quite high.

It is clear that, for all segments of the population, divorce is now a legitimate procedure. It is a recognized option available when a marriage, for whatever reason, major or minor, is regarded as unsatisfactory.

In the upper strata of society, the business leadership, the high echelons of government, and the stars of the entertainment industry, divorces are the rule and lifelong marriages the exception. Democracy may be defined as that system of society in which the poor are free to imitate the vices of the rich. The standards of the upper classes are accordingly percolating down to the middle and lower classes. In fact, many members of the less-favored groups dispense with the formalities of divorce proceedings altogether and simply go their separate ways.

In the past, advocates of women's rights and other libertarians looked forward to the easing of the restraints on divorce as a great step forward in human freedom. Undoubtedly the availability of an easy divorce has broken the shackles of many intolerable unions for men and women who would otherwise have been bound to each other in misery for life. Unfortunately, however, the fatal human weakness that may be characterized as the "pendulum syndrome," the tendency to rush from one extreme to the other, has vitiated many of the benefits flowing from the liberalization of divorce. Only those who conceive of sex relations among human beings as being little more than the copulation of animals in heat can view with equanimity the unchecked rise of divorce and the revolving door of marriage in contemporary society.

We have already had occasion to call attention to the burden of loneliness and misery that is often borne by divorced persons. Indirect evidence for this observation is to be found in the speed with which they remarry when they have the chance. Women, who represent a larger proportion of the population and have a longer life expectancy, find remarriage more difficult to achieve. For them divorce is all too often no blessing at all. As for the third party in many divorce actions, the children, they are generally the victims and rarely the beneficiaries of divorce. This is true because so large a percentage of modern divorces take place for relatively insignificant or transitory reasons. Had a divorce been more difficult or impossible to obtain, many of these couples would have achieved an adjustment and the children would not have been deprived of their parents in a united home.

How can we hope to cope with the problem? Americans have an ingrained tendency to rely on the law to cure the ills of society, but the evidence is clear that even if it were possible, the reimposition of legal restrictions or prohibitions would be of no avail. In the face of the powerful social, economic, and cultural forces weakening the fiber of marriage today that were discussed earlier, the insights of the Jewish tradition are directly relevant to the present situation.

The rabbis of the Talmud allowed a wide variety of reasons for the issuance of a divorce. While, as we have noted, the School of Shammai restricted divorce only to the ground of adultery, the School of Hillel accepted virtually any ground for dissolving the marriage."[4]

The attentive reader will have noticed that the law speaks of the husband's issuing the divorce. From the language of the biblical text, "He shall issue her a bill of divorcement," the rabbis inferred that the husband alone has the power of issuing a divorce. Nevertheless, they added a long list of causes on the basis of which the woman could sue for a divorce before the rabbinical court.[5] Many of these grounds might seem superficial and unimportant to an outsider. Such is the charge that the wife burns the meals she serves, or that the husband suffers from bad breath or from an unpleasant disease, or that his occupation is distasteful to her.

Particularly striking is Rabbi Akiba's statement that a man may divorce his wife "if he finds another more attractive."[6] Rabbi Akiba, it need hardly be added, was not defending promiscuity or the multiple-marriage pattern of some layers of modern society. His own marriage is one of the great love idylls of the Jewish tradition. But in admitting this and other, apparently trivial grounds for divorce, Rabbi Akiba, like Judaism generally, shows a fine psychological perception of the reality of human relations. That such apparently superficial motives would be adduced by either party in order to secure a divorce is evidence of a deeper clash of personality between husband and wife, testimony that the community of spirit, which is the essence of marriage, has ceased to exist.

A more liberal stance on the subject is scarcely to be imagined. When a marriage has failed and all efforts to achieve compatibility and work a reconciliation prove useless, Judaism regards divorce as legitimate, without insisting that one of the partners must be guilty.

In sum, Jewish law regards divorce, not as a punishment for a crime, but simply as the frank admission of a failure. The grounds upon which a divorce is issued are therefore not limited to adultery. The fact that both parties recognize that they cannot live together happily, or at least tolerably well, constitutes the strongest ground for issuing a divorce, not for denying it.

Once it becomes clear that the marriage is beyond remedy, Judaism recognizes that the union has lost its sanction and its sanctity, for love and mutual respect are the only marks of God's presence in a home. When these conditions do not obtain, the husband and wife are no longer joined together by God in any meaningful sense, and society stultifies itself by trying to ignore the truth.[7]

Nor does the presence of children necessarily mean that the marriage must be preserved at all costs. There is mounting evidence today that the happiness of the children, too, is often better served by a divorce than by a hate-ridden, quarrel-filled marriage.[8] Here again, Jewish tradition has manifested a deep insight into the realities of human nature, a level of understanding which our age has scarcely begun to attain.

While the official Halakah gave the husband unlimited power to divorce his wife and the wife considerably-more-restricted rights, the customary law in the talmudic and medieval periods went much further. Considerable evidence has come to light that both in Egypt and in Palestine, and over a period of fifteen centuries, a woman was able to demand and receive a divorce when she found her marriage intolerable. In some instances, as will be noted below, she had merely to declare, "I do not love him."[9] It thus becomes clear that incompatibility was an adequate cause for divorce, universally recognized for the husband and, more irregularly, admitted for the wife.

Nevertheless, the traditional Jewish attitude is poles apart from the accepted mores of our time. Even with the trend toward liberalizing divorce laws in the various states of the union, as well as abroad, the dissolution of a marriage is still a costly and complicated procedure. On the other hand, contemporary society regards divorce as normal and certainly free from stigma. In some circles, indeed, a divorce is carried about as a badge of honor, like going to a psychiatrist. The contemporary American attitude toward divorce may be summarized as *official severity in law and total laxity in life*. It is the consequence of the tragic paradox in attitude which regards marriage as a necessary evil and divorce as a punishment for trying to escape the evil!

Traditional Judaism adopts the diametrically opposite attitude toward divorce. Instead of *severity in law and laxity in life*, Judaism establishes the contrary balance: *the attitude in life toward divorce is strict*, thus underscoring the need for the couple to strive earnestly for the permanence of the marriage bond, but *the law on divorce is liberal*, offering release where life together proves truly intolerable. All the resources of the tradition, the sanctity of its ideals and the solemnity of its ritual, are invoked to make husband and wife recognize the sacred character of their union. "He who divorces his first wife —even the Temple altar sheds tears for him," the rabbis declared.[10] The *Ketubbah*, or marriage agreement, which required a cash payment on the dissolution of a marriage, was instituted to hinder easy divorces. The same motive led to a complicated ritual with regard to the issuance of a bill of divorce *(get)*.[11]

The effect of the Jewish law of divorce must be seen within the context of traditional Jewish life. In the Jewish community, powerful religious and social factors operated to heighten the sense of the sanctity of marriage and the conviction that a marriage was normally a permanent status. As a result, divorce was rarely resorted to, and only after all efforts at mutual adjustment and reconciliation had proved abortive. Trivial disagreements were not likely to serve as causes of dissolving a marriage in the face of the social pressures to maintain it. Indeed, there was every inducement for the couple to iron out even more significant differences.

While traditional communities tended to segregate the sexes, thus minimizing the possibility of heterosexual contacts, they did exist. But they were not likely to lead to extramarital liaisons, given all the human and religious factors operating to make marriages permanent and viable. Thus, a fine balance existed between life on the one hand, which stressed the sanctity and permanence of marriage, and the law on the other, which had a remedy available in case of dire necessity, if all else proved fruitless.

Today, divorce is not the problem; marriage is. Divorce is not a disease; it is a symptom. Society is sick and in danger of losing its soul. The childish notion that the accumulation of material possessions and the instant gratification of desires constitute the royal road to happiness lies at the root of most of the dislocations of contemporary life, including drugs, crime, and the corruption of our political and economic order. The erosion of genuine values threatens to destroy the family by subverting the institution of marriage, which has, for most of recorded history, been the best instrument yet discovered for the protection of children, the socialization of their behavior, and the satisfaction of the physical and emotional needs of men and women.

Secular law can deal only with the external and overt aspects of the marriage relationship to the extent that it can be helpful in limiting the abuse of the weak by the strong. In such areas as divorce settlements and the custody of children, it should be utilized to the full. Every effort should be made to bring the law into conformity with the best insights of psychology and the highest dictates of a humane conscience.

But the law cannot deal with "matters entrusted to the heart," the intangible feelings and attitudes that are the results of nature and nurture. There is no quick and easy panacea for halting the headlong plunge to a maximum number of divorces on which our generation seems bent. A psychologist addressing a group of young mothers was asked at what age the child's education should begin. His answer was, "Twenty-five years before the child is born." In the face of prevailing fashions, with the trends being set for the lower classes of society by the jet set and other groups who modestly call themselves "the beautiful people," no quick remedy is in sight. Only a lifelong process of education can avail. The example of the home will prove far more efficacious than formal teaching in the classroom or eloquent preachment in the pulpit.

The Midrash declares that when the wife of the Egyptian nobleman Potiphar tried to seduce Joseph, who was her husband's steward, the lad was tempted by her beauty to yield. Then the image of his father, Jacob, appeared before him. The moral standards in which he had been reared reasserted themselves and he was able to resist her blandishments.

All resources must be mobilized in order to inculcate an ideal of marriage that will reckon with human limitations and do justice to human aspirations. Nothing less will avail to rescue humankind from the morass of degradation and misery into which it is being plunged today.

The moral imperative of Judaism is to strive to re-establish the sense of the sanctity of marriage as the noblest condition available to a man and a woman. The Jewish tradition regards the single state, even when it takes the form of continence or celibacy, as inferior to marriage. With its penchant for honesty and frankness, the Talmud declares, "If a man reaches the age of twenty and is unmarried, his days are spent in sin . . . or in the thought of sin."[12] It may be argued that the utterance reflects conditions in the semitropical Orient, where sexual maturity comes earlier than in the West. This may or may not be true.

Undoubtedly, the economic facts of modern life make early marriages difficult, if not impossible, for most people. Moreover, the extended period of education and intellectual maturing that American youth undergo suggests that early marriages may not be advisable today. When a marriage takes place before the partners have fully developed, they are exposed to the hazards of disaffection and mutual alienation as they grow older, and may grow apart from each other. Hence, the rabbinic injunction cannot be applied to the modern scene, but its basic insight into the value of marriage remains unassailable. The human personality fulfills itself most truly in marriage, which permits love to be united with responsibility, stamps it with the attribute of permanence, and demonstrates the truth that sex and love are indivisible. It is pre-eminently in marriage that sex becomes holy and love becomes real.

8

BIRTH CONTROL, GROUP SURVIVAL, AND THE POPULATION EXPLOSION

In our discussion of the negative attitude toward sexual relations in the New Testament, it became clear why the Roman Catholic Church has steadfastly opposed birth control. Nevertheless, in spite of the Papal denunciation of the practice, contraception is practiced almost as widely among Catholics as among other segments of the population. The issue, like that of divorce, poses grave problems for the future authority of the Church in the Catholic community.

What is the attitude of Judaism toward planned parenthood? Does the Jewish tradition also condemn the practice?

With increasing vigor an effort is being made in some quarters to insist that Jewish tradition is opposed to family limitation. This judgment may be categorically described as untrue. A balanced examination of the subject is definitely in order.

As has already been noted, Jewish tradition is unequivocal in regarding children as a blessing. The desire of Abraham and Sarah for offspring remained a constant Jewish experience. The Psalmist expressed his basic goal in these words:

> Lo, sons are a heritage from the Lord,
> the fruit of the womb, God's reward.
> Like arrows in the hand of a warrior
> are the sons of one's youth.

> Happy is the man who has
> his quiver full of them!
> He shall not be put to shame,
> when he confronts his enemies in the gate.
>
> (127:3–5)

Many similar quotations from biblical and rabbinic literature can be cited without difficulty.

In part, this desire for progeny was based on the fact that children were a source of economic help to their parents, both in rural and urban surroundings, even during the time that their parents were physically active. During old age, children were a source of sustenance and support. But there was a deeper emotional need that cried out for fulfillment. In the face of the inevitability of death, children were recognized as constituting a passport to immortality, an assurance that the parent would live on beyond the span of his earthly existence.

This factor may have been somewhat submerged in the modern world, with its emphasis upon the immediate personal gratification of desires, but it still operates powerfully in the human breast, at least on the subconscious level. It may well surface again in the years ahead.

That children are a blessing was maintained by the rabbis of the Talmud with equal vigor: "Four are considered dead, the poor, the blind, the leper, and he who has no children."[1] This conviction the rabbis maintained, in spite of their clear awareness of the difficulties in raising children and the frustrations and disappointments that inevitably accompany the process. There is a world of realism and compassion in the rabbinic term which has no analogue in other cultures, *tsa'ar giddul banim,* "the pain of rearing children."

The classic passage in Genesis affirms that the procreation of children is both a duty and a blessing:

> And God blessed them, and God said to them, "Be fruitful and multiply, and fill the earth and subdue it; and have dominion over the fish of the sea and over the birds of the air and over every living thing that moves upon the earth."
>
> (1:28)

However, the full implications of the passage have not been adequately noted. The verbs, "be fruitful and multiply," are in the plural and are addressed to "them," clearly a reference to the verse preceding:

> So God created man in his own image,
> in the image of God he created him;
> male and female he created them.

What emerges is that the passage, whether it is primarily a blessing, as seems to be the case, or is a command, is addressed to both the male and the female. The rabbis, who were sensitive to every nuance in the biblical text, nevertheless concluded that women are not duty-bound by the commandment to procreate children and that the obligation is limited to men only.[2] The practical implications of this observation for birth control will become clear below.

Another passage frequently invoked in the discussion occurs later in Genesis. Judah, the son of Jacob, sired three sons, Er, Onan, and Shelah. He married Er off to a woman named Tamar. The narrative then continues:

> But Er, Judah's first-born, was wicked in the sight of the Lord; and the Lord slew him. Then Judah said to Onan, "Go to your brother's wife, and perform the duty of a brother-in-law to her and raise up offspring for your brother." But Onan knew that the offspring would not be his; so when he went in to his brother's wife he spilled the semen on the ground, lest he should give offspring to his brother. And what he did was displeasing in the sight of the Lord, and he slew him also.   (38:7–11)

From this passage the rabbis derive that it is a sin "to spill one's seed in vain," though the act is not punishable by human agency. Thus, coitus interruptus and masturbation would be regarded as sinful and prohibited. It should be noted in passing that Judaism never evinced the morbid preoccupation with masturbation that has characterized some Christian religious circles virtually to our day.

However, if we read the biblical narrative on its own terms, we may well conclude that Onan's sin was not his method of intercourse but his unwillingness to fulfill the sacred duty of the levirate.[3] The practice was both ancient and widespread that when a man died childless his brother was obligated to marry his widow and bring a child into the world to perpetuate his name among the living. When, after Onan's death, Judah keeps his youngest son Shelah away from Tamar, she takes extreme measures to have the rite fulfilled. Arraying herself as a harlot, she traps Judah into having intercourse with her and giving her progeny. Judah's judgment upon her highly unorthodox procedure clearly indicates the spirit and tenor of the narrative: "She is more righteous than I, for I did not give her to Shelah, my son." (Gen. 38:26)

Even if a condemnation of spilling one's seed in vain is found in the narrative, it is clear that the rabbis did not maintain that sexual activity is permissible only when the act can lead to procreation. As we have seen, the Halakah urged people who were ill, old, or sterile to marry.[4]

Moreover, talmudic law permits a woman to sterilize herself permanently, like the wife of the Sage Rabbi Hiyya who "drank a cup" to render herself incapable of childbearing because she could not stand the extreme pain involved.[5] Rabbinic law also permitted women to avoid pregnancy if they had immoral or degenerate children and feared bringing others of a similar kind into the world.[6]

The Talmud contains a classical passage on the subject of birth control.[7] It is repeated no less than six times.[8]

> Rabbi Bebai recited a Tannaitic passage in the presence of Rabbi Nahman. Three types of women use an absorbent (to prevent conception), a minor, a pregnant woman and a nursing mother; the minor, lest she become pregnant and die; a pregnant woman, lest her embryo be injured and become a (fish-shaped flat) abortion; and a nursing mother, lest she wean her child too soon and it die.
>
> Who is meant by a "minor" (*ketannah*)? From the age of eleven years and a day to twelve and a day. Below this limit

and above it she cohabits in the normal manner, so says Rabbi Meir. The Sages say that *(ahat zo ve' ahat zo)* both within this limit *(i.e.,* from eleven to twelve years), and outside of it (below or above), she cohabits in the normal manner, and Heaven will have pity and protect her, as it is said, "The Lord guards the simple."   (Ps. 116:6)

From a straightforward reading of the text, it is clear that, with regard to the pregnant woman and the nursing mother, there is no disagreement at all. They differ only on the first category, the minor (from the age of eleven to twelve). In this case, Rabbi Meir demands the use of a contraceptive, while the Sages trust to Providence to prevent her death from pregnancy. In the ancient Orient, child marriages were fairly common but were opposed by the rabbis.

The post-talmudic commentators differ as to whether these three types of women *may* practice family limitation (and others may not), or whether these categories *must* do so (and others may).[9] The latter is the prevalent interpretation.

There are, of course, varying positions on the subject to be found in the vast Responsa literature of the past millennium and a half, with authorities differing on the time and the type of contraception that may be employed.[10] Some opponents of birth control have introduced another element—sexual intercourse must be "natural" to be legitimate. Hence, chemical contraception would be permissible while mechanical devices would be forbidden. Paradoxical as it may seem, the latter-day stress upon this distinction may be the result of Catholic influence. Right-wing traditionalists have, in several other instances as well, set aside the clear intent of Jewish traditional sources in order not to appear more permissive or liberal than the Pope. Be this as it may, the basic talmudic passage clearly deals with an absorbent, which is a mechanical form of contraception.

No matter how these various questions are resolved, it is clear that the Talmud provides a strong sanction for contraception. Thus, a child-wife, a nursing mother, or a pregnant woman is either commanded or permitted to practice family limitation, because of possible danger to the mother or to the embryo, or to a child already born.

As in any system, the law can be construed narrowly or broadly. It seems reasonable that the health of a mother or a child cannot properly be limited to surviving acute disease or total hunger. A human being has other needs inseparable from his human status. Chronic malnutrition or inadequate housing, a lack of educational opportunities or of recreation—all these constitute a genuine threat to the health of a child. Moreover, health must include mental health. If a mother or her child is deprived of these essentials of human existence, or is perpetually worried about them, the psychological trauma induced in the mother is a palpable health hazard.

In sum, Judaism regards the procreation of children as a God-given duty. It may, however, be set aside when it conflicts with the supreme Divine imperative, "He shall live by them —and not perish by them," which commands us to preserve existing human life and to enhance it.[11]

The evidence is undeniable that normative Judaism in its classical period was not opposed to family limitation. Yet the large families that have characterized traditional Jewish families in past generations testify that this attitude did not prevail after the talmudic era. What led to the development of this negative attitude? The answer is to be sought in history. Several factors conspired to transform the attitude toward family limitation by Jewish leadership during the Middle Ages and beyond. Throughout these centuries, persecution, spoliation, expulsion, and massacre made great inroads in the Jewish population. The physical hazards of disease and malnutrition also decimated the ranks of children.

Faced by these perils, medieval Jewry saw its preservation dependent on a high birth rate, without restriction or qualification. The imperious demand for group survival made no allowance for individual desires or family welfare. Only through children and more children could the Jew hope to overcome the tragically high mortality rate. Thus the instinctive wish for progeny was intensified by overpowering religio-national motives.

Hence the view of the Halakah that the birth of two children fulfills the requirements of the law was ignored. Parents were encouraged to bring as many children into the world as possible, with the hope that many, if not most of them, might survive the rigors of malnutrition, disease, and persecution, and attain to maturity.

This driving need explains the extraordinary treatment that the talmudic passage received at the hands of post-talmudic interpreters. Some of the commentators set aside the clear meaning of the text and interpreted it to mean that only Rabbi Meir permits or requires the child-wife, the pregnant woman, and the nursing mother to practice contraception, while his colleagues prohibit it for all three.[12]

Moreover, this basic talmudic passage on birth control was totally ignored and passed over in silence in the medieval codes. It is not referred to in the Mishneh Torah of Maimonides or in the authoritative *Shulhan Arukh* of Rabbi Joseph Karo.[13] A distinguished modern Orthodox scholar writes that "the codes, *rather surprisingly*, omit any direct reference to contraception altogether."[14] Actually, the attitude is entirely explicable in terms of the Jewish historic experience.

The same motivation came into play on a related subject. The Talmud frequently voices strong objections to the marriage of young children.[15] The medieval authorities set these objections aside and urged that marriage engagements be entered into whenever practicable. They justified their action by calling attention to the rigors of the exile, which included the perpetual threat of physical attack and economic insecurity.

A deep-seated opposition to birth control has become dominant among right-wing traditionally minded Jews, in spite of Jewish tradition. However, in the rabbinic Responsa of the eighteenth and nineteenth centuries, more liberal viewpoints are met with, side by side with more rigorous ones. Nevertheless, the spirit of the Jewish tradition, as expressed in its classic sources, remains clear.

Family limitation has one other great virtue, of which Judaism is particularly conscious—it permits earlier marriages. Our economic system often demands that both husband and wife work, at least for the first few years of their marriage. As we have already seen, the rabbis of the Talmud were refreshingly free from the modern hypocrisy which shuts its eyes to the moral dangers of late marriages and which, until very recently at least, has pretended that most men and women can and will remain continent for many years without negative consequences.

Traditional Judaism would have no sympathy for men and women who are physically and economically capable of rearing a family and refuse to do so because of selfishness or indolence. But it would also not ignore the contention that it is better for reluctant parents not to bring unwanted children into the world.

Today, modern Judaism unequivocally reaffirms the obligation to perpetuate the human race through the medium of the family as a basic and general goal. But it recognizes also that family planning is often a necessity of modern life, in view of complex moral, hygienic, and economic factors.

As we have seen, Jewish law approaches the issue of birth control, as does the average family, from the standpoint of the individuals involved. In our day, however, two new factors of overriding importance have entered into the situation. One is the worldwide population explosion.[16] United Nations experts estimate that in the year 2000 there will be 6 billion people on the earth. This is double the present total, which itself is three times the size of the world population at the beginning of the century! The U.S. Bureau of the Census projects a population of 378,219,000 for the United States in the year 2000.[17]

The population explosion threatens the underdeveloped countries with total disaster. Their present food supply, already stretched thin, will be still less able to keep pace with the growing population tide, even if food resources are increased. The specter of widespread hunger and disease affecting hundreds of millions on this planet is therefore a virtual certainty if present trends continue.

Even the prosperous industrialized nations, who may be able to cope with the food problem (though this is doubtful), are confronted by major difficulties. The land available will not grow in extent. As a result, the problems of overcrowding and noise, of water and air pollution, which already constitute a massive complex of problems for our urbanized civilization, will become insoluble.

Faced by this menace, governmental programs of birth control have been launched in India and China, as well as in Pakistan, South Korea, Taiwan, Malaysia, and Egypt, Tunisia, and Kenya. Latin America, which has the largest rate of population growth in the world (2.8 percent a year against a world average of 2 percent), has lagged in birth-control efforts. According to the Population Council, Latin America has resisted birth control "in part because of the predominantly Catholic religion and in part because of the countries' traditional image of themselves as under-populated, with large areas capable of new settlement."[18] There are signs, however, that this situation may be changing. Government-supported family-planning campaigns have been launched in Chile, Honduras, Venezuela, and Peru. In Colombia, a nongovernmental birth-control drive has started.

It is clear that birth control is essential if the population explosion is not to destroy man nearly as effectively as the nuclear bomb or the antiballistics missile, or the new forms of chemical and germ warfare. Failure to employ birth control in the face of this menace may well represent the final transgression in the long catalogue of sins that will bring the human race to the brink of extinction.

On a smaller scale, but equally perilous for those concerned, is the opposite threat facing the Jewish people—not overpopulation but genocide from within and without. As the most highly urbanized group in the Western world, Jews have long exhibited a birth rate lower than that of their fellow citizens. Many factors play a part in this phenomenon. There are the limited living quarters available in apartment dwellings, coupled with a desire for a high level of material comfort. Where the wife's earnings in the labor market are essential, her enforced absence from her job, especially during pregnancy and the early years of a child's life, proves a major deterrent to childbearing. Moreover, the high standards for education and personal development which most Jewish parents wish for their children makes the rearing of a child under modern conditions very expensive. The cost of a four-year college education of average quality in the United States today is estimated as in excess of $25,000. Given several children of college or near college age, a family finds the burden economically insupportable. The wish for personal freedom in the life style of the husband and the wife leads them to seek to minimize their obligations, particularly the onerous duties involved in child-raising.

Finally, another motive rarely avowed, but undoubtedly present in many instances, is the conviction that bringing a Jewish child into the world exposes another human being, not merely to the petty annoyances of normal anti-Semitism, but to the potential horror of a new Holocaust. The isolation in which the State of Israel has been placed by the unrelenting hostility of the Arabs, abetted by the greed and cowardice of the other members of the United Nations, is felt by Jews the world over to be not merely a ploy in international affairs; they recognize it in a mortal threat to their own physical and spiritual survival.

Now these varied factors are not all on the highest ethical plane. Yet neither commendation nor condemnation will radically change the fact that the Jewish birthrate is lower than that of the general population.

This long-standing demographic threat to Jewish survival has been immeasurably aggravated by two new factors entering into the picture in the twentieth century. The first is the decimation of the Jewish population in the Nazi Holocaust, which destroyed six sevenths of European Jewry, more than a third of the Jewish people. The other is the threat to Jewish survival due to the mass defection of Jews from Judaism in an open society through countless forms of alienation, of which intermarriage is only one. To be sure, sociologists, ecologists, and political leaders, concerned by the explosion of population during the second half of the twentieth century, have been urging a zero population growth for the future. On the other hand, there is bitter irony in the fact that Jews have already contributed far more than their share to zero population growth, thanks to Hitler and his allies on both sides of the Second World War. In 1939, the world Jewish population stood at nearly 17 million. In 1948, it had been reduced to 11 million. Nearly thirty years later, in 1974, it has grown to 14 million, still far below its level of four decades ago, and this in an era when the world population has increased 40 percent from 2 1/2 to 3 1/2 billion.[19]

The instinct for individual self-preservation through children, coupled with the desire to keep alive the Jewish identity and the Jewish tradition, still beats powerfully in the Jewish breast. These impulses demand that the falling birthrate be halted and, whenever possible, reversed. Jewish families in the future are not likely to run to eight or ten children each, but neither should they be limited to one or two. Since it requires 3.6 children merely to keep the population unchanged, three or four children should be adopted as the minimum for Jewish families. Parents should be encouraged to bring a larger number of children into the world within their capacity and the scope of their desires. Though the cost of raising a child in modern society is high, modern Jewish couples should increase their family size as a matter of Jewish loyalty and social policy, if they are at all able to afford it economically, physically, and culturally. They will be richly rewarded as they forge a lifeline to immortality for themselves and their people.

In sum, we have here once again an instance of the creative

tension between traditional Jewish law, which is permissive in its attitude toward birth control, and the contemporary social needs and standards of the Jewish community, which point to the need for larger families. The final decision falls within the category of *d^e bharim hamm^e surim lallebh,* "matters handed over to the heart," which each family must decide for itself.

There is no real contradiction between urging the practice of birth control upon many nations in Asia, Africa, and South America, in order to meet the menace of overpopulation, and calling for larger families in the Jewish community. Birth control is not an end in itself. Where it serves to advance human welfare, as in the case of the underdeveloped areas beset by overcrowding, grinding poverty, disease, and the lack of economic resources, the practice of family limitation is a necessity. Where families have become too small even to reproduce themselves, as is the case in the Jewish community, birth control should be used sparingly and only when warranted by conditions. In this crucial area, the Jewish tradition with its blending of realism and idealism once again points the way to the good life for all people.

9

ABORTION

Major Wrong or Basic Right

Undoubtedly the most highly charged issue in the area of sexual ethics in our time is abortion. The question is by no means limited to the United States. Controversy has swirled around the problem everywhere, in Catholic Italy, in the State of Israel, and in Communist China, to cite only a few instances. In Italy, the long struggle by the Roman Catholic Church against legalizing abortion proved unavailing and the Parliament adopted a highly permissive law on the subject. In the State of Israel, a recent study claimed that 46.7 percent of all Israeli women had had at least one abortion by the time they reached forty. Estimates of the number of abortions in the country range from forty to seventy thousand a year. The Orthodox rabbinate fought strenuously against legalizing the practice. Its efforts ended in failure, when the Israeli Knesset adopted an abortion law January 31, 1977, the provisions of which will be discussed below. In Communist China, abortion is recognized not merely as legal but as an act worthy of praise as a service to the revolution.

In the United States, as we have seen, there has been a steady rise in the rate of *reported* abortions in recognized hospitals and by reputable physicians, ever since the practice was legalized in most of the states of the union. The adjective in italics is important because its significance has often been overlooked in heated discussions on the subject. Available data indicate that legal abortions are on the increase among both married and unmarried women. For the former, it serves as a method of family limitation, especially after the birth of a number of children. The rate of abortion has been rising even more rapidly in the case of unmarried women, for self-evident reasons.

From a purely rational point of view, one would have imagined that abortions would have declined in popularity in view of the ready availability of contraceptive means, which do not entail the destruction of incipient life. In this connection, one would have thought that the old adage applied: "An ounce of prevention is worth a pound of cure." Nevertheless, the fact is that hundreds of thousands of women, and the number is increasing, are undergoing abortions. The reason may be ignorance or negligence, or the fact that sexual intercourse had not been expected and the partners, therefore, were not prepared with contraceptives. One must also suspect that the rapid rise in abortions and the call for abortion on demand point to another disquieting factor—a lack of sensitivity with regard to the moral issues that may be involved.

During the past few decades, many states of the union have legalized abortion within their borders, some with various limitations. These statutes have been challenged in the courts, but they were upheld by the Supreme Court in 1976; the Court reaffirmed the right of a woman to decide whether she will undergo an abortion. Many of the restrictions subsequently imposed by state legislatures have been declared unconstitutional on the ground that they were basically efforts to circumvent the original Court decision.

The victories that the right-to-abortion forces have achieved in legislatures and the courts has stimulated the unfortunate tendency, to which Americans are particularly prone, of identifying the legal with the moral and concluding that what the law permits is, therefore, ethically sound. This fallacy is particularly disastrous in the area of personal morality and family ethics.

The acceptance of abortion as legitimate is, of course, far from unanimous. On the contrary, it has evoked passionate opposition from the Right to Life movement and other groups whose original impetus derived from Catholic theology but whose ranks include people of other persuasions as well. What the anti-abortion movement may lack in numbers and practical influence is largely compensated for by its zeal and dedication. All Americans, including those who do not share its position, owe the movement a debt of gratitude for reminding the American people that moral issues cannot be settled merely by a majority in the legislature or by the decisions of judges.

Catholicism has been confronted by some special theological problems. For many centuries Catholic theologians have debated the casuistic question of "ensoulment," i.e., just when the soul enters the foetus. The consensus among Catholic theologians, at least up to the present, has been that the soul enters the foetus at the moment of conception, so that the destruction of the embryo is tantamount to murder. Moreover, since Augustine, the Church has taught that an embryo must be baptized if it is not to suffer eternal damnation. These theological attitudes explain the passion with which the Catholic clergy and many of the laity react against abortion.

In view of the heat with which the issue is argued today, it is of interest to note that Catholic teaching on the subject has fluctuated through time. In the fourth century, St. Basil condemned abortion at any stage, but the Code of Justinian in the sixth century exempted abortions during the first forty days from penalty. This position was reaffirmed repeatedly by Papal decree for nearly ten centuries. In 1588, Pope Sixtus V declared all abortions to be murder, but less than three years later, Gregory XIV rescinded his decree. Not until 1869 was the prohibition reinstituted by Pope Pius IX.[1] It is this position that is now official Catholic doctrine.

What are the facts on the attitude of Jewish tradition toward abortion? The first point to bear in mind is that Catholic theological problems such as ensoulment and baptism have no counterpart in Judaism. In Jewish sources random speculations as to when life begins are to be encountered, but they play no significant role in connection with abortion. In fact, Jewish law has a variety of time periods applicable to different issues as to when a newborn child is *bar kayyama*, "independent and viable." To cite one familiar example, the *Pidyon Haben*, "the Redemption of the First-born," does not take place until the thirty-first day of the baby's life. What is fundamental is that the Halakah explicitly recognizes that the foetus is not a viable being while it is in its mother's womb, since its life cannot be sustained outside its natural shelter there.

The basic sources on abortion in the Bible and the Talmud are very sparse. In Exodus 21:22–25 we read: "When men strive together and hurt a woman with child, so that there is a miscarriage, and yet no harm follows, the one who hurt her shall be fined, according as the woman's husband shall lay upon him; and he shall pay as the judges determine. If any harm follows, then you shall give a life for a life, an eye for an eye, a tooth for a tooth, a hand for a hand, a foot for a foot," etc. In other words, the Torah commands that if the woman is not injured and only the foetus is destroyed in the encounter ("no harm follows"), there is to be financial compensation to the husband for the embryo. But if the woman is killed or hurt ("if any harm follows") as a result of the quarrel, the assailant is guilty of a capital or major crime. The destruction of the foetus is clearly not treated as co-equal with the death of the mother in the text of the Hebrew Bible.

However, an alleged biblical source for a prohibition of abortion has been derived from this same passage, on the basis of an enigmatic and an almost certainly erroneous translation of the Hebrew text in the Septuagint. This ancient Greek version renders the Hebrew word *'ason*, "harm, injury," inexplicably as "form, shape," a meaning for which scholars are unable to offer a warrant or even a credible explanation.[2] The passage then emerges as "But if it [the embryo] be perfectly formed, you shall give a life for a life."[3] This dubious rendering has been used in the Christian Church as a biblical support for treating abortion as murder.

The second passage bearing directly upon the subject of therapeutic abortion occurs in rabbinic literature. The Mishnah reads: "If a woman is having difficulty in childbirth (so that her life is endangered), one cuts off the embryo, limb by limb, because her life takes precedence over its life. If most of the foetus (or the head) has emerged, it may not be hurt, for we do not set one life aside for the sake of another."[4] This classical passage clearly embodies the principle that the foetus is a limb of its mother.[5] In Rashi's words, "The life of the mother in childbirth takes precedence over that of the embryo to the very last moment of pregnancy."[6]

Maimonides, who summarizes this provision of the Mishnah in his code, adds an explanation which has had the practical effect of limiting the permissibility of abortion among some later authorities. He explains that the permission to destroy the embryo set forth in the Mishnah is due to the fact that the embryo is "like a pursuer seeking to kill the mother."[7] This explanation would seem to permit abortion only when and if the mother's life is in danger. This interpretation of Maimonides, which Feldman rightly calls "a surprising position,"[8] is clearly more restrictive than the talmudic provision.

I would suggest that the reason that Maimonides and other medieval codifiers diverge from the Mishnah may inhere in the same conditions that led them to disregard the clear talmudic warrants for birth control. They were leaders of a community perpetually engaged in a desperate struggle for survival against disease, expulsion, and massacre. They felt keenly the necessity for bringing many children into the world and thus preserving the Jewish people against extinction. Since group survival took precedence over individual well-being, they sought to limit such practices as abortion and birth control, or to forbid them altogether, in spite of the clear provisions in the Mishnah and the Talmud.

Many later authorities attempted to explain away Maimonides's limitation and to harmonize it with the broader principle laid down in the Mishnah, a discussion that has continued to the present.[9] While some would restrict the provision permitting abortion to only when the mother's life is in danger, the majority of decisions recognize that physical injury to the mother, even if death is not involved, should also be a legitimate ground for abortion.

Other factors also command impressive rabbinic support. Some authorities explicitly permit an abortion if the pregnancy adversely affects the feeding of an existing child.

The dominant attitude of the Halakah, which is derived from the Mishnaic statement already quoted, is summarized by Rabbi Ben-Zion Uziel, former Chief Rabbi of Israel, who declared that abortion is permitted even for "a very thin reason," such as avoiding pain for the mother.[10] The mother's anguish at the possibility of bearing a defective child is also admitted as ground for abortion. So is the element of disgrace and the threat of suicide by a woman who has been raped or has become pregnant as a result of adultery. The twentieth-century authority Rabbi Yehiel Weinberger ruled that "the authorities who differ with Maimonides are *in the majority,*" and he, therefore, agreed with Rabbi Jacob Emden in permitting abortion to spare the mother pain.[11]

In spite of the luxuriant variety of views and nuances to be found in rabbinic sources, it is clear that the Halakah on abortion may be fairly described as lenient. It surely cannot be regarded as establishing a blanket prohibition. Indeed, the broad interpretation of the rabbinic attitude is entirely justified, since it is a fundamental principle of the Mishnah, amply confirmed by modern medicine, that an embryo is not an independent living being.

The rabbinic discussions on the subject are primarily concerned with *therapeutic abortions.* There are several types of abortion that may be described as extensions of the therapeutic category into the mental area. On these, a broad consensus of agreement probably exists in contemporary society, except possibly for some of those bound closely to Catholic dogma. Earlier Jewish authorities devote little attention to the problem of women who become pregnant as a result of incest or rape, yet, undoubtedly, both of these evils existed in the past. Perhaps we are more conscious of these crimes today because of a greater recognition of women as independent personalities. Whatever the reason, it will be generally agreed that the victims of such atrocities have already undergone major psychological trauma even if they did not suffer physical violence.

To permit such a pregnancy to run its course means to bring into the world a permanent reminder of the terror and the shame that the woman experienced at the time the crime was committed. Furthermore, the child would forever bind her to one who had viciously violated the sanctity of her person. Moreover, the child himself, who is totally free from guilt, would carry a stigma almost too heavy to bear throughout his life. Moreover, since a human being is an amalgam of spirit and body, the mental well-being of the mother is as important as her physical health.

There is warrant in rabbinic Responsa for permitting abortion if the mother is deeply concerned about the health of her unborn child.[12] If, therefore, there is a possibility that the child may be born defective because the mother is a drug addict or has taken some medication with aftereffects dangerous to the offspring, the pregnant woman's worry is sufficient ground for an abortion because of the debilitating effects psychologically or otherwise on her well-being. Under any of these circumstances, few would be disposed to oppose abortions designed to prevent a major traumatic episode from being converted into a lifetime tragedy. These instances may fairly be regarded as falling within a broadened category of therapeutic abortion.

While therapeutic abortions are by no means negligible in number, the gravamen of the struggle today lies in the area of *non-therapeutic abortions,* where the woman simply does not wish to have the child born—so-called abortion on demand. Her motive may be the size of her family or the fact that she is unmarried or simply a desire not to be burdened by the responsibility of child-raising.

On the one hand, it may be argued that there is no urgency to permit such non-therapeutic abortions, particularly in view of the variety of moral issues that have been raised with regard to the right to life of the unborn foetus. On the other hand, we have seen that such issues as ensoulment and the baptism of unborn infants are strictly dogmatic in character and are applicable only to believing Catholics.[13] For other elements of the population in general, and for Jews in particular, the weight of authoritative opinion, both religious and scientific, does not regard the foetus as a viable and independent human being or abortion as murder.[14]

When, therefore, a woman asks for an abortion for one of the reasons mentioned, we cannot in justice ignore several other aspects of the situation that are of valid social and ethical concern. What destiny awaits a child who cannot be properly cared for, because he is being born into a family where there are already far too many mouths to feed? What about a child who is not wanted because he is the result of extramarital intercourse? In the latter case, does the mother deserve lifelong punishment for a single indiscretion? What about the handicaps for a child growing up in a home without a father, from which the mother is often absent, with no one to supervise and guide the youngster because she must work for a living? Think what we may of a woman who does not wish to bear and raise a child simply because she consults only her own convenience and comfort, what environment awaits an unwanted child born under such circumstances? A study of the mounting tide of child abuse and child murder by parents might well disclose this attitude as a motive for crime.[15]

Finally, we cannot, in all honesty, ignore the fact that all too often the issue is not whether or not an abortion is to take place but under what circumstances. Will it be done through proper procedures by experts, or under unsanitary and dangerous conditions by incompetents or charlatans who threaten the life or health of the mother? We cannot overlook the fact that the affluent and the well-educated have always had access to abortions on demand. All that is being asked for is to make the same procedures available to the poor and the underprivileged as well. In effect, opposition to legalizing properly performed abortions on demand amounts to a flagrant form of economic discrimination. Not altogether unjustly, therefore, the movement against legalizing abortion is often charged with being both hysterical and hypocritical.

No wonder, too, that the liberalization of abortion laws is proceeding space throughout the world. In 1976, a United Nations study found that two thirds of the world's population lived in countries where legal abortion was relatively easy, as compared with only one third five years earlier. During the last decade, thirty-three countries have liberalized their abortion laws, and twelve permit abortion on demand during the first three months of pregnancy. The record discloses that no democratic nation has ever moved to make abortion more restricted.[16]

Do these considerations effectively dispose of the case against abortion on demand and justify the practice? Such a conclusion would be premature.

The alleged right of abortion on demand is generally supported by the argument that a woman has rights over her own body. This is a contention which Judaism, and indeed all high religion, must reject on both theological and ethical grounds as being essentially a pagan doctrine. It is basic Jewish teaching that no human being is master of his own body, because he did not create himself; male and female alike have been fashioned by God in His image.

This conviction lies at the heart of the Jewish insight that in addition to *mitzvot bein adam lamakom,* "commandments between man and God," and *mitzvot bein adam lahavero,* "commandments between man and man," we may posit another category, *bein adam l'atzmo*, "obligations and prohibitions between man and himself." These include debasing one's character through degrading habits and demeaning actions, injuring one's body through addictive drugs or excessive drinking, or other sins of the first magnitude. When the human body and the human spirit are injured, a sin is committed against the handiwork and the property of God. This is the root of the religious prohibitions of suicide and of self-mutilation.

Moreover, abortion on demand is a threat to a basic ethical principle which Judaism enunciated centuries before Albert Schweitzer. An embryo in its mother's body is not actually a living creature, but it is potential life, not to be lightly cast aside. Obviously what is only potential must be sacrificed when necessary for saving what is actual, but where no such threat exists, potential life too must be safeguarded. When an embryo is aborted, we are, in the fine rabbinic phrase, "diminishing the Divine image in which man is fashioned."[17]

In sum, while the law does not categorically rule out abortion since it is not "murder," the spirit of Judaism, reinforced by a realistic understanding of human motivation, must look askance at any blanket provision for abortion on demand. Long before Albert Schweitzer enunciated his justly famous ethical doctrine, Judaism sought to inculcate in its adherents —and largely succeeded—reverence for life and hatred of violence and bloodshed.

This all-important principle is imperiled today. If the law were to remove all conditions and restrictions, the increased practice of abortion on demand would further erode reverence for life, which has already been tragically weakened in our violence-riddled society. It cannot be denied that the casual attitude toward potential life implied in the practice is one more instance among many of the cheapening of life in contemporary society.

Are we confronted once again by an insoluble dilemma? On

the one hand, refusal to legalize abortion is obviously discriminatory; on the other hand, permitting abortion on demand means sanctioning a practice that at best is ethically dubious and socially corrosive, undermining what is perhaps the most sacred value in the Hebraic tradition, the sense of life as holy.

Actually, the contradiction involved in balancing opposite positions and opposing what is legally permitted is only apparent. It can be understood as an extension of the traditional rabbinic doctrine of *seyag,* "a fence around the law," already discussed in this volume, a "margin of protection" to safeguard a fundamental article of faith or practice.

It may also be suggested that here we have another illustration of the valuable tension between law and society that has been noted in the attitude of the Jewish tradition toward divorce and birth control. The law on abortion is and should be liberal, to meet genuine cases of hardship and misery that are not soluble in any other way. But society has an obligation to educate its members to ethical standards that rise above the level of abortion on demand. In other words, abortion should be legally available but ethically restricted, to be practiced only for very good reasons. Men and women must be persuaded that though the abortion of a foetus is not equivalent to taking an actual life, it does represent the destruction of potential life and must not be undertaken lightly or flippantly.

Until the day comes when ethical standards suffice to govern the actions of men and women without the use of external restraint, how is this tension to be resolved? We must have recourse to secular law, which alone has the power to enforce its norms. Here blanket permissibility would be almost as morally and socially catastrophic as a total ban.

On January 31, 1977, the Israeli Knesset adopted a new law on abortion that was strenuously opposed by the Orthodox rabbinate and did not please Israeli feminists. Nevertheless, the provisions of the law are both realistic and humane, and might well serve as a model for other countries. Under the

Israeli law, abortion is permitted if carried out in a recognized medical institution, with the woman's approval, and according to one or more of the following criteria: if the birth would endanger the woman's life or injure her physical or emotional health; if it can be determined that the child would be born either physically or mentally handicapped; if the pregnancy was the result of rape, incestuous relations, or intercourse outside of marriage; if the woman is below the age of sixteen or over forty.

Obviously, there can be no totally satisfactory solution to the abortion problem, which is itself a symptom of a tragedy. The choice of the lesser of two evils must be the goal in guiding society to a rational decision.

So long as we must depend upon a legal system rather than upon the human conscience to enforce an ethical code, it is clear that the best solution lies in preserving a basically liberal attitude toward abortion with conservative safeguards. That is to say, proper facilities for an abortion should be generally available to all classes of the population, while precautionary procedures must be established in special cases.

Over and above its intrinsic value, such a system of checks and balances would represent a protest against the pagan notion that human beings are absolute masters, either of the world about them or of their own persons, or of burgeoning life within them. The triumph of paganism, today as in the past, must lead to moral catastrophe and the destruction of civilization.

10

HOMOSEXUALITY AND
THE HOMOSEXUAL

Nowhere else is the confrontation between the classical religious tradition and emerging contemporary attitudes sharper than with regard to homosexuality. Biblical law and biblical life are completely at one in condemning the practice. The sexual codes in the Torah describe male homosexuality as an "abomination" punishable with death like other major infractions of the moral code, such as incest and sexual contact with animals (Lev. 18:22; 20:13).

The practice is clearly regarded as worse than rape, as is evident from an incident narrated in Chapter 19 of Genesis. Two strangers, who are actually angels sent by the Lord to survey the sinful city of Sodom, are given hospitality by Lot, Abraham's nephew. When the townsmen hear of the strangers in their midst, they besiege Lot's house and demand that he turn the wayfarers over to them for homosexual abuse. Horrified at this breach of the ancient custom of hospitality, Lot offers instead to send out his two virgin daughters to the mob to do with as they wish. When the mob refuses the offer and tries to storm the door of Lot's house, it becomes clear that the city is beyond hope, and its destruction is decreed by God.

A similar tragic incident, going back to an early, lawless period shortly after the conquest of the land, is reported in

Chapter 19 of the Book of Judges. A traveler passing through
the town of Gibeah in Benjamin is denied hospitality by the
townspeople. Only one old man gives lodging and food to the
stranger, his concubine, and his animals. When the Benjaminites learn that the stranger is being housed among them, they
gather and demand that he be handed over to them for sexual
purposes. The host remonstrates with them in vain, offering to
turn over his daughter and his guest's concubine to satisfy
their lust. When the mob does not desist, the guest takes his
concubine and pushes her out of doors. They rape her and
abuse her all night and leave her lifeless body on the threshold.
The book of Judges goes on to narrate the punishment visited
upon the Benjaminites, leading to the virtual extinction of that
tribe from the household of Israel.

There are many instances where rabbinic law has modified
biblical attitudes in the direction of greater leniency, but this
is not true of homosexuality.[1] Here the attitude remains
strongly negative, though the practice receives relatively little
attention in the Talmud, probably because the rabbis believed
that "Jews are not suspected of committing homosexuality and
buggery."[2]

This persistent feeling of revulsion toward homosexuality
was nourished by a variety of historical causes. During the
biblical period, the fertility cults that were widespread
throughout the Middle East included intercourse with sacred
male prostitutes at the pagan temples. From the Canaanites
these practices, along with idolatry in general, penetrated into
the religious practices of the Hebrews during the early days
of the Davidic kingdom. These functionaries were finally banished from the precincts of the Temple, but only after repeated and determined efforts by several Judean kings, Asa,
Jehoshaphat, and Josiah.[3]

During the Greco-Roman era and beyond, the opposition to
homosexuality by Jewish rabbinic leadership was a reaction to
its widespread presence in the ancient world, where it was
furthered and encouraged by pagan society and religion.

Homosexual liaisons played a significant role in the social and cultural life of the ancient Greeks and Romans. Indirect evidence of the strong hold that homosexuality had on the Greco-Roman world is to be found in Paul's Epistle to the Romans. In the strongest of terms he castigates homosexuality as "dishonorable" and "unnatural." That he places homosexuality at the head of a list of offenses would suggest that the practice was widespread. It is also noteworthy that he first levels his attack against the women and only then turns to the men as "likewise" engaging in these "shameless acts." (1:26,27)

This negative attitude toward homosexuality has been maintained by Jewish tradition to the present time. It regards homosexuals as flouting the will of the Creator, who fashioned men and women with different anatomical endowments and with correspondingly distinct roles to play in the sexual process.

All these objections to homosexuality in Judaism were intensified in Christianity because of several additional factors. Most of the converts to the early Christian Church were former pagans who had been exposed to the presence of homosexual practices in their previous environment. Paul, as well as the Church after him, therefore felt it incumbent to attack the practice with all the power at his command. Moreover, as we have seen, classical Christianity was basically unhappy with the sexual component of human nature in general. It had to concede that sexual contact was legitimate, first because the instinct cannot be successfully suppressed by most men and women and, second, because it is essential for procreation. Since this last factor is obviously lacking in homosexual activity, there is no justification for yielding to "unnatural lust."

In sum, both Judaism and Christianity, in spite of differences in their approach to sex, have regarded homosexuality as a violation of God's will and a perversion of nature.

The subsequent weakening of religion and the growth of secularism in the Western world did little to reduce the sense of hostility toward homosexuality. The new emphasis on the cultivation of the body and the development of athletics in the modern period underscored the goal that men should be men. Nowhere is masculinity revealed more unmistakably than in sexual potency. Psychoanalytic theory, particularly in its classical Freudian formulation, saw male and female sexuality as the fundamental element in the human personality, which, when diverted from "normal" channels, becomes the source of psychological and physical trauma. In this respect as well, homosexuality ran counter to the values of the age. As a result of all these factors, as well as vestiges of the religious approach, homosexuality continued to engender feelings of revulsion going beyond the bonds of rational response.

Perhaps the most sensational manifestation of this reaction came at the end of the nineteenth century. In 1895, the brilliant and gifted English dramatist and poet Oscar Wilde was prosecuted by the Crown for having homosexual relations with Lord Alfred Douglas. Wilde was convicted, imprisoned for two years, and emerged from this experience a man physically broken and creatively ruined.

Wilde is by no means the only example of talent or genius to be found among homosexuals. More or less plausibly, many distinguished figures of the past and the present have been described as homosexuals. It is likely that lesbianism is as common as male homosexuality, but it is felt to be less offensive because its manifestations seem less blatant.

The hostility of society to homosexuals is reflected in the statute books. Homosexual behavior is treated as a crime in China and the Soviet Union; in the United States, homosexual soliciting is a criminal act. To be sure, such laws have often not been enforced in this country, particularly in the recent past.

By and large, the penalties accorded to homosexuals have been social and economic rather than legal.[4] Homosexuals have been driven underground and have had to suffer all the psychological traumas associated with a closet existence. They have been forced to deny their desires and to pretend to interests and feelings not their own. Always there is the human propensity to cruelty, of which the twentieth century has made us painfully aware. Add to it the negative attitude toward homosexuals in the religious tradition and in secular law and you have a moral base for flagrant discrimination and hostility toward homosexuals in housing and employment.

The alleged effeminacy in dress and demeanor of homosexuals has been the butt of ridicule and scorn in public and in private, on the printed page, the radio, television, the screen, and the stage. This in spite of the alleged high percentage of homosexuals in the artistic, literary, and entertainment worlds.

Only within the past two decades has the public attitude begun to change. The general weakening of traditional religion has diminished the influence of biblical and post-biblical teaching on the subject. In addition, sexual experience without regard to procreation has increasingly been accepted and glorified as a good in itself, if not as the *summum bonum* of existence. Hence, homosexuality has lost some of the horror it conjured up in earlier generations. Above all, in our age, the drive for new and exciting experiences, however untried and even dangerous they may be, has led to new patterns of sexual conduct, like sexual communes and wife-swapping, not to speak of various forms of perversion. Advocates of homosexuality have, therefore, felt free to argue that they are simply practicing an equally legitimate life style, a variant pattern to the dominant heterosexuality of our culture. Some have maintained that 10 percent of the population are homosexual, a figure that can neither be demonstrated nor disproved.

Substantial success has already crowned the efforts of the various organizations in the gay-liberation movement to remove disabilities in employment and housing from homosexuals in the United States. In France, Italy, Sweden, Denmark, Switzerland, Mexico, and Uruguay, the practice has long been decriminalized. Great Britain took the same step in 1967 and Canada in 1969.[5]

What approach toward homosexuality should modern reli-

gion sanction and modern society adopt? No excuse can or
should be offered for the cruelty that traditional attitudes toward the practice have engendered in the past. Nevertheless,
the classical viewpoint of Judaism and Christianity, that homosexual conduct is "unnatural," cannot be dismissed out of
hand.

Here a brief theological digression is called for. That the
goal of the universe and, by that token, the purpose of existence are veiled from man has been the conviction of thinkers
in every age. Koheleth in the Bible and the medieval philosopher Maimonides are at one with the Hasidic teacher Rabbi
Bunam of Pshysha, who found his beloved disciple Enoch in
tears. The rabbi asked him, "Why are you weeping?" and
Enoch answered, "Am I not a creature of this world, and am
I not made with eyes and heart and all limbs, and yet I do not
know for what purpose I was created and what good I am in
the world." "Fool!" said Rabbi Bunam. "I also go around thus."

Nevertheless, we may perhaps catch a slight glimpse of the
purpose of the Creator, or, if secular terms be preferred, the
direction and goal of the life process in the universe. The
lowest creatures in the evolutionary ladder, the single-cell
organisms, multiply by fission, the splitting of the cell into two
equal parts. As a result, each of the two new beings possesses
exactly the same attributes as the parent, no more, no less, no
change. Only with the emergence of multicellular organisms
does bisexuality appear on the evolutionary ladder. Fission is
now replaced by bisexual reproduction, which becomes the
universal pattern. This fundamental change seems to indicate
that the Author of life has intended the life process to be not
a perpetually static repetition of the old but a dynamic adventure, with new combinations of attributes constantly emerging through the interaction of a male and a female producing
a new organism different from both its parents. It therefore
follows that, in purely secular biological terms, homosexuality
is an aberration from the norm, a violation of the law of nature.

It may be objected that since man is not merely a creature

of nature and is free to modify his environment and perhaps even his heredity, what is natural is not the sole touchstone of what is right for man. There is, however, good reason for believing that homosexuality is a violation not only of nature but of human nature as well. No attribute is more characteristic of humanity than the gift of speech. Language is probably the greatest intellectual achievement of primitive man. Imbedded in the structure of all languages is gender, a recognition of bisexuality, which, by extension, is applied to every object in the real world. Gender remains basic to language and to thought for the most sophisticated of moderns.

For later stages of human development, it may be noted that no society has made homosexuality its basic or even its preferred pattern of sexual conduct. This is true even of predatory groups that could have replenished their ranks through captives taken in war.

Transposed into theological language, heterosexuality is the will of God. It therefore follows that homosexuality is a violation of His will, for which the traditional term is "sin." The concept of sin in general may seem outmoded to modern ears and, in any event, too harsh a term to apply to homosexuality. But the etymology of the Hebrew word *het,* like its Greek counterpart, *hamartia,* is derived from marksmanship and means "missing the mark," as has already been noted. Sin means a turning aside from the right path that can and should be followed. Consequently the Hebrew *teshubbah,* generally translated as "repentance," means "returning" to the right road.

Judgments and attitudes aside, what are the facts about homosexuality? In spite of the vast interest in the phenomenon, very little is really known about its origin and nature or any possible treatment. Modern psychologists may be correct in believing that latent homosexual tendencies are to be found in most people. If this is true, it would seem that homosexual patterns of behavior become dominant for some men and women because they are stimulated by personal contact with homosexuals. If, therefore, homosexuality is culturally induced, it would be a flagrant example of a conscious and often conscienceless distortion of normal human nature. On the other hand, homosexuality may be the product of a genetic disturbance. In this case, it must be regarded as a biological abnormality. Whether the practice is the result of heredity or of environment, or of both, intensive research is needed to discover the etiology of homosexuality and then to search for a remedy, or at least for methods of treatment.

For centuries, society, abetted by religion, has been guilty of condemning as a sin and punishing as a crime what should have been recognized as an illness. In fact, physical illness in general was regarded as a Divine visitation, a punishment for sins for which the sufferer himself was responsible. This attitude is not altogether dead today. Recently, the president of a mammoth bank in New York demonstrated that he is obviously afflicted with massive spiritual myopia. He declared that physical illness is a crime against society committed by those who are ill, and that therefore society has no obligation to provide medical care and other social services to the sick poor.

If homosexuality is an abnormality or an illness, as has been maintained, a parallel to our problem in several respects may be found in alcoholism. So long as the alcoholic was regarded as an incorrigible sinner, little progress was made in curing this major malady. It is only in our day, when alcoholism is being recognized as a disease, probably genetic in origin though socially stimulated, that genuine progress has begun to be made in overcoming it.

The analogy is helpful in another respect as well. Experts are agreed that the will to recover, as expressed in total abstinence, which is encouraged by such programs as Alcoholics Anonymous, plays an indispensable role in the treatment of alcohol addiction. It is also known that only a fraction of all alcoholics, somewhere between one third and one half of all patients who undergo treatment, recover fully or substantially.[7]

At the present level of our knowledge, the percentage of homosexuals who can be "rehabilitated" is almost surely lower than that of alcoholics. To a substantial degree, this is due to the varying attitudes of contemporary society toward two phenomena. While alcoholism is universally recognized as a liability, homosexuality is often defended as a normal life style, a legitimate alternate pattern to heterosexuality. The gay-liberation movement has vigorously opposed the older traditional view of homosexuality as a sin. It is not more kindly disposed to the more modern concept of homosexuality as an illness. It uses every available means to propagate the idea that homosexuality is an entirely proper life style.

Nevertheless, if we are not to fall prey to the old prejudice or to succumb to the new fashion, we must insist that homosexuality is not normal. To the extent that men and women cannot control their homosexual desires, they are suffering from an illness like any other physical disability. To the degree that they can hold the impulse in rein and fail to do so, they are committing a sin, a violation of the will of God or, in secular terms, an aberration from the norm.

However, a basic caution is in order. Ignorant as we are of the etiology of the disorder, we are in no position to determine to which category a given act belongs. Hence, homosexual activity, when carried on by adults in private and violating no one's wishes and desires, should be decriminalized on the statute books. The practice belongs to the rabbinic category of an act that is "free from legal punishment (by human agency), but forbidden."[8] The homosexual in contemporary society has a just claim to be free from legal penalties and social disabilities.

Yet there are some critical areas where blanket removal of all restrictions against homosexuals may be unwise. Such a decision should be reached without panic or prejudice, on the basis of a careful investigation of all the relevant factors. Sensing the widespread erosion of conventional moral standards everywhere, homosexual groups are pressing for much more than freedom from discrimination and harassment. They are demanding that homosexuality be recognized as a legitimate and normal alternative to heterosexuality.[9]

Some Christian theologians, troubled by the tragic and undeniable fact that Western society has been grievously lacking in compassion for homosexuals, have attempted to give a Christian justification for homosexuality. One Catholic writer explains away the biblical condemnations of homosexual practices as "Old Testament legalism."[10] A Protestant theologian takes his point of departure from the Christian doctrine that salvation is directed to all mankind, so that all human beings are equally sinful in the eyes of God. He, therefore, leaps to the non sequitur that "no absolute or ultimate distinction can be made between homosexuality and heterosexuality." He goes even further and declares that "no human condition or life style is intrinsically *justified* or righteous—neither heterosexuality nor homosexuality, closed nor open marriage, celibacy nor profligacy." He proceeds to express doubts as to whether the family centeredness of contemporary Christianity can be justified theologically, since both Jesus and Paul were suspicious of family ties! He concludes that there are three life styles open to men and women intrinsically equal in moral validity: marriage, celibacy, and homosexuality.[11]

The lengths to which sympathetic souls may be led are evident in the secular sphere as well. In fact, like the generous Irishman who was asked, "Isn't one man as good as another?" and answered, "Sure, and a whole lot better, too," some advocates have argued that homosexuality is not merely as good as heterosexuality but better, since it avoids the possibility of increasing the population! The same logic would lead to the conclusion that sterility is healthier and more beneficial than fecundity.

It is perhaps a sign of the times that a recent radio broadcast referred to a sado-masochist liberation movement, which calls itself the Til Eulenspiegel Society. This group, whose size was not indicated, demands "equal rights" for the practice of sexual perversion, including such forms as flagellation and sodomy, which, they insist, are also legitimate alternatives.

Having mastered the modern art of lobbying, homosexuals carried on a campaign among the members of the American Psychological Association and, in 1974, succeeded in having homosexuality removed from the list of abnormal patterns of behavior. An effort is being made in some quarters to reverse the ruling of the American Psychological Association. The argument advanced by gay-liberation groups is that homosexuals are basically healthy, well-adjusted individuals who do not seek medical or psychiatric treatment because they do not need it. Spokesmen for homosexuality, aware of the widespread frustration and unhappiness with conventional marriages, have urged the claim. In a growing number of cases, homosexuals have asked the clergy to officiate at homosexual "marriages." No comparative study is available of either the permanence of homosexual unions or of the quality of life of homosexual couples.

On the other hand, testimony has been advanced to show that the self-acceptance and satisfaction with life expressed by many homosexuals is often only a façade for resignation and despair, all the more hopeless because it cannot find channels of expression. In their youth, it has been maintained, homosexuals have suffered from rejection and unhappiness, which are integral to their condition. In adult life, they continue to experience conflict, anguish, and pain which they deny even to themselves. It has also been argued that the growing militant assertion of "gay pride," coupled with the A.P.A. declaration that homosexuality is normal human behavior on the one hand and the generally negative attitude of society on the other, has intensified their unhappiness. That there is so much heat and so little light demonstrates only how slight is the authentic scientific knowledge available on this important issue.

There have been some specifically religious aspects to the campaign for equal rights for homosexuals. In 1976, the Episcopal Bishop of New York ordained a woman to the priesthood who stated publicly that she was a lesbian. The act raised considerable protest among many communicants and clergy. Some time ago, on the West Coast, a group of Jewish homosexuals organized themselves into a congregation and were admitted into membership in the Union of American Hebrew Congregations. In the East, a "Gay Synagogue" holds Friday evening services in New York City that are announced by *The New York Times* each Friday.

How should the Jewish community react to a call for special worship facilities for homosexuals? The answer would not be difficult to reach were the issue not beclouded by so much passion on both sides of the barricade. Men and women suffering various disabilities do not organize special synagogues. The only exceptions are facilities for worship for the blind and the deaf, dictated by the necessity of finding alternate modes of communication. Jewish male and female homosexuals are Jews and should always be made welcome among their people. In the discussion engendered by the West Coast group, it was explained that homosexuals wish to be able to kiss one another publicly after the conclusion of Sabbath services. Evidently, they believe that this type of greeting is a law of Moses from Sinai. But missing a kiss in public hardly justifies founding a synagogue. Undoubtedly, other and weightier motives play their part as well.

As is so frequently the case, truth and justice in this troubled area lie, not with the extremes, but with the center position. We can no longer accept the traditional religious reaction to homosexuality as a horror and an abomination. On the other hand, the fashionable doctrine being propagated in our time —that it is an alternate life style of equal value and legitimacy —must be decisively rejected. Homosexuality is an abnormality, an illness which, like any other, varies in intensity with different individuals. Until more efficacious means are discovered for dealing with their problem, homosexuals deserve the same inalienable rights as do all their fellow human beings— freedom from harassment and discrimination before the law and in society.

There can be no question that homosexuals are entitled to more than justice before the law. It is not enough merely to remove the various kinds of legal disability and overt hostility to which they have long been subjected. Whatever evaluation is placed upon their condition, be it moral, medical, or psychological, they are human beings, our brothers and sisters, who deserve compassion and love from their fellow men and, above all, from their brothers in kinship and in faith.[17]

11

SEX WITHOUT MARRIAGE
Center of the New Life Style

However sensational homosexuals may be, they represent a small minority of the population. A more common manifestation of the new morality lies elsewhere, in the growth of free sexual relations between men and women outside of marriage.

Obviously, extramarital relations are not a modern invention. Casual meetings between men and women leading to strong mutual attraction and culminating in sexual intimacy are as old as human experience itself. In the past, an effort was generally made to keep such episodes secret, and usually they were of brief duration. The higher echelons had several additional options open to them, as befitting their privileged position. Besides such casual encounters, rich and powerful men were often able to have their will with women who were slaves or servants in their households. In addition, upper-class society was frequently characterized by long-standing liaisons outside of marriage between men and women of approximately equal social standing. Finally, a man could establish a relationship with a woman of lower rank whom he kept as his mistress. These various types of connections were usually kept secret, or at least were officially ignored in the circles in which the participants moved.

The present situation differs from the past in at least three respects. First, such long-term relations are no longer limited to the upper classes. They offer a striking confirmation of the cynical definition of democracy as that social order in which the lower classes are free to imitate the vices of the rich. Second, the number of such arrangements has increased tremendously, as the practice has been "democratized." Third, little or no effort is generally being made today to keep them secret since contemporary society, if it does not actively approve, tacitly acquiesces in them. Increasingly, extramarital relationships tend to be regarded as an alternate life style of almost equal legitimacy with marriage.

The new patterns of sexual intimacy fall into two major categories. The first (premarital sex) consists of many couples who are formally or informally engaged and plan on marriage in the near future, as soon as economic and other conditions are propitious. The second (non-marital sex) consists of young people (and older ones as well) drawn to each other sufficiently to wish to live together, though they have no intention of marriage and make no long-term commitment to each other. The arrangement may last a few weeks or months, or even longer, but what is decisive is the absence of any element of mutual obligation. This residential and sexual pattern is what the euphemism of the day calls "a meaningful relationship." Its basic nature is expressed in the words of a song, "It's the friendliest thing you can do."

Obviously there can be no hard and fast statistics with regard to the increase and extent of these two types of non-marital relations in our time. A partial clue may be found in the number of brides who are not virgins at the time of their marriage and in the percentage of children born out of wedlock. Nearly half of all unmarried American women have had sexual intercourse by the time they are nineteen years old. Of the births to teenage girls that result from first pregnancies, 45 percent are illegitimate and six in ten of the legitimate births among girls in this age group were conceived before marriage. "To marry and then to conceive is the exception among teenagers." In 1950, illegitimate live births represented 3.9 percent of all births; in 1955, 4.5 percent; in 1960, 5.3 percent; in 1965, 7.7 percent; in 1970, 10.7 percent; in 1971, 11.3 percent; in 1972, 12.4 percent; in 1973, 13.0 percent. In the last seven years, the number of non-marital relationships in the U.S. has doubled.

Undoubtedly, young men have always tended to exaggerate their sexual prowess to their peers. In an age of equality, women may perhaps be doing the same. Hence claims put forward in this connection may be greater than the reality. After all, there have always been examples of brief sexual encounters outside of marriage among the lower classes. Such episodes have also been characteristic of those groups in society who are their "betters," whose claim to the title is clear from the greater finesse with which they make their arrangements in this area. However, after due allowances are made for factors such as these, there is little doubt that premarital sex is much more prevalent today than it was in the past, the practice being both the cause and the effect of the new morality.

The process became general about two decades ago when young unmarried men and women began moving out of their parents' home and setting up their own "pad" so that they "could do their own thing." Then came a demand that college dormitories for girls abolish the limitations on visiting hours and be open at all hours to male friends. Where this demand was granted, it was followed by a call for coed dormitories, with all their appurtenances. This step has not yet become the universal rule. On some advanced campuses, an enthusiastic medical staff spends a good deal of its time and energy providing counseling and contraceptive pills designed to facilitate sexual intimacies for male and female students.

Many a modern mother, suspecting that her daughter going out on a date may engage in sexual relations, has been confronted by the dilemma of whether or not to advise her daughter on the use of a contraceptive before she leaves for the evening. In most cases, the mother has opted for discretion as better than faith. It is not altogether uncommon for a girl of middle-class background to bring a boy friend home to her parents for a weekend and take it for granted that they will share a common bedroom. It is clear that the rising tide of sexual relations outside of marriage shows no sign of receding. Has the time come for religion to abandon its long opposition to premarital sexual experience? Have new circumstances of contemporary life radically changed the norms by which lives should be governed?

Before we attempt to deal with this question, it is worth pointing out that in its long and varied history the Jewish people has already encountered the two principal categories of non-marital sexual experience we have described. The actual response of Jewish tradition to both, to the sexual activity of engaged couples expecting to be married shortly and to the long-term relationships of men and women outside of marriage at all, may appear astonishing.

There is no need to emphasize that Judaism maintains the principle that sexual relations are proper only within the marriage bond. Moreover, the standard of chastity before marriage and fidelity within it was alive and well among the masses of Jews who lived by the traditional patterns, so that aberrations from the norm were relatively few.

Hence Jewish leadership rarely felt called upon to admonish or to castigate the masses of the people with regard to liaisons outside the marriage bond. Preoccupation with the subject of fornication, which, many Catholic writers declare, has characterized the Catholic pulpit and the confession box, has no counterpart in Jewish experience. During a lifetime of attendance at the synagogue, I do not recall one sermon on the subject. It is significant that there is no Hebrew equivalent for the Christian concept of "living in sin," which is applied to unmarried men and women who share a common home.

Here the Halakah is highly significant. While Judaism objects to all extramarital intimacies, it does not equate a relationship with an unmarried woman as being on a par with adultery or treat it as an equally serious infraction of morality. Thus Jewish law does not regard a child born to an unmarried mother as illegitimate, though he obviously has an inferior social status.[2]

A much more frequent problem, it would appear, is that of intercourse by engaged couples. According to the codes, intimate relations between engaged couples are prohibited, not biblically, but only rabbinically.[3] According to the Talmud and the Geonim, there was substantial freedom in the relations of engaged couples as early as the period of Ezra and Nehemiah (fifth century B.C.E.).[4] In Tannaitic times, private companionship for couples before marriage was permitted in Judea, though not in Galilee.[5] The stricter Galilean rule became the norm in talmudic and post-talmudic law.[6]

That the practice existed on a fairly wide scale is clear from the fact that it led to a major change in the Jewish marriage ritual. The traditional Jewish marriage ceremony consists of two sections, each of which is climaxed by the sharing of a cup of wine by the groom and bride. The first section is the *kiddushin,* the setting aside or betrothal of the bride exclusively to the groom; the second, the $n^e su'in$, is the marriage proper, which permits the couple to cohabit. In the Middle Ages, these two parts of the ceremony did not take place at the same time. An interval of several months, or longer, might exist between them. However, because of the possibility of intimacies between the engaged couple after the *kiddushin,* rabbinic authorities changed the marriage procedure drastically by having both stages take place at the same time, and this is the current practice.[7]

On this subject, a striking talmudic statement, not devoid of humor, is reported in the name of Rabbi Levi: "He who eats *matzah* on the eve of Passover [i.e., before the advent of the Festival] is like a man who has relations with his betrothed in the house of his father-in-law [i.e., before marriage]. He who is guilty of this offense [i.e., the eating of *matzah*] is punished by flagellation."[8] We may note the insight into human frailty underlying the analogy between the two acts. Yet in spite of its sympathy for the weaknesses of the flesh, Jewish tradition expresses its negative judgment by the penalty that is prescribed in the Talmud and the codes. When even this deterrent was not completely effective, Jewish practice, as we have seen, was modified, so as to obviate the problem. But there was none of the frenetic condemnation of the practice that has characterized some other religious traditions.

In cases where marriage is not contemplated, non-marital relations are vigorously opposed by Judaism. Yet here too the moral stance was tempered by psychological insight. In the period of the Mishnah, the second-century sage Rabbi Eliezer strongly condemned the unmarried woman who engaged in sexual intimacies.[9] However, his views were not shared by the majority of his colleagues.

The problem took on larger proportions in medieval Spain, where Jews lived in close proximity with the non-Jewish population, both Christian and Muslim. The impact of Islamic culture on Judaism in the fields of philology, poetry, philosophy, history, and the natural sciences was both powerful and beneficial. More equivocal was the influence of non-Jewish mores on Spanish Jews, particularly on members of the affluent classes. Extramarital liaisons among the nobility and the rich, both Christian and Muslim, were common and Jews were not slow to follow suit. The situation was sufficiently widespread to command the attention of the great Spanish authority Nahmanides (1194–1270), who went so far as to declare that relations with an unmarried woman who has no relations with other men are permissible. This extremely lenient attitude was naturally not accepted universally. Thus, Rabbi Isaac bar Sheshet Perfet (1326–1408) was far stricter.[10] He decried the popular saying "An unmarried woman is not forbidden,"[11] but he saw other and greater threats to traditional standards of personal morality in his time.[12] Such liaisons did not abate, even in the face of rabbinical opposition. A well-known authority on Jewish sexual mores remarks: "In vain did the great Maimonides try to prohibit concubinage; not only did the practice continue, but most contemporary and later rabbinical authorities . . . accepted it. Acceptance, of course, did not mean approval."[13]

While no authorities favored such extramarital relationships, those who were less rigorous in their attitude found a basis for according them a quasi-legitimate status in the biblical institution of the *pillegesh*, "concubine" or "secondary wife." The practice is mentioned in connection with the Patriarchs Abraham and Jacob,[14] and in the early period of the Judges.[15] Thereafter, it seems to be restricted to monarchs like David and Solomon, as well as to foreign kings who could maintain large households.[16] The number of biblical references to the practice is small and its precise character is unclear. In the post-biblical era, concubinage is no longer in existence.

Liaisons of the kind we have described ended with the tragic destruction of Spanish Jewry as a result of the expulsion of the Jews from Spain in 1492 and from Portugal in 1497. Thereafter, the earlier and stricter traditional standards became all but universal again, and there no longer was a need to find even a quasi-legal basis for extramarital relations.

With this historical perspective as a background, we may address ourselves to the basic issues involved in premarital sex today. On the subliminal level, let it be confessed, there lurks the feeling among some of the elders that a good time had by the young is immoral per se and should be prohibited on general principles. Be this as it may, it should be obvious that the basis of the Jewish approach to the problem cannot be the prevention of happiness.

The new life styles we are discussing have been defended from two distinct, indeed contradictory, points of view. One school of thought maintains that premarital sex is an excellent preparation for marriage. It affords the young people an opportunity to learn to know each other well, discover their strengths and weaknesses, and decide how compatible they are. In short, the practice makes it possible for the couple to test out married life without marriage, so that if the experiment is unsuccessful, the principals avoid the heartaches and the complications incidental to a legal divorce. Thus, a premarital relationship can help to buttress the marriage institution.

The argument is ingenious and is no doubt sincerely advanced by many of its proponents. The theory recalls the "companionate or trial marriage" idea advocated in the 1920's by Judge Ben Lindsey.[17] His proposal called for a legal marriage agreement to be entered into by the couple, who would practice birth control during their period of cohabitation. The arrangement stipulated unhindered separation at the will of either partner if there were no children.

During its heyday, the trial-marriage plan was urged on the ground that it would make it possible to test the relationship of the two people involved and avoid the trauma of divorce complicated by the possible presence of children.

The Lindsey plan was, of course, closer to legal marriage than are the contemporary patterns of living together. Yet even then it was recognized that the Lindsey plan was not a successful surrogate for marriage and, therefore, not a true test. For the essence of the marriage relationship is the element of mutual responsibility on a permanent basis, involving a long-term, if not a lifetime, commitment. In other words, the only way to know whether a marriage will work is to get married. For only then do the young people have the incentive to work out their differences, adjust to one another, compromise their different goals, and, in general, submerge the desires of the "I" into the goals of "we." As in every human enterprise, rewards cannot be won unless the risks are run. In the words of Rabbi Akiba's parable: "The shop is open and the dealer gives credit. The ledger lies open and the hand writes. Whoever wishes to borrow may come and borrow, but the collectors regularly make their daily rounds and exact payment from each person, with or without his consent, for they have what they can rely on in making their demand. The judgment is a judgment of truth and everything is prepared for the feast."[18]

As a body of experience with regard to premarital relations has accumulated, it is becoming clear that the partners do not avoid most of the problems and difficulties associated with traditional marriage. Marriage counselors in New York and California estimate that fully 10 percent of their caseloads consist of couples living together without benefit of clergy. All too often, their mutual adjustment in taste and temperament leaves much to be desired, and leads to quarrels and bitterness of spirit. One observer comments, "As the unwed couples in counseling have come to realize, you don't have to be married to suffer."[19]

In addition, unwed couples face one other major source of difficulty inherent in their uncertain situation. As one authority explains, "Unmarried couples are less securely anchored. There's more tentativeness about the capacity of the other to endure hostility or a rocky period."[20]

Far from strengthening the institution of marriage, a premarital relationship undermines it at its most basic. If marriage is to survive in spite of all its liabilities, it must be endowed with one unique attribute characteristic of it and of it alone—*it must be the only theater for experiencing the most intimate interplay of love and sex.* Marriage must have this special quality in order to survive the limitless challenges and temptations of modern life in a free and open society. Never have these hazards been as ubiquitous and as powerful as they are in society today. By robbing marriage of this unique character, premarital sex weakens its staying power. Premarital sex transforms the sexual act from being an expression of the highest level of intimacy and love into a run-of-the-mill sensual experience, casual or irregular, available at any time and with any partner.

Even for a couple who are engaged and are planning to be

married, the significance of the marriage state is vitiated by premarital sex, because the pattern of their life together before and after the marriage ceremony is virtually indistinguishable. Nothing in their behavior has been changed by the intervening ceremony. As a result, the sanctity of marriage, that is to say, its claim upon loyalty and permanence even in the face of inclination and desire, is gravely weakened, if not destroyed.

When young people who have had sexual intimacies together marry and live happily after—and this does happen—the best that can be said is that the premarital relationship did not destroy their marriage; it cannot be regarded as strengthening the bond.

Nor is this all. Premarital sex robs the love act of its full potential for joy. Intercourse always carries with it the possibility of conception. This is true even today with the various contraceptive devices available, as the mounting tide of illegitimate births and abortions testifies. When the act of supreme intimacy takes place outside of marriage, it must inevitably be beclouded by concern and anxiety, instead of bringing total joy and release to the participants.

There is another subtle yet vital aspect of love at its highest —the desire, indeed, the need, of the lover to announce to all the world his pride in his beloved and his joy in their relationship. While love is a private matter, it does not reach its fullness unless it is publicly expressed. In all ages, poetry and music have not only given voice to longing, desire, and courtship, they have also served as instruments for love's proud proclamation to the world—in the words of the beloved in the Song of Songs, "This is my lover, and this is my friend, O daughters of Jerusalem." Whatever inhibits the full avowal of love, forces it to dissemble or makes it surreptitious, constricts the relationship and impugns its quality. Love that is limited is love in chains.

Proof of this truth scarcely needs to be offered, as anyone who has ever been in love knows out of his own experience.

However, a recognition of this insight has recently come to light from an unexpected source, the memoirs of the English writer Virginia Woolf. During the first two decades of the twentieth century, she was one of the leading members of the Bloomsbury Circle, a group of talented writers and artists well-connected, successful, free-living, politically enlightened, and sexually emancipated. In a memoir written at the end of her life, she comments on an engagement she had observed in her family many years earlier:

> It was through that engagement that I had my first vision —so intense, so exciting, so rapturous was it that the word vision applies—my first vision then of love between man and woman. It was to me like a ruby; the love I detected that winter of their engagement, glowing, red, clear, intense. It gave me a conception of love; a standard of love; a sense that nothing in the whole world is so lyrical, so musical, as a young man and a young woman in their first love for each other. I connect it with respectable engagements; unofficial love never gives me the same feeling. "My love's like a red, red rose, that's newly sprung in June"— that was the feeling they gave; the feeling that has always come back, when I hear of "an engagement"; not when I hear of "an affair."[19]

It is a sad fact that contemporary marriage is beset by many difficulties, often economic in nature. The solution lies in meeting those problems directly, whether by parental assistance or government subsidy, or other means. It is essential to facilitate marriage for people in love and minimize the dangers that arise from economic need afterward.

Here it is important to distinguish between "quick" marriages and early marriages. It is true that quick marriages (after a short period of acquaintanceship) have a high mortality rate. Society might well consider the advisability of adopting a rule similar to the practice of "publishing the banns" in the Catholic Church. An extended period of six months or a year might be required from the time that an intention to marry is registered until a marriage license is issued. But postponing marriage causes physical and psychological problems, and is therefore not the solution.

In all honesty, it must be recognized that premarital relations are not designed to strengthen the marriage institution, nor do they achieve that objective.

Generally, the pattern of living together outside of marriage is defended on totally opposite grounds—not that such a relationship helps build a better marriage, but that it constitutes an alternate and superior pattern for meeting the sexual and social needs of men and women.

In this connection, we need not be detained long by the newly advanced contention that the federal income-tax laws are designed for the benefit of single people, so that if both the man and the woman are gainfully employed, the argument runs, their income tax is less than if they are married and file a joint return. Obviously this consideration can be raised only by those who are impervious to the deeper implications of marriage. If the tax laws affecting married people are inequitable, the obvious course is to amend the laws, not to abolish marriage.

There are, of course, far less trivial reasons offered in defense of permanent extramarital relations. In essence, the new life style represents a major challenge to the institution of marriage, which basically is designed to establish a permanent relationship. The new competitive pattern raises the question whether monogamous marriage, like the feudal system, has outlived its usefulness and should now be consigned to the dust heap of history. Perhaps traditional marriage has been foisted on the human race by a combination of force and guile and has been preserved through deep-seated fears and superstitions, from which the human race is now emancipating itself.

In response to these questions, we need to recall that the tradition of monogamous lifetime marriage is by no means the only pattern of sex relations with which the human race has experimented. Polygamy and polyandry have existed in many older societies and may have been far more prevalent than our surviving records indicate, as many anthropologists maintain. Free sex liaisons have been traditional among many primitive tribes. Sacred prostitution practiced in temples was, in effect, a form of free sexual encounter with no strings attached. Group marriage also has its analogues in some earlier societies.

The dissolution of a marriage by a simple declaration by one of the partners with no complications has been in practice in widely different cultures. For example, it has been the law in Islam, where women are legally bereft of basic rights and only the husband's statement is required to dissolve a marriage. It was attempted in the early years following the Communist revolution in Russia, but was later abandoned and replaced by rigorous standards.

In sum, society has experimented with many sexual behavior patterns. Stripped of their contemporary trappings, it is the new types of alternate life styles being urged upon us today that are old. They have been tried and found wanting, and it is they that represent the debris of history. Monogamy has prevailed over all other patterns, through no dark conspiracy, but because, while it is not a perfect arrangement—none can be—it offers the best hope for the well-being of the greatest number of men, women, and children.

To be sure, there are problems and difficulties associated with the marriage institution, some inherent to the human condition always and everywhere, others the result of the new and rapid transformations in society described earlier. We need the combined resources of the wisest, most sympathetic, and most knowledgeable scientists, scholars, and thinkers available to analyze the difficulties and suggest proposals for their amelioration. Some suggestions will be set forth in later chapters of this book. But if men and women are to enjoy a truly meaningful relationship, to use a contemporary cliché meaningfully, their best chance lies in monogamous marriage. If the Bible is right in declaring, "It is not good for man to dwell alone," the religions that are rooted in Scripture are justified in upholding the pattern of traditional marriage and defending it against attack.

Yet it must be admitted that however effectively we may present the case for premarital continence, the trend is in the opposite direction. In continuing to advocate the traditional ideal, are we not voices crying in the wilderness?

History indicates that morals ebb and flow and that trends have been reversed time and again. There have been eras of great permissiveness, such as the Restoration period in England in the seventeenth century, followed by ages of more rigorous standards, like Victorian England. As we have seen, significant segments of Spanish Jewry felt free to contract long-term liaisons with women outside of marriage. Nevertheless, in succeeding ages, these looser standards of behavior virtually disappeared from Jewish life. The pendulum may well swing in the other direction, if only because of the incurable human tendency to tire of the old and seek out the new. Action and reaction is as much a part of human nature as the systole and diastole are of the human heart.

But whatever the future may hold, we cannot honorably abandon our standpoint in order to be in style and curry favor with the masses. If we are convinced of the validity and value of the traditional ideal of love, sex, and marriage, we have no choice but to make it part of our teaching and counseling, and embody it in the way of life we advocate. As Milton declared in the *Areopagitica,* "Let truth and falsehood grapple. Who has ever known truth to be worsted in a full and free encounter?"

But these are long-term considerations. How are these theoretic principles to be translated into the agonizing nitty-gritty problems confronting parents and children today? What should parents do in the face of the widespread pattern of youthful rebellion? How should they react to the news that a son or a daughter is involved in an extramarital relationship? It is perhaps easier to say what they ought not to do. At all costs, they must avoid both extremes. On the one hand, they should not become hysterical and hostile and drive the young people out of the family orbit. On the other hand, they must not surrender their own standards on the fallacious notion that everybody is doing it, because they are afraid of being stigmatized as old-fashioned. They must not condone the fact and certainly not facilitate the conditions for premarital relations. There should be no question in the young people's minds where their parents stand on the issue. All too often the problem arises because the parents have no firm anchor in the tradition. Even a rebel needs a standard against which to rebel.

Basically what is required is a combination of two qualities that superficially appear to be contradictory—firmness and love. Parents must have the courage to stigmatize premarital relations as wrong. They should make it clear that they are motivated, not by some irrational and outmoded taboos, but by solid reasons—because it undermines the uniqueness of marriage and threatens the long-term happiness of the principals. At the same time, parents must demonstrate in every conceivable manner that their love and sympathy for the child remain unimpaired. The child must never be in doubt regarding the strength and sincerity of the moral commitments maintained by his parents or of the depth of the love they bear him.

Whether the values of the tradition will succeed in overcoming the pull of currently fashionable life styles cannot be foretold. But a war is not over until the last shot is fired. The struggle for the happiness and the well-being of humankind must go on, as long as the race survives, for there is no higher commandment.

12

ADULTERY AND ILLEGITIMACY

Of all the concepts encountered in this volume, none may strike the modern reader as more outmoded and archaic than that of adultery. The term occurs in the statutes governing marriage and divorce in our legal system, but it does not possess the deep emotional impact it had in the past. In many cases, extramarital affairs are no longer clandestine. Politicians find them no bar to public office. Artists and actors describe their romantic attachments for the benefit of their public-relations image. More private persons, like business leaders, professional people, and workers, also contribute their quota to liaisons outside of marriage. Such relationships become matters of public record only when divorce proceedings are initiated and adultery is the legal ground for the petition. It is fair to say that the present attitude condones, if it does not applaud, such patterns of behavior—a far cry from the standpoint that has characterized most societies during the greater portion of recorded history.

In the past, adultery was always regarded as the most heinous offense in the realm of sexual conduct. Adultery is listed in the Egyptian Book of the Dead in the "Protestation of Innocence" which each man must pronounce when coming before the judgment of the gods in the hereafter. It is condemned in the Wisdom literature of the ancient Babylonians. It bulks large in the criminal codes of the Greeks and the Romans.

It is, of course, well known that adultery was regarded as a sin of the greatest gravity in biblical thought. It is the only sexual offense included in the Decalogue, occurring as the Seventh Commandment immediately after the prohibition of murder. With great circumstantiality, biblical law prescribes death for both partners in an adulterous act.[1] It is one of the major sins repeatedly condemned by the Prophets in their excoriation of the corruption of society in their day.[2] Because of its relative accessibility to the wealthier levels of society, who alone were blessed with the leisure and the means to indulge their desires, the writers of the Book of Proverbs, who were the teachers of upper-class youth, devote considerable attention to warning their youthful students against its hazards.[3] In his great "Confession of Integrity," Job declares his freedom from this sin:

> If my heart has been enticed by a woman,
>   and I have lain in wait at my neighbor's door;
> then let my wife grind for another
>   and let others bow down upon her.
> For that would be a heinous crime;
>   an iniquity to be punished by the judges;
> a fire which consumes unto Abaddon,
>   and burns to the root all my increase.
>   (31:9–12)

In the New Testament, where divorce is generally prohibited, the only ground recognized as permitting or requiring the dissolution of a marriage is adultery. The Catholic Church has enshrined this dictum in canon law. As we have already noted, it has also entered into the secular legal systems of the West, being embodied in the divorce laws of various states in the union and many other countries.

While the increase in quasi-public non-marital sex patterns is of recent vintage, the phenomenon itself is as old as marriage. Many factors enter into the picture. There are the perennial problems of incompatibility and difficulties of adjustment between husband and wife. A biblical Wisdom teacher warned against the attractiveness of "forbidden waters." (Prov. 9:17) Recent research has demonstrated that psychological changes induced by the aging process may lead men and women to violate their oath of fidelity and to seek new and exciting relationships outside the marriage bond in a futile effort to deny the inevitable march of time.

To be sure, the role of male dominance is clearly evident in all ancient law. Adultery is limited to a violation of the marriage obligation by a married woman; the man's status is irrelevant. It seems clear that originally adultery was recognized as an injury to the property of the husband. Nevertheless, this lenient attitude toward the male partner in an adulterous affair was not due simply to the idea that a married woman was a chattel possession of her husband, as some writers have been quick to assert. Another consideration entered into the picture—the fact that the man was not limited to one woman, being free to contract several marriages in a polygamous society. It is noteworthy that in spite of the letter of the law, the Bible stigmatizes as adultery any extramarital relationship involving either partner (Hos. 4:14). The earlier sense of a property violation gave way in Judaism to a recognition of adultery as a deep moral sin, an offense against God, not to be atoned for merely by financial compensation.

In rabbinic law, the death penalty for adultery is no longer imposed, both because of the rabbis' negative attitude toward capital punishment in general and because of the loss of judicial power by the Jewish community. Nevertheless, the stigma and the penalty for adultery remain very great. When a woman is guilty of unfaithfulness, her husband must divorce her and she is forbidden to contract a marriage with her paramour as well.[4] A child born to a married woman committing adultery is illegitimate and suffers great disabilities. According to the Torah, a *mamzer*, "bastard," is unfit to marry a member of the Jewish community and "even to the tenth generation shall not enter into the assembly of the Lord." (Deut. 23:3)

The stringency of these prohibitions reflects the strong conviction that adultery is a direct onslaught on marriage and a major moral catastrophe. Opposition to extramarital sexual relations has remained strong and unrelenting through every period of Jewish history.

In modern society, the freer and closer relationship between the sexes has immeasurably increased the opportunity for free sexual adventures. Does an episode of adultery mean that the marriage must be dissolved? This is clearly the thrust of rabbinic law, as embodied in the talmudic and the great medieval codes.

However, I have called attention elsewhere[5] to the fact that by the side of codified law in Judaism, there is another category, that of "customary law," new evidence for which is constantly coming to light.[6] As we shall note in the next chapter, the official Halakah took several highly significant steps in order to enlarge the rights of women in a male-dominant society. However, customary law went considerably further in the direction of equalizing the status of women in Jewish society.

One important area in which codified and customary law diverge is that of adultery. To be sure, the severe attitude toward adultery embodied in the biblical codes prescribing death for the adulterous pair was mitigated in talmudic law, which requires only the dissolution of the marriage. Nevertheless, a woman divorced by her husband under such a cloud would be socially ostracized. She would also be highly vulnerable economically, particularly in an age when gainful employment for women was virtually nonexistent.

On adultery, customary law adopted a less severe stance. In the biblical book bearing his name, the prophet Hosea tells of a tragic marital experience that he has undergone.[7] He has entered into marriage with a woman he dearly loves. Though she bears him three children, his hopes for happiness are blasted by her shameless adulteries. Hosea's first reaction is one of indignation, and he proceeds to drive his faithless wife from his home in disgrace. Soon, however, his love for her triumphs over his hostility and pain. He goes out to persuade her to return, so that after a period of penance they might rebuild their love relationship. The prophet, of course, does not recount this episode out of a penchant for autobiography. In his own tragic experience of love, betrayal, estrangement, and reconciliation, Hosea sees an analogy for the relationship of God and Israel. He is, therefore, able to bring to his wayward people the message that love, forgiveness, and new hope always await a people returning to God.

Biblical scholars differ with regard to their understanding of Hosea's marital episode.[8] Some believe that Hosea became a prophet as a result of his sad experience. It is more probable that, being a prophet already, he was sensitive to the broader implications of his wife's infidelity. In either case, it is almost universally agreed that we are dealing with a real-life situation. Here we are interested in the clear implication that the restoration of marital ties after adultery is not merely legitimate but praiseworthy.

The same basic attitude emerges from an incident of an earlier age, the period of the Judges, already referred to in another connection (19:1–3). A Levite living on the slope of Mt. Ephraim married a concubine who "played the harlot against him,"[9] and then left him to return to her father's house. Out of his love for her, the husband went after her to persuade her to return to him. The tragic aftermath of the journey prevented the resumption of their relationship, but that is not our present concern.

These incidents have come down to us in spite of the fact that they clearly contradict the provisions of codified biblical law. They demonstrate that, even after flagrant adultery, customary law did not enjoin the total rejection of the wayward spouse and demand the permanent dissolution of the marriage. But even without this explicit evidence, we may be sure, in view of human nature, that forgiveness and reconciliation took place and the marriage relationship was re-established in many cases of adultery that have left no record behind them. The innately humane spirit of Jewish law emerges clearly in the Responsa literature (legal decisions) of later rabbinic authorities. As has been noted, the Halakah requires that a husband divorce an adulterous wife. Hence Rabbi Ezekiel Landau (1713–93) decided that if a man confessed to having had relations with a married woman over an extended period, the husband must be told of his wife's guilt. However, other authorities who cited the decision and discussed it ruled against informing the husband, an act that would have broken up the marriage. Thus the distinguished talmudist and Hasidic master of Sanz in Galicia, Rabbi Hayyim Halberstam (1793–1867) decided against informing the husband, adding that this was the practice of "the great Hasidic masters of the generation" when they were confronted by similar cases. The important Sephardic authority Rabbi Joseph Hayyim of Baghdad (1835–1909) advised likewise. This attitude is all the more striking in view of the fact that rabbinic decisors during the past two centuries have tended to adopt a severe stance on questions posed to them.[10]

The testimony of the tradition is, therefore, not univocal. Under the vastly changed circumstances of modern life, with the greater temptations to which men and women are exposed, what attitude should modern religion adopt?

In the case of an isolated extramarital episode or even an extended liaison, *when the illicit relationship has been terminated,* I believe that modern Judaism should adopt the more compassionate rather than the more rigorous attitude. Every effort should be expended to restore the family relationship when the erring partner genuinely regrets the infidelity, and the husband and wife both cherish a regard and affection for each other. Such an approach is surely to be preferred when there are children, especially young children, in the family.

Though this means going beyond the traditional position of codified Jewish law, it can be validated in practice by several norms within the official Halakah. In Jewish law, conviction for a major crime requires the presence of two competent witnesses of the act, who in fact must explicitly issue a warning before the act is committed. Now adultery is rarely committed in public! In the absence of witnesses, therefore, the "wronged " party would not be obliged halakically to divorce the erring partner. Even a confession of the sin committed would have no legal standing because of the fundamental rabbinic principle that, in the case of major crimes, "no one makes himself out to be wicked."[11] Hence, even the confession of adultery by the party involved would be thrown out of court.

There is additional warrant in Jewish historical experience for adopting a less rigorous approach. As we have seen in the previous chapter, during the medieval Spanish period, sexual mores, which were much freer in general society, had an impact upon Jewish conduct as well. Confronted by the problem of extramarital relations, some rabbinic authorities, though by no means all, accepted such liaisons, though they strongly disapproved of them. They sought and found a basis for giving a quasi-legitimate status to a "secondary wife," in the ancient biblical category of the *pillegesh,* "concubine."

In our day, such a procedure is completely out of the question. Obviously the *pillegesh* could be sanctioned only in a polygamous society, such as that of Islam, where Jews were legally free to have more than one wife. Moreover, this condoning of extramarital relations on the part of the husband is based upon the double standard, which is totally unacceptable today. Medieval rabbis would have been horrified if a woman had insisted upon equality and demanded the right to have two husbands simultaneously! Today, a sex code laying claim to ethical validity must apply the concept of adultery equally to the husband and the wife—infidelity by either is equally heinous. The experience of Spanish Jewry is cited here only in order to indicate that, in the past, rabbinic authorities did not feel compelled to terminate a marriage because of a breach by one of the partners if a basis still remained for rebuilding the relationship.

There is another consideration that militates against a punitive approach to adultery. In many, if not most, cases of adultery, right is not exclusively on one side. Generally, there have been sources of tension and dissatisfaction of greater or lesser urgency before the adultery is committed. The trouble may be physical or psychological, involving any aspect of the marriage. The crisis of an extramarital experience may prove salutary in getting both husband and wife to reassess their attitudes toward each other and scrutinize their own shortcomings.

If the couple feel that they cannot solve their problem unaided, they should seek the help of religious teachers, psychologists, and marriage counselors. Obviously, when the breach in the marriage bond is permanent, a divorce is called for, since the marriage has really ceased to exist.

Adultery often proves the cause of one of the most painful aspects of the Jewish sexual code. As we have seen, when the forbidden relationship leads to the birth of a child, he is a *mamzer*, "bastard," with a tragic and irremediable status in Jewish law.

The Hebrew term is obscure, with no satisfactory etymology. The only two biblical passages in which the word occurs suggest a possibility that it may refer either to some foreign stock or to one carrying some deep stigma.[11] But speculations such as these are really irrelevant. For millennia, Jewish law has interpreted the term as referring to the offspring of an incestuous union or of an act of adultery. A bastard has, therefore, been regarded as ineligible to marry into the Jewish fold.

The rabbis were very much troubled by the injustice involved in inflicting lifelong punishment and virtual ostracism on a child for an offense he did not commit. They sought every possible road to leniency, but generally they felt frustrated by the uncompromising character of the text. Their deep sympathy is expressed in a poignant passage of the Midrash:

> Daniel the Tailor interpreted the passage in Ecclesiastes (4:1) as referring to bastards: "*Here are the tears of the oppressed.* If the parents of these bastards committed a transgression, what fault is it of these poor sufferers? So too if this man's father committed incest with a woman forbidden to him, what sin has he himself committed and what fault is it of his? *With none to comfort them and with power in the hands of their oppressors.* This refers to Israel's great Sanhedrin, that comes to them with the power derived from the Torah and excludes them from the community because of the commandment, 'A bastard shall not enter into the Assembly of the Lord.' *With none to comfort them.* The Holy One, blessed be He, says 'It shall be my task to comfort them, for in this world there is a stigma attached to them. But in the world to come, as the prophet Zechariah has said: "I saw them all seated upon thrones of gold." ' "[13]

In earlier periods of Jewish history, when extramarital relationships were rare, the number of illegitimate children likely to be affected by the rigors of the law was limited. Of course, the hardship imposed on each victim was severe. Today, however, the problem has grown tremendously. Whatever our judgment on the morality of extramarital relations, the lot of the innocent offspring should be a subject of deep ethical concern to Judaism.

Fortunately, the structure of the traditional Halakah suggests a procedure for removing the penalty enjoined by the law upon the illegitimate child and permitting him to marry within the Jewish fold.

As we have noted, the kind of legal proof of a criminal act required by the Halakah makes it virtually impossible to demonstrate an act of adultery. Even a confession is inadmissible, since Jewish law does not admit self-incrimination as evidence. By applying these canons of Jewish law, it is possible to free the child from both the stigma and the punishment commanded by the letter of the law. In the eyes of the Halakah, an actual case of illegitimacy, as a result of adultery, in which the offspring would be excluded from marrying another member of the Jewish community would practically never arise.

There is, however, one category of adultery and the resultant illegitimacy that cannot be met by these specific principles of the Halakah. The problem, one of the tragic legacies of the Nazi Holocaust, has been repeated more than once. A woman is informed that her husband had been killed in a concentration camp or a crematorium. In complete honesty and innocence she proceeds, some time later, to enter into a second marriage, on the assumption that her first has been terminated by the death of her husband. It happens, however, by one of the accidents of modern life, that her first husband has not died, and he reappears. Her second marriage is now technically an adulterous union and the children born of it are illegitimate. A few years ago, a furor was created when the official rabbinical court in the State of Israel declared a brother and a sister, who were the offspring of such a second marriage, to be *mamzerim* and forbade them to marry into the Jewish community. Ultimately, the rabbinical court in Israel, in spite of its reputation for rigidity, was able to remove the stigma from the principals because of other factors that came to light.

In general, however, the Halakah, when applied with sympathy and courage in such cases, can prevent the anguish and suffering that would come to one who is technically illegitimate. As we shall note below in connection with women's rights, there is solid talmudic authority for the power of the rabbinate to annul a marriage. This principle can justly be invoked in cases such as this, particularly since no real adultery is involved. An annulment of the first marriage by the rabbinical court would have the effect of making the second marriage valid, thus purging the children of any taint of illegitimacy.

The traditional Jewish law on adultery and illegitimacy is ancient and reflects attitudes and conditions radically different from those prevailing today. Nevertheless, the Halakah possesses inner resources, as we have seen, that make it possible to maintain the letter and the spirit of Jewish law. The letter is important in order to preserve the continuity of the Jewish tradition and the unity of the Jewish people. At the same time, we must be responsive to its ethical spirit, which is marked by sensitivity to the weaknesses of human nature and a deep compassion for the ills of the human condition.

Every effort should be made to penetrate to the motives and impulses that lead men and women to commit adultery. Such an understanding is a prerequisite for a broad-based, long-range campaign for educating men and women at every age level to adopt and live by a code of personal ethics that will be in conformity with their own noblest ideals and the traditions of Judaism at its highest. In view of the far-flung temptations and stresses to which modern marriages are exposed and from which no one is exempt, couples should be encouraged to re-establish the marriage relationship if there is a chance of repairing the damage caused by infidelity.

But the principle laid down in the Decalogue cannot be abandoned. "You shall not commit adultery" is a categorical imperative if marriage is to survive and men and women are to fulfill the highest dictates of their nature.

Problem Areas
in Modern Judaism

13

WOMEN IN JEWISH LIFE
AND LAW

There is no lack of major problems confronting the Jewish community today. High on the list is the issue of the position of women in tradition and law. On the one hand, apologists for the status quo insist that women have always enjoyed positions of high regard and influence in Judaism and that the various forms of discrimination which seem to be imposed upon them by the Halakah are more apparent than real. They are designed simply for the purpose of providing channels for the different roles assigned to women by God and nature. On the other hand, advocates of women's liberation have called attention to many disabilities under which women labor in civil, family, and ritual law, as well as in custom.

These opposing attitudes are possible because each group reckons with a different set of facts. As the rabbi's wife discovered, in the old story, both are right and wrong. The key to the contradiction lies in the gap between law and life, and the tension that inevitably exists between the codified practice of the past and the emerging ideas of the present. As we have already noted, life is perpetually in flux, with certain advanced sectors of society serving as the cutting edge of progress and change. On the other hand, the law is basically static, concerned with preserving norms which emanate from the past, and thus is a bastion of conservatism. A truly comprehensive view of the position of women in Jewish life and law must, therefore, reckon with both facets.

Women as Persons

Readers of the Bible cannot fail to be struck with the vivid personalities of the women in its pages. At the dawn of biblical history, one is impressed by the resourcefulness and vigor of the wives of the patriarchs Abraham, Isaac, and Jacob. The matriarchs Sarah, Rebecca, Leah, and Rachel know what they want and get it.

Actually, they are not the first women in Genesis to exhibit initiative and an openness to innovation, whether for good or for ill. In the Garden of Eden, it is Eve who takes the lead in eating the forbidden fruit, and influences her complaisant husband to do the same. Many generations later, Tamar, the daughter-in-law of Judah, adopts extreme measures in order to beget a son who will bear the name of her dead husband (Gen. 38).

Women are to be found in the ranks of the Prophets, exhibiting outstanding traits of leadership. Miriam, while still a child, makes herself responsible for the safety of the infant Moses floating in a basket among the bulrushes of the Nile. Later she rallies the womenfolk in a song of triumph and thanksgiving after the destruction of the Egyptians at the crossing of the Red Sea (Ex. 15:20–1). During the desert period, her outspoken nature leads her to attack her brother Moses, for which she is punished (Num. 12:1–16).

After the entrance into the Promised Land, when the Israelites are threatened by a powerful combination of enemies and by their own disunity and lethargy, it is the Prophetess Deborah who rallies the tribes to resistance and literally shames their leader Barak into taking up the gauntlet of battle (Jud. 4–5). Centuries later, in 621 B.C.E., while repairs are being carried out on the Temple in Jerusalem, an ancient Book of the Law is discovered in the foundations. It is the Prophetess Huldah who underscores the importance of the discovery and thus leads King Josiah to undertake the most far-reaching religious reformation in biblical history (II Ki. 22:14–20). Two women have given their names to the books describing their exploits, one in the Bible and the other in the Apocrypha. Both Esther and Judith occupy positions of honor among the saviors of Israel.

The Bible is far from regarding women as plaster saints or as paragons of virtue. Its pages contain unforgettable portraits of evil women as well. Most notable of all is Jezebel, the Phoenician princess who becomes the wife of King Ahab.[1] She is unrelenting in pursuing her ends, whether it be the extirpation of the worship of the God of Israel, or the expropriation of a peasant's vineyard (I Kings 21). Everywhere she proves herself a doughty opponent of the Prophet Elijah.

Her royal dignity does not desert her to the very end of her life. After her husband's death, when Jehu comes into the royal courtyard in order to kill her, she adorns herself in all her finery and calls down to him from her window, "How goes it with you, murderer of your liege lord?" After she is thrown from the window and killed, her mortal enemy offers his grudging admiration, "See now to this cursed woman, and bury her; for she is a king's daughter." (II Ki. 9:30–4).

There are other women whose names have not come down to us who played decisive roles in the affairs of their day and thus refute the assumption that they were mere chattels. In the period of the Judges, when the ambitious Abimelech lays siege to the city of Shechem, it is a woman who throws a millstone down from the walls and crushes his skull, thus bringing to an end the threat of royal tyranny (9:53). In the latter days of King David's reign, it is a wise woman of Tekoa who is skillful enough to mitigate the brokenhearted king's anger against his wayward son Absalom (II Sam. 14).

More important than specific incidents is the general attitude toward women in the biblical period. The Song of Songs reflects an attitude of comradeship and equality between the lover and his beloved, both in their distinctive roles and in their attitude to each other. Neither partner is reticent in avowing his desire for the other and in initiating their love relationship, with no hint of subservience or inferiority. The great song of praise to the "woman of valor" in Proverbs pictures her as the efficient mistress of her household, providing food and clothes for her family. In addition, she is active in business, and is respected everywhere for her qualities of charity, kindness, and piety.[2] The same biblical book offers vivid vignettes of the "loose" woman, tempting young men to adultery,[3] together with warnings against the prostitute who brings disaster in her wake.[4] The injunction to respect both parents in the Decalogue and in the Holiness Code was re-enforced by the Wisdom teachers.[5] The widespread prevalence of monogamy already referred to also testifies to the position of dignity and influence which women enjoyed in the biblical period and which remained basic in Jewish life.

Women's Disabilities in Jewish Law

When we turn to the status of women in biblical or post-biblical law, the picture is radically different. Here their status of inferiority is clearly evident. A girl may be sold into marriage by her father solely according to his will (Ex. 21:7). If she makes a vow, it may be annulled by her father before she is married and by her husband afterward (Num. 30:2-17). Inheritance is the prerogative of sons; only in the absence of male issue do daughters inherit from their father.[6]

That the power to initiate a divorce rests with the husband and that the wife is compelled to accept it was deduced by the rabbis of the Mishnah from the passage in Deuteronomy 24:-1-3, which they interpreted to mean: "When a man takes a wife and marries her, if then she finds no favor in his eyes, because he has found some indecency in her, he shall write her a bill of divorce and shall put it in her hand and he shall send her out of his house."[7]

Except for very special cases, women were regarded as incompetent to testify in lawsuits, thus occupying a position identical with that of minors, deaf-mutes, and the insane.[8] When a girl is violated and her own innocence is established, it is her father who is compensated for the injury (Deut. 22:29).

Provisions such as these cannot be ignored in establishing the position of women in Jewish law, but they do not tell the whole story. There is one very important fact referred to several times in this book that has hitherto not been noted. Both biblical and post-biblical law fall into two categories. There is the codified or official law, specific enactments to be found in the legal sections of the Torah and in the Mishnah and the Talmud, as well as in the later codes. This body of law, from which the provisions cited above are drawn, tends to be basically conservative, reflecting the legal inferiority of women.

In addition, however, Jewish life was governed by another category, that of customary or unofficial law. It was not assembled in the recognized codes, and our information about it is fragmentary, but it is quite clear that it operated in Jewish society. We are not in position to establish the parameters, either in time or in space, within which provisions of customary law were maintained, but the evidence suggests that it was operative over wide periods and in various communities.

Women's Rights in Customary Law

While biblical and rabbinic law gave to the father alone the power of marrying off his daughter, in practice the mother played an important role in this decision. In the Apocryphal book of Tobit, when the father Raguel arranges for the marriage of his daughter Sarah to Tobias, he calls her mother and tells her to "bring a book and write an instrument of cohabitation."[9] This document is obviously the *ketubbah* or "marriage contract," probably in an earlier form than our present version.

Inheritance in customary law was not limited to sons and brothers. The closing verses in Job inform us that Job gave his daughters "legacies together with their brothers." (42:15) Similarly, Judith, left a widow, inherits her husband's estate (8:7).

The Book of Ruth describes the business transaction in which Naomi offers the fields belonging to her dead husband and sons for sale to their kinsmen.[10] Clearly, Naomi is legally as competent to sell as the woman of valor is competent to buy (Proverbs 31:14–18).

The rich cache of documents found in Elephantine in Egypt constitutes the archives of a Jewish military colony in Egypt in the fifth century B.C.E.[11] It has brought to light a large number of documents regarding the extensive business transactions, as well as the marital complications, of a redoubtable Jewish businesswoman named Mibtahiah. She is only one of a long line of Jewish women down to modern times who have shown extraordinary ability and energy in practical pursuits, frequently serving both as breadwinners and as home builders for their families. At the same time, their "husband is known in the gates where he sits with the elders of the land" (Proverbs 31:23), or engages in advanced talmudic studies, as was common in Eastern Europe until the Holocaust.

The most radical extension of women's rights, the power to initiate a divorce, has not become normative in traditional Judaism, at least not yet. But, as has already been pointed out, at various periods and in different communities a woman was able to demand and receive a divorce when she found her marriage intolerable.[12] This virtual equality of the sexes with regard to divorce was achieved by a variety of procedures.[13]

It should be kept in mind that these divergences from the codified, official Halakah did not emanate from dissident sects. They constituted the everyday practice of Jews living in accordance with normative Judaism, validated in many cases by the leading rabbinical authorities of the time.

The Extension of Women's Rights
in Rabbinic Law

We have thus far dealt with three aspects of our subject: (a) women as persons, (b) their liabilities in biblical and rabbinic law, and (c) their level of activity and authority in customary law.

The fourth element in the situation, and probably the most significant, still remains to be presented. In spite of the inherent conservatism of codified law, the entire thrust of the Halakah was in the direction of achieving a greater measure of equality between the sexes. This objective was to be achieved by the double process of extending the rights of women on the one hand and limiting the powers of men on the other. The impetus for this trend derived from a constantly growing recognition that a woman is a personality with rights, desires, and wishes of her own.

The Mishnah, to be sure, speaks of the three modes by which a woman is "bought" in marriage.[14] But the innate conservatism of language, especially in legal and technical spheres, should not obscure the fact that in rabbinic law a woman was no chattel and that her role in both marriage and divorce was that of an active and influential personality. The Bible had already moved substantially beyond the original rightlessness of women that characterized primitive and ancient societies. The process was carried considerably further in rabbinic law, which achieved a great expansion of their rights as daughters, wives, and mothers.

The end result of the double process of extending feminine rights and limiting masculine prerogatives was the attainment of a virtual equality of the sexes before the law. To be sure, this equality was often not manifested in traditional Jewish life. However, this condition was due, not to the letter of the law, but to the general climate of society, in which women's inferiority was taken for granted both by them as well as by their male counterparts.

The process of the growth of women's rights may be illustrated by two examples, one of largely historical interest, the other of practical significance today. The first is the institution of the levirate (from the Latin word "*levir*," "brother-in-law"). A widespread practice in early societies throughout the world provided that when a man died without issue, his wife was taken in marriage by a brother or other close relative, so that the first child born of the new union would "carry the name of the deceased on his inheritance." This all-but-universal practice was not limited to brothers of the dead man but extended to other relatives in many societies. It was an expression of the deep-rooted horror of extinction that came when a man died with no offspring to carry on his family line. Hence the rite of the levirate was compulsory; it could not be set aside either by the dead man's male relation or by his widow, whether because of personal feelings between the principals or other factors.

The first instance of *yibbum*, "levirate," in the Bible occurs in Genesis 38, in the case of Tamar, already discussed in another connection. Tamar is married to Judah's son Er, but he dies without issue. Judah orders his brother Onan to perform the duty of the levirate with Tamar. Onan fails to perform his duty toward his dead brother and dies. Understandably Judah is loath to expose his youngest son, Shelah, to the hazards of marriage with a woman who has already lost two husbands, and he refrains from doing so. After the passage of considerable time, Tamar disguises herself as a harlot, entices Judah to have relations with her, and becomes pregnant. When she is about to be executed for immorality, Tamar reveals to Judah that he is the father of her twin sons, and he declares, "She is more righteous than I, for I did not give her to my son Shelah." One of the twins, Perez, is the ancestor of King David.

At this stage in the institution, the basic obligation is the marriage of the dead man's widow to his brother. Hence even the extreme measure adopted by Tamar is felt to be justified.

The next stage in the levirate is set forth in the legislation in Deuteronomy.[15] The rite has now been considerably constricted. It is now limited to "brothers dwelling together," with no hint that the obligation also falls upon other, more distant relatives. Moreover, even for the brothers, *yibbum* no longer is obligatory, though it is clearly the preferred procedure. A brother may avoid the duty if he is willing to be exposed to a measure of public indignity and have his family carry some stigma, the severity of which we cannot judge.

In rabbinic Judaism, the recognition of personal desires and the play of human likes and dislikes affecting both the brother-in-law and the widow increasingly came to the fore. The Mishnah declares: "*Yibbum* took precedence over *ḥaliṣah* ['casting off the shoe,' a symbolic divorce of the widow] in earlier times when men were concerned with fulfilling the Divine commandment. But now that men are not concerned with fulfilling the Divine commandment, *ḥaliṣah* takes precedence over *yibbum*."[16] Undoubtedly, the rarity of polygamy, even in talmudic times, also militated strongly against the practice of *yibbum*, since most adult men were married. In the talmudic period, all the resources of rabbinic hermeneutics were mobilized to limit and, where possible, to prevent the consummation of the levirate.[17]

In the tenth century, the *taqqanah* of Rabbi Gershom Ben Judah of Mainz and his synod forbade polygamy for European Jewry, so that henceforth *ḥaliṣah* became the only permissible mode of procedure in Western countries. *Yibbum* continued to be permissible only in Muslim countries where polygamy was not prohibited.[18]

Yibbum is no longer practiced in Judaism, since monogamy is now universal and the rights and predilections of the individual men and women involved are being increasingly recognized. The levirate is a striking illustration from history of an institution that can be traced from its earliest stage, when it was virtually compulsory, until the present, when it has totally disappeared.

On the other hand, divorce is of continuing practical and

contemporary concern. The history of Jewish divorce reveals the same pattern of expansion of women's rights. As we have already noted, the biblical text, as interpreted by the rabbis, gave the complete and exclusive initiative in divorce to the husband. In ancient times, when no employment opportunities or social contacts were possible for women outside the home, the divorced woman was in a very difficult position. Her only recourse was to return to her father's house, assuming that he was still alive. Even more important, she would be economically destitute. To hold her husband's hostility in check and reduce the incidence of hasty divorce, Simon ben Shetaḥ established the *ketubbah*, "marriage contract," used in traditional Jewish marriages to the present day.[19] It provided for a payment in cash of two hundred zuz (a figure often increased voluntarily by the parties), to be paid either upon the death of the husband or upon his divorcing her. The obligation to produce a payment in cash in an age when legal tender was scarce was designed, in the language of the Mishnah, to ensure "that it would not be easy for him to divorce her."

This limitation on the prerogative of the husband was accompanied by a parallel extension of the power of the wife to demand a divorce. As we have seen, our sources indicate that the customary law, maintained in Egypt and Palestine during several widely different periods, gave a woman the right to sue for divorce, even on the broad ground "I do not love him." There is no reason to assume that the practice was limited to these times and places.

But even official law, as codified in the Mishnah, granted women a substantial measure of initiative. When the grounds for divorce commended themselves to the judges, they would "pressure the husband until he would say, 'I am willing [to issue the divorce].' "[20] The rabbis were convinced that his consent was genuine, because they held that fundamentally all people are decent and law-abiding, so that his deepest wish, even if unconscious, was to obey the teaching of the Sages!

Throughout the Middle Ages, rabbinical courts were able to mitigate the rightlessness of women by compelling husbands to obey the court, using the threat of excommunication and other penalties.

In addition to utilizing these instruments of community discipline, the rabbis in the Middle Ages introduced other modifications of the law in order to mitigate the tragic plight of the *agunah,* "the chained wife." This term was applied to a woman whose husband had disappeared with no evidence of his death, so that technically she remained married to him and could never enter into a new relationship. Thus the rabbis accepted the testimony of one witness or even of the woman herself that her husband was dead as sufficient to set her free.

Women's Rights in Judaism

The problem of women's disabilities became acute in the modern age with the Emancipation and the breakdown of the authority of the Jewish community. Now the Jewish community possessed no legal or judicial power to enforce its decisions. Recalcitrant husbands were free to disregard rabbinical courts and their edicts.

In modern times, the incidence of the *agunah* and the tragedy of her lot were greatly intensified. Three categories came into being. The first, that of husbands absconding, was originally rare. However, the mass migration of Jews from the great centers of Jewish population to all corners of the world made desertion a much more frequent phenomenon. In the early decades of the twentieth century, Yiddish newspapers in America carried as a regular feature a "Gallery of Disappeared Husbands," containing pathetic appeals to the readers to help find them. Modern warfare, too, with its massive annihilation of combatants of whose bodies nothing remained, added to the number of *agunot.*

With the wholesale breakdown of religious observance, civil

divorce has become the norm. All too often, the husband defiantly refuses to grant his wife a *get,* or religious divorce, out of either greed or malice, or both. Thus she is left with the alternatives of lifelong loneliness or committing bigamy in the eyes of Jewish law, with tragic consequences for the status of children born of a second marriage. The lot of these unfortunate women is graphically described in Chaim Grade's powerful novel *The Agunah.*

Through the years many proposals for dealing with the ethical and human problem of the deserted wife emanated from sensitive, farsighted scholars. Unfortunately, these individuals have remained largely voices crying in the wilderness, and the collective leadership in the Orthodox rabbinate has taken no comprehensive steps thus far to mitigate this manifest injustice. One exception may be noted. Following the tragic loss of life in the Yom Kippur war, when hundreds of young men were missing in action, some members of the Israeli rabbinate found ways and means of freeing young wives from perpetual widowhood.

Paradoxical as it seems, the establishment of the State of Israel has diminished the chances that a halakic solution to this evil will emerge from these circles. In Israel the government recognizes the jurisdiction of the Orthodox rabbinate in the areas of marriage, divorce, and personal status generally, and uses its police power to enforce decisions of the established rabbinical courts. Hence, recalcitrant husbands, when they can be found, may be punished by imprisonment and compelled to issue a *get* to their estranged wives.

The urgency of the *agunah* problem is, therefore, not felt to be acute by Israeli rabbis. They are able to overlook instances of men who disappear with no witnesses to their death available. Nor are they confronted by the most frequent and exasperating cases of all, the recalcitrant husband outside the State of Israel who has a civil divorce and refuses to grant a *get* to his former wife for whatever reason.

Practical measures for dealing with the problem on a comprehensive basis within the framework of the Halakah law have virtually been limited to Conservative Judaism. A series of steps in this direction were undertaken during the past four decades.

In 1935, the Rabbinical Assembly adopted a plan proposed by the late Rabbi Louis M. Epstein, which, though complicated in practice, was halakically sound. Basically, the plan called for the appointment of agents by the husband at the time of the marriage to execute a conditional divorce (*get 'al tnai*) under certain circumstances. These would include his disappearance or his refusal to issue a Jewish divorce after having secured a civil divorce, or his being reported missing in military action.

It was to meet the practical problem involved in the last category that the Epstein plan was put into practice during the period of the Second World War. In all essentials, it was also adopted by the Orthodox Rabbinical Council of America during the same period.

Subjected to a barrage of misrepresentation and proving unwieldly in operation, the Epstein plan, after being put into practice in many cases, fell into disuse. But the principle of an active concern for the *agunah* and a determination to act on her behalf persisted. The Rabbinical Assembly then proceeded to adopt a procedure worked out by the eminent rabbinic authority Professor Saul Lieberman. It consists of a codicil added to the traditional marriage contract in which husband and wife solemnly agree to abide by the provisions of Jewish law. The theory is that this commitment includes the issuance of a *get*, should that become necessary in the future. If the husband then fails to honor his promise, the civil court could be asked to enforce performance of the contract. The plan raised several major questions. Is it wise to involve the civil authorities in a basically religious issue? Would the courts be willing to accept jurisdiction and enforce compliance?

The Rabbinical Assembly then decided to utilize several resources of the traditional Halakah available for dealing with the problem, by putting into practice existing provisions for conditional marriage and divorce in the Talmud.[21] The Committee on Law and Standards of the Rabbinical Assembly turned to the talmudic principle "Whoever contracts a Jewish marriage does so under the authority of the rabbis."[22] This is not merely an abstract principle. It is applied in the Talmud itself and by post-talmudic authorities to annul a marriage when circumstances require it. In the words of the Talmud, "The rabbis retroactively break the husband's marital contract."[23] Even the presence of children born to the couple does not prevent the application of this principle, since their legitimate status in Judaism is not impugned by the annulment.

In putting this procedure into practice when all other expedients fail, the Beth Din of the Rabbinical Assembly has followed the clear precedents to be found in these talmudic and post-talmudic law formulations. When a marriage has been civilly dissolved and all pleas and warnings addressed to the husband requesting him to issue a *get* prove unavailing, the Beth Din proceeds to annul the marriage and thus sets the woman free from a lifelong enchainment. Often the husband's knowledge that a remedy is at hand impels him to adopt the right course of action and to grant the *get*. If he remains adamant, the remedy of rabbinic annulment is available. Thus, Jewish law helps fulfill the great injunction in the Torah, "You shall do what is just and right in the sight of God." (Deut. 6:18)

Woman's Role in Religious Life

Less important, perhaps, than the *agunah* problem, but affecting a far larger number of women, is a series of questions relating to the religious status of women in Judaism. All too often in discussions of this question, it is overlooked that women have always played a significant role in Jewish religious life. The entire structure of *Kashrut*, upon which the physical life and the spiritual health of the family depended, was pre-eminently the woman's special sphere of activity. Her participation in all the rituals of Jewish home life through the year, the Sabbath, the festivals, the Passover seder, made her her husband's co-partner in building the Jewish home. In our day, the domineering Jewish woman as wife and mother has become a stock-in-trade among some writers and comic entertainers—and the two categories are not always to be told apart. These caricatures are distortions of the active and positive role Jewish women have played in maintaining the Jewish family, supporting its members, educating the young, and preserving traditional standards of adherence to Torah and *mitzvot*. Unfortunately, the erosion of Jewish values in the home in our time, a process which must be reversed if Judaism is to survive in any meaningful sense, has obscured the central role of the woman in Jewish religious life.

It must be confessed, however, that all these activities and prerogatives were limited to the private sphere. The woman's public role in Judaism, whether in the community or in the synagogue, was greatly restricted.

In 1975, the Rabbinical Assembly voted to permit (not to compel) individual rabbis and congregations to count women for the *minyan,* or quorum, in prayer. There is also the growing practice in Conservative congregations to extend to women various religious honors, like being called to the Torah. This last practice, it should be added, is expressly sanctioned by the *Shulhan Arukh,*[24] but has been a dead letter in practice. As the recent controversy on the subject demonstrates, the practice marks a significant advance in the religious enfranchisement of women in traditional Judaism.

It is necessary to understand the full extent of the issues involved and the approach needed to meet the issue. Those who oppose counting women in the *minyan* seek to justify their position by referring to the fact that the traditional Halakah exempted women from the *obligation (hiyyubh)* of prayer. This exemption in turn is buttressed by the talmudic principle that "women are free from commandments that must traditionally be performed at specific times."[25] The fact is, however, that even in talmudic and medieval times, the principle was not universally applied. Always there were exceptions, such as the kindling of Sabbath and festival lights, that were held to be obligatory upon women. It is, therefore, a reasonable conclusion that the principle is a generalization from a few specific instances and not a universally binding rule. The application of this role to women's prayer is, therefore, a rationalization rather than a reason, serving to maintain the inferior status of women.

Be this as it may, the argument has even less justification today. In this age of labor-saving devices, a woman who is a homemaker, even if she takes care of a family, has at least as much free time available as her husband, who is a worker, a businessman, or a professional. As for the woman who is gainfully employed outside the home, she is in exactly the same position as her male counterpart.

The American historian James Harvey Robinson once said that every event in history has a good reason and a real reason. In the case of the *mitzvah* of prayer for women and their exclusion from the *minyan*, the real reason is not good and the good reason is not real.

Throughout the Western world, women's-rights groups are demanding with ever greater militancy the right to serve in the clergy and are encountering strong opposition by upholders of the status quo, clerical and lay. The Episcopal Church and several other Protestant denominations have ordained women to the ministry, not without substantial opposition within their ranks. The vigorous demand by some Catholic women, including nuns, to be ordained to the priesthood has, thus far, been countered by an equally emphatic "no" from the papacy, but the agitation continues to grow in strength. In Judaism, the call has gone out for the ordination of women.

Reform Judaism has had no real problem on this issue and was able to extend equality in religious life to women virtually from its inception, primarily because it did not recognize the binding power of the Halakah and, therefore, had no traditional obstacles to contend with. Several women have been ordained as rabbis by the Reform and Reconstructionist seminaries, but the prejudice against this public role for women is still strong, not only among many men, but among many women. The question of the ordination of women to the rabbinate is becoming a live issue in Conservative Judaism. It has thus far not surfaced in Orthodoxy.

Undoubtedly, the rate of progress has been far slower than advocates of women's rights in Judaism would have wished. This is, of course, true of society as a whole; witness the slow and painful progress through the state legislatures of the Equal Rights Amendment. But if the progress that has been achieved is not breathtaking, it is by no means negligible.

In the field of ritual, a significant change was introduced as far back as 1945 in *The Sabbath and Festival Prayer Book*, issued by the Prayer Book Commission of the Rabbinical Assembly and the United Synagogue, on which the writer had the honor of serving as chairman. The commission rephrased the three Preliminary Blessings in the morning service which had long been the subject of discomfort and controversy. These three blessings read as follows in the Orthodox prayer book: "Blessed art Thou, O Lord our God, King of the universe, who has not made me a Gentile, a slave, or a woman." In the Conservative prayer book these three blessings are expressed in the positive: "Blessed art Thou, O Lord our God, King of the universe, who has created me in His image, has made me free, and has made me an Israelite." Incidentally, there is warrant in rabbinic sources for these formulations, as an appendix in *The Sabbath and Festival Prayer Book* makes clear.

The modified text is not merely less open to objection per se; it expresses a fundamental religious and ethical insight of the Jewish tradition. As is clear from the first chapter of Genesis, every human being, male or female, is created "in the image of God," and possesses an innate worth and an inalienable dignity. The two succeeding benedictions articulate in positive terms the joy of Jewish belonging and the privilege of human freedom.

To revert to our basic theme, the solution to the issues of justice and equality for women in Judaism can be met only by an approach to Jewish tradition that is both sympathetic and reverent. At the same time, it must be aware of the millennial experience of the Jewish people and sensitive to the conditions and ethical insights of the contemporary world. Traditional Jewish law arose in the ancient world and developed during the medieval period. During both eras, women occupied a position of inferiority everywhere in society, both in life and in law. The glory of the traditional Halakah is that, nevertheless, it took giant steps to extend the range of women's rights and to circumscribe the originally unlimited powers of men.

That the process was not completed by the Halakah in the past is not surprising. Even modern society still has a long way to go before the full equality of women is achieved. What is remarkable is not that women still suffer various disabilities in Jewish law today but that so much progress has been registered.

It is to be hoped that work in this area will be carried forward by Halakic authorities from various groups in association with all those elements of the Jewish community who accept the authority of the Halakah and are dedicated to making it viable in the modern world. The record of the past suggests that there is movement in human affairs. In Galileo's words, *eppur si muove.*

Jewish tradition possesses important resources for advancing the process, if the insights available from history, sociology, and psychology are utilized, as well as the inherent wisdom and humanity of the Halakah. The struggle for justice, freedom, and equality, in this area as everywhere, which goes back almost to the dawn of history, is not yet over, but the final outcome cannot be in doubt.

14

INTERMARRIAGE
AND THE JEWISH FUTURE

We have sought to bring the insights of the Jewish tradition to bear on the various aspects of sexual morality confronting all men and women, whatever their religious or ethnic backgrounds. There is one issue which, strictly speaking, is not part of sexual morality in general, though it does have important ethical implications. It is intermarriage, a problem as old as the Jewish people itself. Because it is of overriding significance for the survival of Judaism and the Jewish people, it cannot be overlooked in any discussion of love, sex, and marriage from the standpoint of Judaism.

Motives for Opposition

In order to understand the Jewish attitude toward intermarriage, one must recognize that there have been two powerful yet antithetic tendencies at work throughout Jewish history. On the one hand, Judaism has always had strong theoretic objection to the practice of intermarriage. It is true that all that lives normally strives to continue its existence, but the Jewish struggle for survival has always been characterized by a passion and a sense of urgency unparalleled elsewhere. Its tremendous emotional force derives from a conviction as old as the Jewish people itself, that it is a small enclave in an alien world and that its faith is a tiny island buffeted by the waves of a pagan sea. Both the Jewish people and Judaism are, therefore, perpetually exposed to the danger of annihilation. Intermarriage is a royal road to the absorption and disappearance of the people and its traditions.

It is noteworthy that this conviction is expressed in the Torah immediately after the prohibition of intermarriage with "the seven nations of Canaan":

> It was not because you were more in number than any other people that the Lord set his love upon you and chose you, for you were the fewest of all peoples." (Deut. 7:7)

The grounds for this millennial Jewish objection to intermarriage are twofold. Most fundamental is the *religious rationale,* the classical expression of which is to be found in the same passage:

> When the Lord your God brings you into the land which you are entering to take possession of it, and clears away many nations before you, the Hittites, the Girgashites, the Amorites, the Canaanites, the Perizzites, the Hivites, and the Jebusites, seven nations greater and mightier than yourselves, and when the Lord your God gives them over to you, and you defeat them; then you must utterly destroy them; you shall make no covenant with them, and show no mercy to them. You shall not make marriages with them, giving your daughters to their sons or taking their daughters for your sons. For they would turn away your sons from following me, to serve other gods. Then the anger of the Lord would be kindled against you, and He would destroy you quickly. . . . For you are a people holy to the Lord your God; the Lord your God has chosen you to be a people for his own possession, out of all the peoples that are on the face of the earth.

That the danger of paganism was not imaginary, the Israelites had learned through their experience with the daughters of Moab, who led them into idolatry and licentiousness, a stratagem which the Torah attributes to Balaam.[1]

As in most areas, rabbinic Judaism carried forward the biblical prohibition against intermarriage. The biblical text was invoked to prohibit marriage for all time with the Ammonites, the Moabites, the Edomites, and the Egyptians.[2] However, a problem existed with Ruth, who was a Moabite, and Na'amah, the mother of King Rehoboam, King Solomon's son and successor, who was an Ammonite (I Ki. 14:21). Both were the ancestresses of the royal Davidic line. The rabbis, therefore, declared that the biblical prohibition applied only to the males of Ammon and Moab, but no such exemption existed for Edom and Egypt. The general principle in talmudic law is that intermarriage with all other nations is forbidden.[3]

To be sure, the overwhelming majority of Gentiles were still pagans in the period of the Mishnah. It has, therefore, been argued in some quarters that marriages with non-Jews who are not pagans would, therefore, not be forbidden.[4] The contention has no merit. Even if we recognize the monotheistic character of Christianity and Islam, there still would be strong religious objection to intermarriage. Loyal and informed Jews wish to perpetuate Jewish monotheism and Jewish *mitzvot* and are committed to the preservation of the entire Jewish world-view and way of life, which is far from identical with those of its daughter religions.

Besides, it has been generally overlooked that the religious concern is not the only motive for the Jewish objection to intermarriage. There is another which is as old as the patriarch Abraham—*the national or ethnic-cultural factor.*

The patriarch Abraham opposes Isaac's marrying one of "the daughters of the land," and is equally firm in forbidding Isaac to leave the Promised Land at the behest of his wife:

> Abraham said to his servant, the oldest of his house, who had charge of all that he had, "Put your hand under my thigh, and I will make you swear by the Lord, the God of heaven and of the earth, that you will not take a wife for my son from the daughters of the Canaanites, among whom I dwell, but will go to my country and to my kindred, and take a wife for my son Isaac." The servant said to him,

"Perhaps the woman may not be willing to follow me to this land; must I then take your son back to the land from which you came?" Abraham said to him, "See to it that you do not take my son back there. The Lord, the God of heaven, who took me from my father's house and from the land of my birth, and who spoke to me and swore to me, 'To your descendants I will give this land,' he will send his angel before you, and you shall take a wife for my son from there. But if the woman is not willing to follow you, then you will be free from this oath of mine; only you must not take my son back there."[5]

In Deuteronomy 23:4, the Ammonites and the Moabites are forbidden admission to "the congregation of the Lord forever," because of their hostile acts against the Jewish people.

After the Return, Ezra, with the active cooperation of Nehemiah, denounces the people and particularly the leadership for their mixed marriages with the inhabitants of the land. They are not described as heathen either in belief or practice. The only specific offense which is charged to these marriages is national-cultural: "In those days, also, I saw the Jews who had married women of Ashdod, Ammon, and Moab; and half of their children spoke the language of Ashdod, and they could not speak the language of Judah, but the language of each people."[6]

Thus the Jewish opposition to intermarriage is as old as the Jewish people and relates directly to the dual character of Jewish belonging, which is both religious and national. In sum, the strength of this attitude of opposition cannot be gainsaid.

Intermarriage in Jewish History

However, as against the theoretic prohibition of intermarriage in the Jewish tradition, there is the undeniable evidence that intermarriage was widespread in Jewish history. Joseph may be described as the first "modern" Jew, because he lived in two cultures, Hebrew and Egyptian, and married into the Egyptian aristocracy. The Bible reports that Moses married not only the daughter of a Midianite priest but apparently also an Ethiopian woman, an act which would represent an interracial alliance. There is, incidentally, no opposition in the tradition to the marriage of a white and a black Jew, a clear implication of the biblical narrative.[7] There were, of course, the "normal" dynastic marriages by the royal house, certainly not limited to David and Solomon. The Israelites absorbed many material and cultural aspects of Canaanite civilization, which included the plastic arts, architecture, music, and even language. Such intimate day-by-day contacts must undoubtedly have led to friendship, love, and marriage.

Modern writers frequently remind us that, in the passage quoted above, the Israelites were commanded to exterminate the inhabitants of the land. What is generally overlooked is that, though undoubtedly there were casualties in the course of the Conquest and during the period of the Judges with the ebb and flow of military operations, there is no record of a campaign of extermination against the Canaanites ever being carried out. On the contrary, the historical sources specifically indicate that Canaanites continued to dwell in the southern, central, western, and northern sections of the land.[8]

If the Canaanites were not wiped out physically and yet ultimately disappeared from history, it is clear that they were absorbed into the Jewish people by intermarriage. The ancient tradition of a Moabite ancestry for David is not limited to the books of Ruth and Chronicles. It may lie at the basis of the incident reported in the Book of Samuel that David sent his parents to Moab for safety (22:1–4). Ezekiel tells Jerusalem, "Your father is an Amorite, your mother, a Hittite." (16:3, 45) In sum, history validates the brilliant observation of Rabbi Joshua ben Hananiah that since the days of Sennacherib all national groups have been intermingled.[9]

Conversion in Judaism

To fall back on the three Hegelian categories, the thesis of opposition to intermarriage and the antithesis of its practice led to a synthesis—the development of the rabbinic concept of *giyyur,* "conversion," which incorporated the first and reckoned with the second. Conversion became an important resource for the preservation of Judaism. While it was not established merely or even primarily for cases of intermarriage, it nevertheless served to prevent the loss of Jews through absorption into the majority culture. At the same time, it took into account the realities of non-Jews entering the Jewish community. Ruth became the prototype of the righteous proselyte and therefore worthy to be the ancestress of King David. That Jews took pride in accessions to their ranks from without is clear from the traditions in rabbinic sources that many of the greatest of the Sages were the descendants of non-Jews, in fact, enemies of Israel. Rabbinic tradition makes this claim for Shemaiah and Abtalion, Rabbi Akiba[10] and Rabbi Meir.[11]

In the last two pre-Christian centuries, the old pagan religions in the Mediterranean area were disintegrating and losing their hold on their devotees. A large-scale effort was now made to spread the teachings of Judaism throughout the ancient world, particularly in the Greek-speaking Diaspora. An extensive apologetic literature came into existence. Much of it has survived in the Apocrypha and Pseudepigrapha, and in the writings of Philo and Josephus, as well as in the various Greek translations of the Bible.

It is a matter of sober record that Judaism was not always opposed to missionary activity. On the contrary, in a noted passage, the New Testament complains that the Pharisees, who were the leaders of Judaism at the time of the birth of Christianity, "travel over the land and sea to make one convert." (Mat. 23:15) The vast extent of accretions to Judaism may be judged from the estimate of Harnack that 4 million, fully 10 percent of the population in the Mediterranean area, accepted Judaism in the first century. Salo Baron set the figure higher, at 6 million. Obviously, a substantial proportion of these Jews were accessions from the Gentile world.

As was to be expected, varying attitudes toward these new converts are to be met with among the Sages of the Talmud, depending upon their personalities and the circumstances of their time. Thus the patriarch Simeon ben Gamaliel, who was head of the Palestinian Jewish community, declared it a duty to welcome a proselyte seeking shelter "under the wings of the Divine presence."[12] A later Sage, Eleazar ben Pedat, went so far as to state that the Jewish people were exiled and dispersed in order that they might gain converts.[13]

At the other end of the spectrum was the opinion of a little-known scholar, Helbo, whose name rarely occurs in the Talmud. He declared: "Proselytes are as hard for Israel as leprosy." This harsh verdict is not to be taken too literally, since it is based on a play of words which the rabbi was unable to resist *(saphah, sapahat)*. It is ironic that the biblical passage he uses as his basis speaks in glowing terms of non-Jews as "attaching themselves to the house of Jacob."[14] What is more important, Rabbi Helbo's standpoint was not accepted as normative by his colleagues. To be sure, a negative attitude toward converts persisted in certain quarters throughout later periods, but that was the result of adverse historical factors.

Actually, talmudic law made detailed provision for the acceptance of proselytes. While Rabbi Eliezer required the rite of circumcision for converts, and Rabbi Joshua the rite of immersion, the majority of the Sages made both rituals obligatory, a decision with momentous consequences for the future of Judaism.[15]

The tradition in the Halakah recognized two principal types of converts. The first were the semiproselytes, called in Greek sources *phobomenoi tou theou*, "fearers of the Lord," who accepted the fundamentals of Jewish practice without undergoing the full process of conversion, especially circumcision, which they would put into practice with their newborn children. The second were the *gerei tsedek*, "righteous proselytes," who fulfilled all the Halakic requirements and were completely integrated into the Jewish people.

The missionary efforts of Paul on behalf of Christianity were directed in substantial measure to the semiproselytes. They would find particularly congenial his amalgam of Jewish faith, pagan concepts, and mystical salvation, together with the elimination of the halakic standards insisted upon by Judaism.

Nonetheless, many, if not most, of the proselytes remained loyal to Judaism. Aquila, the translator of the Bible into Greek; Poppaea, the wife of Nero, who was known as a Judaizer; and Helene, queen of Adiabene, and her household represented instances of conversion to Judaism that penetrated even to the highest strata of society. Obviously many more new adherents to Judaism came from the other strata of society.

When Christianity became the official religion of the Roman Empire in the early part of the fourth century C.E., Jews were forbidden to carry on missionary activity. The Emperor Constantine prohibited the marriage of a Jew and a Christian in 339 C.E. In the Middle Ages, severe punishments were visited upon Jewish communities that accepted converts from Christianity. Hospitality to proselytes was fraught with peril for Jews.

In spite of these difficulties, however, accessions continued to the ranks of "the despised faith," as Judah Halevi called it, even in the darkest days of the Middle Ages. Bodo, a former bishop of the Catholic Church who had served as the confessor of Louis the Pious of France, adopted Judaism in the ninth century. Another proselyte was a Crusader who had gone to Palestine with Geoffrey of Bouillon. On accepting Judaism, he adopted the Hebrew name of Obadiah and wrote his autobiography in excellent Hebrew. One of the French Tosaphists is called Rabbi Abraham the Proselyte. Many other proselytes could be mentioned. The most beloved of all in Jewish legend was a seventeenth-century Polish count, Valentine Potocki, who paid with his life at the stake for accepting the Jewish faith.

The greatest mass movement of proselytization was the Khazar kingdom in central Russia. In the eighth century the royal house, dissatisfied with the paganism in which its members had been reared, cast about for a new and better religion. Advocates of Christianity and of Islam sought to win the royal family for their respective creeds, but the king and his household, followed by the court and eventually by a large part of the people, accepted Judaism. For several centuries, until Khazaria was overrun and conquered by the Russians, there was a large and independent Jewish state in Europe. There is one striking fact about it worth underscoring. While religious bigotry and persecution were common everywhere else in the world, the only instance of complete religious tolerance and equality for Christians, Mohammedans, and Jews alike was to be found in the Khazar kingdom.

After its destruction in the tenth century, the Khazars fled westward and were accepted into the Jewish communities of Poland and the Baltic region. Historians have always been aware of the influx of Khazars into Jewish communities in Eastern Europe. Hence modern Jews probably number some of these converts to Judaism among the thousands of their ancestors. This fact has recently been exaggerated and sensationalized by Sir John Glubb, the creator of the famous Jordanian Legion, and subsequently by Arthur Koestler, the former for use as anti-Zionist propaganda.[16] Both seek to establish the indefensible thesis that Ashkenazic Jews are entirely or predominantly Khazar in origin, and are not the physical descendants of the ancient Hebrews. Obviously the Khazar refugees could not have found shelter in western Russia and Poland unless there were Jewish co-religionists already living there to receive them. That the language of Eastern European Jews is not Russian or Polish but Yiddish is decisive testimony that they are the descendants of Jews coming from

German-speaking lands. Finally, the absence of statistical data regarding the Jewish population at the time in general and the number of Khazar refugees in particular deprives the entire theory of any scientific basis whatever.

In sum, three factors enter into the historical Jewish attitude toward intermarriage: (a) a deeply rooted, psychologically powerful opposition to the practice, (b) widespread evidence of its existence, and (c) the mechanism of conversion.

Intermarriage in the Modern Period

Modern intermarriage is quite different in motivation, character, and extent. In the ancient and medieval periods, what was crucial was conversion, which might or might not be followed by the marriage of a former non-Jew to a Jewish partner. In the modern period, intermarriage is the decisive element, which may or may not entail conversion. In other words, in the earlier periods, the phenomenon was basically religious; in the new age, it is primarily sociological.

The Emancipation Era, which was marked by the dissolution of the power of the Jewish community and the breakdown of the authority of Jewish law, brought Jews into close contact with non-Jews in every area of society. As Jews were admitted to political citizenship and civic equality, and found opportunities for economic advancement and cultural expression, intermarriage in its modern sense came into being. In modern intermarriage, two people of varied religious background or of none enter into marriage on the basis of mutual attraction or other motives, not necessarily taking into account their group origins.

There are many cases where the emotion of love becomes so strong that it overrides every other consideration, including even a deep commitment to faith and community on the part of the young people themselves. In a democratic society marked by a progressively greater degree of acculturation, these personal factors will continue to operate in ever larger degree. Young men and women will meet each other and be attracted to one another in school, in business, in the social sphere, and in public life, unless Jews are prepared to ghettoize themselves—and no one has seriously suggested this course of action.

The only possible exceptions are self-segregating groups, like the Hasidic community in New Square, near Monsey, New York, and concentrated Hasidic neighborhoods in Williamsburg, Crown Heights, and Borough Park in Brooklyn. Yet even these groups are not prepared to surrender the political rights and economic advantages of an integrated society. They have, in fact, demonstrated great skill and energy in fighting for their objectives in the political arena.

Nearly two centuries after the French Revolution, it has become clear that the Emancipation did not usher in the Messianic era of universal brotherhood. It produced a society that was largely open but not genuinely free, since it denied Jews the basic right of spiritual self-determination. In Mordecai Kaplan's precise formulation, the modern world gave the Jews the right not to be Christians, but not the power to be Jews. It imposed on them a variety of disabilities, brutal or subtle, overt or covert, legal or social, if they sought to retain their Jewish loyalties.

The existence of the hydra-headed monster called anti-Semitism exerted a strong influence on ambitious and able Jews to cut their links with the Jewish community and become totally absorbed into the dominant majority. In Europe, conversion to Christianity, with varying degrees of conviction on the part of the convert, became a widespread phenomenon, particularly in the upper levels of Jewish society. Many Jews were not deterred by consideration of *noblesse oblige*, as was Gabriel Riesser, or by sensitivity to the intellectual dishonesty and the moral weakness often involved in surrender. This was particularly true in Central and Western Europe, Germany, Italy, France, and Britain. Ahad Ha'am correctly described these Jewish communities as living in a status of "slavery within freedom," spiritual bondage and inferiority within a framework of political liberty, civic equality, and economic opportunity.[17]

In the United States, where the separation of church and state was a deeply ingrained characteristic of American society, formal conversion, while by no means absent, was not a *sine qua non* for personal advancement. Quite by accident, the Cabinet of President Jimmy Carter serves as a showcase of assimilation at work. His Cabinet numbers two converts to Christianity and one Jew who has married out of his faith.

Intermarriage is a far more attractive option than conversion to Christianity. Marrying a non-Jewish partner avoids the necessity of a formal act of apostasy and "painlessly" integrates the Jew into the dominant culture, particularly through his children and grandchildren. The intermarriage rate in Imperial Germany was estimated at an overall figure of about 25 percent, and was constantly growing during the days of the Weimar Republic. Jacob Leschinsky set the figure for 1921–30 for Berlin at 25 percent, the rest of the country at 15.8 percent. Figures were higher for Scandinavia, Italy, Czechoslovakia, and Hungary.[18] Where the process would end was projected by the German sociologist Felix A. Theilhaber in the title of his book, *Der Untergang der Deutschen Juden.* The advent of Hitler replaced this gradual process of automatic and "impersonal" assimilation with the bloody horror of the Holocaust.

In the United States, the same phenomena have been in evidence. Undoubtedly, the American-Jewish experience is unique in many respects. But, it is becoming clearer each day, not in respect to assimilation, conversion, and intermarriage. The American Jewish community was built up through successive waves of immigration. It was born in the seventeenth century with a trickle of Sephardic Jews, who set the earliest pattern of synagogue polity in accordance with their tradition. The eighteenth century was marked by a stream of emigrants from the German-speaking culture sphere, particularly after the failure of the revolutions of 1848. They created the organizational structures of Jewish life in America, both synagogal and philanthropic, that have survived to the present. After 1881, with the adoption of the infamous May Laws in Russia, came the tide of Eastern European Jews, which reached its peak in the three decades ending in 1910. They brought strong Jewish loyalties into the American scene and are the dominant factor today in the American Jewish community. Following the overthrow of Hitler came a small but still substantial current of survivors from Central and Eastern Europe who, for obvious reasons, are the least acculturated to the American scene.

Intermarriage had played a notable role in depleting the ranks of early Sephardic Jewry. With the passing of time, the same forces became operative, first with German and now with Eastern European Jews and their native-born descendants. The full extent of intermarriage has become widely apparent in the second half of the twentieth century.

Sociologist Erich Rosenthal of Queens College studied the admittedly atypical Jewish communities of the state of Iowa and of the nation's capital, Washington, in 1953–59. He found that in the Greater Washington area the intermarriage rate for males in the first immigrant generation was 1.4 percent, for males of the first native-born generation 10.2 percent, and 17.9 percent for males of the second native-born generation.[19] The most disconcerting of his findings attracted relatively little attention at the time—in each category the intermarriage rate doubled for college graduates, going from 1 percent to 15.6 percent to 37 percent in the three generations surveyed. Since nearly 90 percent of young American Jews are college-trained, the figures cannot be described as less than ominous. To be sure, the figures have been disputed or explained away, but the spiraling trend toward intermarriage really needs no statistical confirmation.

More recent studies have disclosed an intermarriage rate of about one third. In 1975, Dr. Fred Masarik of the University of California reported to the Council of Jewish Federations and Welfare Funds that between 1966 and 1972 mixed marriages accounted for 31.7 percent of all Jews presently married.[20] It seems clear that an overall figure of 25 percent for American Jewry today is not far from the mark.

Obviously intermarriage is by no means the only threat to Jewish survival. However, because it avoids the psychological and moral problems many Jews would encounter in formal conversion, it is a major challenge both to the Jewish people as a recognizable entity and to Judaism as a living religious tradition. Thus, the same dual problem which motivated opposition to intermarriage from the beginning of Jewish history has surfaced in our day.

Granted that the basic objectives remain the same, the radically different conditions of modern life make it imperative that we not approach the problem in the simplistic terms of earlier periods. There is great wisdom in the insights of the past, but even greater wisdom is needed to apply these insights to the present and the future. What shall be the attitude toward intermarriage in our time? Once again, a variety of views are to be found in the Jewish community.

The Reasons for Intermarriage

Assimilationists have favored intermarriage on *theoretic* as well as on *pragmatic* grounds. At the end of the nineteenth century and in the first decades of the twentieth, there were voices in the Jewish community, including some rabbis, who actively favored intermarriage as a way of solving the Jewish problem "painlessly" by bringing about the disappearance of the Jewish group. While the great Reform scholar Abraham Geiger vigorously opposed the practice and declared, "Every intermarriage is a nail in the coffin of Judaism," some of his colleagues in the rabbinate were willing and even happy to undertake the task. Before we castigate them unduly, we should recall that, at one stage in his career, Herzl seriously thought of a dignified procession by the Jews of Vienna under the leadership of their rabbis to St. Stephen's Cathedral for a mass conversion, thus eliminating "the Jewish problem." To be sure, no one today, particularly in the post-Hitler era, is naïve enough to believe that this goal can be achieved through intermarriage.

On a pragmatic basis, however, there are countless individuals who, being concerned with their own personal advancement and well-being, are seeking to cast off the burdens of the Jewish heritage; they opt for intermarriage with or without formal conversion. Undoubtedly other factors play an important role, such as social contiguity and, above all, personal attraction. But even the most gifted psychologists would be hard put to analyze the extent to which the desire to "pass," conscious or unconscious, influences the attraction. Many a Jewish wife is cast off by her ambitious husband in favor of a non-Jewish consort, whether his goal is social, political, or academic advancement.

The higher incidence of intermarriage among the richest elements of the Jewish community is no novelty. The same situation prevailed in prewar Germany, France, and England, as well as in Russia, Hungary, and Poland. Reading the society news and the obituary pages of *The New York Times* makes it abundantly clear that intermarriage is particularly common, in America as well, in the upper echelons of American Jewry, among government officials, business executives, academicians, scientists, entertainers, musicians, and artists.

These people are not suffering from overt discrimination. It is the subtler forms of acceptance they want, whether consciously or unconsciously, and intermarriage offers a less painful form of "passing" into the major group than baptism. The novelist Robert Nathan tells the story of a wealthy Jew who converted to a prestigious Christian denomination. His loyalty to the church was exemplary and his benefactions for the mission funds and other causes outstanding. When he died, he was naturally admitted into the Christian heaven without hesitation. The experience proved to be less rewarding than he had hoped. "You see," he explained, "it's not being kept out that hurts. It's being let in and made to feel out."

The various kinds of subtle disability which still affect and afflict these Jews induce a marked sense of inferiority among many of them, particularly for those for whom which the terms "Jew" and "Judaism" are empty designations, possessing no positive content. Jews represent not merely a minority group, but, with the exception of the blacks, the most conspicuous minority in the Western world. While blacks and other non-whites have suffered grievously because they are physically conspicuous, Jews have been exposed to persecution and discrimination on a worldwide scale that has persisted for millennia. Moreover, much of it has been perpetrated "in the name of God," "the social revolution," "anti-colonialism," "anti-racism," and other lofty ideals. In sum, there is a vast complex of pressures on Jews to desert the Jewish community, together with a rich supply of idealistic rationalizations to justify the move.

The Psychological Background of Assimilation

In his classic work *Juedischer Selbsthass*, Theodor Lessing collected a large number of examples of Jewish self-hate that have characterized important figures in the most creative of all modern Jewish communities, the German culture sphere, which included all of prewar Austria, Germany, Hungary, and the surrounding territory. Otto Weininger, the brilliant young philosopher who committed suicide in Beethoven's lodgings in Vienna at the age of twenty-three because he could not stand himself as a Jew, though he had been converted to Christianity, has analogues in the American Jewish experience. A few years ago, a young American Nazi leader in Queens committed suicide when a newspaper reporter discovered the fact that he was a Jew. Some years earlier, a distinguished American scientist who had won the Nobel Prize, Karl Landsteiner, sued in vain to prevent the revelation of his Jewish origin in a reference work on the ground that it would prove traumatic to his children, from whom the Jewish skeleton in the closet had been carefully kept hidden.

Selbsthass, "self-hate," like every pathological phenomenon, takes many forms, from the most severe to the most trivial. The importance even of tiny little slips has been highlighted by Sigmund Freud in his *Psychopathology of Everyday Life.* An apparently unimportant instance of the Jewish sense of inferiority may be presented. Virtually every American rabbi has, at one time or another in his career, been approached by a congregant before a wedding and told, "Rabbi, we are going to have a Gentile friend at our ceremony." On the other hand, I doubt that many ministers have been "warned" by their communicants that a Jew would be present at the ceremony. The implications are obvious.

In sum, from the trivial to the tragic, from small vulgarities to major psychoses, Jewish self-hatred exists in modern society as a reflex of age-old anti-Jewish prejudices in the non-Jewish majority. It supplies a powerful drive toward intermarriage. Where this motivation exists, there is little that can be done. By the time the case comes to the attention of the parent, the rabbi, the social worker, or the psychologist, it is generally beyond remedy. Even if we meet with the young man and woman in question, we talk past them, not with them or to them. They already are enclosed in a hard protective shell which shields their neurosis or psychosis against penetration. On the underlying realities, there is no communication.

Another psychopathological factor is the phenomena of rebellion, whether against parents or against the entire social order. As has frequently been noted in this volume, modern society is marked by the breakdown of parental authority, the erosion of traditional moral standards among adults, and the emergence of new patterns of behavior, primarily among the young. Intermarriage is often one strand in this pattern of maladjustment and conflict within the contemporary family. We cannot be certain that family conflict is more characteristic of Jews than of others, though perhaps it is, but it is undoubtedly very widespread. The stereotype of the overly ambitious, driving Jewish mother, less commonly the father, is a staple in the analysis of neurotic or psychotic Jews on the psychiatrist's couch.

What is particularly frustrating is that this rebellion against parents occurs even where there is no objective reason to be found in the attitudes and behavior of the parents; often they have sought to imbue their offspring with positive Jewish values through the home and the school, and their attitude toward their children is both loving and tolerant. When, nevertheless, the antagonism develops and takes the form of total self-alienation through intermarriage, it is clearly pathological in origin. Obviously, there are many instances where the actions or attitudes of parents evoke justified hostility and resentment. On the other hand, many "normal" cases of intermarriage are testimony to the power of the free and open society to loosen the moorings of traditional patterns and values.

Even more common is the process by which Jews change their family names—many like Epstein, Ginsburg, Segal, and Cohen, of high and honorable status—for so-called American names of Waspish origin. Names are no longer a clue to personal background. A boy who takes a girl out on the first date will not begin the acquaintanceship by asking, "Tell me, are you Jewish?" By the time the question arises, the initial bond of love may have been forged between them.

One not altogether irrelevant observation on the subject of names that has never been noted may be added. While Jews are generally not aware of it, many of the "biblical" names popular among Jews today are drawn from the New Testament: Matthew, Mark, John, Paul, Stephen, Thomas, Peter, and Andrew. Though Jews do not usually recognize the source of these names, the fact that they find them attractive is itself significant.

Another vital sociological factor making for assimilation and intermarriage is the disappearance of the older Jewish areas of settlement and their replacement with new areas of residence for Jews. In the old ghettos, the streets themselves were filled with the sounds and smells of Jewishness. The odors of Jewish cooking, the sound of the Sabbath eve Kiddush, the light of candles aglow in the windows on Friday evening and on Hanukkah, the ramshackle *succot* built in back yards and on roofs, the echoes of prayers from the synagogues, the funeral processions through the streets, the carrying of Torah scrolls at dedication ceremonies, the presence of bearded patriarchs in the streets—all these impinged on the consciousness of Jews both young and old, even of those who might themselves rarely, if ever, cross the threshold of the House of Prayer. In the new areas, the Jewish street has disappeared. Jewish neighborhoods have given way to neighborhoods in which Jews live.

Undoubtedly, a positive intellectual commitment to Judaism is of the utmost importance. Yet it is obvious that, in a Jewish neighborhood, social contacts and marriages will result. Most adult Jews today did not marry their wives or husbands out of a sense of Jewish commitment. Very few, if any, said, "I am going to look for a Jewish mate, because I want to be a Jew!" It was perfectly natural, indeed, virtually unavoidable, for them to come in contact with Jews, and ultimately to find a Jewish marriage partner. The breakdown of the Jewish neighborhood opened the floodgates to intermarriage.

When these factors making for intermarriage come into play, either singly or severally, they are frequently encountered in disguise. They often do not come to the surface, because they are overlaid with the patina of rationalization, both ideological and personal. The frequently heard argument that the "Jewish princess" is more "demanding" and "aggressive" than her Gentile counterpart is completely a stereotype. It is probably true of some Jewish girls, as it is of some non-Jewish ones. Today, there are thousands of Jewish young women who go to college, who have developed the same intellectual and cultural tastes, who are as spiritually sensitive and ethically concerned as their male counterparts, and who work after they are married. Jewish girls do not all live in ranch houses in suburbia, spend every weekend at the country club, and own three cars. The stereotype is a convenient rationalization to mask deeper, less attractive motives—it is therefore not easily susceptible to rational analysis and refutation.

The same consideration applies to the various ideological rationalizations advanced. Thus the unexceptionable doctrine that "all men are created equal" is used to justify intermarriage and to dismiss objections to it as mere prejudice. College students who offer this explanation have taken courses in logic. They know perfectly well that it is an outrageous non sequitur; yet the point is advanced time and again.

It is not being suggested that intermarriage is always, or even generally, the result of extraneous psychological drives, whether it be total acceptance by the majority, or self-hatred or rebellion against the existing structure of society. To deny the force of increasing personal contacts and mutual attraction would be fatuous, but it would be equally stultifying to overlook the factors we have indicated. In sum, whether intermarriage is based on ideological grounds or, as is more often the case, is purely a practical and individual decision, the practice is favored, or, at least, is not opposed, by substantial segments of the American Jewish community that favor assimilation.

Intermarriage is also favored by some groups of Jewish *survivalists.* They point to the horrible diminution of Jewish ranks as a result of the Nazi Holocaust, which reduced the world Jewish population by 40 percent. They argue that the Jewish community would do well to replenish its human resources by abandoning its objection to intermarriage and doing what it can to win the non-Jewish partner over to Judaism.[21] A substantial minority of Reform rabbis employ this rationale to justify their officiating at interfaith marriages, with or without the participation of a priest or a minister.

Some have gone even further. They have argued that the insistence that a Jewish ceremony can take place only if the non-Jewish partner has been formally converted to Judaism beforehand is actually less halakic than the practice of officiating at an intermarriage, since it violates the principle that the conversion must be free from any ulterior purpose.[22] The expressed hope of rabbis officiating at mixed marriages without conversion is that their presence at the ceremony will serve to win the good will of the couple and assure the Jewish partner that he or she is not being cut off from the Jewish community. Such a sympathetic approach will help bring the non-Jewish partner into the Jewish fold ultimately.

No statistics are available as to the degree of success that this procedure has achieved. Barring hard evidence to the contrary, I would tend to rate the percentage of conversions at a later date as very low. To be sure, proponents of this position do not seem much concerned with formal conversion either, before or after. One writer on the subject defines a Jew as "any person who wishes to be known as a Jew and who is accepted as such by the established Jewish community in the area where he or she wishes to reside."[23] Apply a similar test to American citizenship or to membership in any Christian communion and it is clear why most Jews, here and abroad, would find such a definition of Jewishness totally meaningless.

These two groups of assimilationists and survivalists favoring intermarriage are opposed by the majority of the Jewish community, which regards intermarriage as a major threat to its survival.

Two important caveats must be sounded at the outset. It is important to recognize that since intermarriage is a complex phenomenon, the attempt to think in terms of a single solution is doomed to failure. Any statement on the subject which begins with the phrase "The answer . . ." or "The only answer . . ." is, ipso facto, wrong. A given course of action may be useful in dealing with one element of the problem, major or minor, but it cannot possibly be the total, definitive answer.

The second conclusion, at least equally fundamental, is that intermarriage is part of the price that modern Jewry must pay for freedom and equality in an open society. However unpleasant the conclusion may be, it is clear that intermarriage cannot be eliminated or even reduced to the near vanishing point so long as Jews live in a free, or at least an open, society.

Opposition to Conversion

There are, however, several distinct though overlapping positions as to how the problem is to be met. The first is one of *unrelenting opposition,* including the refusal to facilitate the conversion of the non-Jewish partner. One of the issues that divide the Ashkenazic and the Sephardic Chief Rabbis of Israel relates to the procedures to be employed in the case of converts whose bona fides have been established to the satisfaction of the rabbinical authorities. Rabbi Shlomo Goren wishes to cut the period of time for processing a convert to less than the two years or more now required. Rabbi Ovadia Joseph opposes any speed-up in the procedure.

Grounds for this total opposition are both *theoretical* and *practical.* It is argued that conversion, even if all the halakic rituals are observed, is not genuine and is vitiated by an ulterior motive, the desire to marry a Jew. Thus it has been maintained in some quarters that as soon as the convert fails to observe one of the *mitzvot,* his conversion becomes null and void.[24] It therefore follows that, in virtually all cases of intermarriage, we can only stand by helplessly, wring our hands at the loss the Jewish community has sustained, and count on the "stonewalling" process by the rabbinate to reduce the incidence of intermarriage.

This negative approach is open to grave objections, both practical and theoretical. To deal with the practical aspect first —when intermarriages were few and far between, an attitude of official opposition by the Jewish community and the refusal of its rabbis to facilitate the conversion and officiate at the wedding might conceivably have served as a deterrent. Even this is doubtful, for it has been observed that when theology conflicts with biology, biology generally triumphs. This is even more likely to be the case, as we have seen, when sociology and economics enter into the alliance against theology. If, as a Hebrew proverb has it, "the troubles of many are half a comfort to the sufferer,"[25] it is equally true that "transgressions that are repeated come to be regarded as permissible acts."[26] Neither rabbinical deterrents nor community disapproval will substantially affect the picture today. In the face of the rising tide of intermarriage, the Jewish community simply cannot afford to lose thousands upon thousands of its sons and daughters without making a yeoman effort to reduce—not eliminate but reduce—the defections from its ranks.

This consideration is particularly important, since it is clear that many of those who enter into intermarriage are not necessarily hostile or indifferent to Jewish life. On the contrary, often there is deep personal agony involved in the decision to intermarry.

In most cases, to be sure, intermarriage among young people of varying backgrounds is the consequence of falling in love, coupled with a minimal attachment to any religious tradition. The naïve conviction that "religion won't make any difference to us" all too often proves a costly illusion, but generally there is no active hostility to Judaism in the transgression involved.

On the theoretic level, the halakic principle that the conversion must be free from ulterior motives is unquestionably sound. But it must not be approached in simplistic terms. Human motivation is always complex.

When the non-Jewish partner is prepared to undertake a process of serious Jewish study and then finds that he can conscientiously accept the principles and practices of Judaism for himself, the fact that his original impetus was the desire to marry a Jew can hardly be described as "ulterior." In this instance, it is worth observing that Ruth, the righteous proselyte, is led to this momentous step by personal affection for her mother-in-law, from which she progresses to a desire to join Naomi's people, and only at the end to give her loyalty to Naomi's God. "But Ruth said, 'Entreat me not to leave you or to return from following after you, for where you go I will go, and where you lodge I will lodge; your people shall be my people, and your God my God.' "(1:16)

Moreover, the desire to establish a home that will not be religiously and spiritually divided against itself can hardly be described as unworthy. For a non-Jew to abandon the advantage of being a member of the dominant majority and to throw in his lot with the Jewish community, with all the disabilities and disadvantages thereunto appertaining, is a major test of sincerity. Such a step represents in substantial measure the fulfillment of the traditional requirement that a would-be proselyte must be warned of the disadvantages to which he would be exposing himself by the acceptance of Judaism. The rabbis declare that a candidate for conversion should be asked, "What leads you to desire conversion? Do you not know that Israelites at this time are exposed to pain, harassment, pressure, and spoliation, with calamities constantly coming upon them? If he says, 'I know and I do not find myself worthy,' he is at once accepted and is to be informed of some of the less weighty and the more weighty commandments."[27]

Moreover, I see no merit in the casuistic argument that one infraction of the law invalidates the conversion.[28] A proselyte is expected to affirm his *kabbalat 'ol mitzvot,* "acceptance of the yoke of the commandments." The phrase does not mean "the total and complete observance of every commandment," which would be expressed by a phrase like *shemirat kol ha-mitzvot bekhol dikdukehen uphratehen.*

Obviously, a non-Jew who is converted to Judaism in adult life will, other things being equal, not have the same sense of rootedness in Jewish life that is possible for one born a Jew. But that does not impugn the quality of his loyalty to the Jewish community and tradition. Similarly, an American may be either native-born or naturalized, and there are obvious psychological differences between the two categories. Yet both are virtually equal before the law and have demonstrated equal loyalty to America in war and peace. Moreover—and this is of far-reaching significance—children born to a couple consisting of a native-born Jew and a proselyte can be loyal and dedicated members of the Jewish community with every fiber of their being, as history and experience have demonstrated time and again.

If it is true that intermarriage threatens the life of the Jewish community, the course that must be pursued must include both general and specific measures. Under the first rubric are steps designed to minimize the trend to intermarriage by making Judaism as attractive and meaningful as possible by enhancing the quality of Jewish religious and cultural life. When we seek to integrate Judaism into the personal experience of as many Jews as possible, particularly our youth, we encounter a major roadblock—the major ills that characterize the Jewish community today. Youth may not always be knowledgeable, but it is generally intelligent. It is, moreover, far less willing than elders to compromise with the weaknesses of the Jewish community.

The sharpened denominationalism within the Jewish community, often representing a distinction without a difference, is one obstacle. Equally important is the high cost of affiliation that frequently prices the synagogue and other Jewish institutions out of the reach of young people. When they try to affiliate, they are told they must pledge a sizable sum for the Building Fund, in addition to substantial annual membership dues. In this area of experience at least, it is true that if we cannot have what we want, we end by not wanting what we cannot have.

234 PROBLEM AREAS IN MODERN JUDAISM

There are thousands of dedicated laymen and women who serve the Jewish people on many levels as volunteers with self-effacing sincerity and deep devotion. But there are others who seek to advance their position or prestige through community leadership and constantly propel themselves into public print. All too often, the personal qualities of our "leading citizens" are scarcely calculated to inspire young people to meaningful Jewish commitment.

Fortunately, there are a variety of positive factors that have emerged, some older, others of recent origin. For a growing segment of our youth, there is a greater openness to the content of Judaism in the areas both of belief and practice, in its world-view and its way of life. Strikingly positive results have been achieved by various dedicated groups and individuals whenever the tradition has been presented with sincerity, sympathy, and skill.

There are far better facilities available today for Jewish education on every age level. In spite of its inherent weaknesses, elementary Jewish education, whether through supplementary schools after public-school hours or in religious schools over the weekend, has greatly improved in quality. The Day School is unquestionably the major contribution of Orthodox Judaism to the survival of the tradition on the American continent. Today it has spread into a sizable network of Conservative Day Schools and is gaining a foothold in Reform circles as well. Particular significance inheres in the increasing number of schools for boys and girls of high-school age.

The Jewish camp movement has brought new vitality and love of Judaism to tens of thousands of youngsters who attend Zionist, fraternal, Orthodox, Conservative, Reform, Hebraic, or Yiddish-speaking summer camps, where they are able to experience total Jewish living in a virtually ideal ambience.

The proliferation of Judaic studies on college and university campuses throughout the United States has brought untold thousands of Jewish collegians into contact with Jewish religion and culture, of which many of them were totally ignorant beforehand or from which they had long been estranged.

Adult Jewish education cannot yet be described as a mass movement of major proportions, but it is increasingly taking hold in communities throughout the country. It must cease being regarded as a frill or a private hobby of the rabbi and a few laymen, and be presented and campaigned for vigorously and effectively.

Finally, and far from least, is the immeasurable impact of the State of Israel as a source of Jewish knowledge, inspiration, and commitment. This holds true of hundreds of thousands of American Jewish youth who have not visited the land of Israel themselves but who find pride and self-respect in its presence and progress. It is, of course, a far more pervasive influence in the lives of many other thousands of American youth who go to Israel for extended periods of study or for other reasons. Like Antaeus in the Greek myth, who regained his strength when he touched Mother Earth in his battle with Hercules, Jewish young people, like their elders, replenish their Jewish vitality by contact with the sacred soil of the land of Israel.

These aspects of the contemporary scene, looking to the enhancement of the quality and content of Jewish life in general, will, it is to be hoped, strengthen Jewish loyalty among the youth and their elders. Though indirect, they can make a highly effective contribution toward a reduction in the incidence of intermarriage.

More specific measures for dealing with the problem are also available.

When the various aspects of personal morality are discussed, the issue of intermarriage should be frankly and fully analyzed. The fact should be underscored that objection to intermarriage does not stem from any sense of racial superiority or xenophobia. The basic motivation is the passionate desire to preserve the Jewish identity and the Jewish religious and cultural transition as a highly valuable element in world culture. The contemporary Jew, young or old, must be shown that by making Judaism his personal commitment he is not isolating himself from the modern world or resigning from the twentieth century, but, on the contrary, is preparing himself to serve mankind best by giving it his best.

A major instrument for dealing with the problem is discussed in the closing chapter of this work, the creation of counseling centers in all organized communities throughout the country, patterned after the Consultation and Information Center on Judaism, which this writer established under the auspices of the New York Board of Rabbis. A volunteer panel of rabbis—Orthodox, Conservative, and Reform—has been set up, each dedicating one day per month to the offices of the New York Board of Rabbis. Here they offer wise and sympathetic counsel, in person or on the telephone, to all who come, young and old, Jew and non-Jew alike. The center functions without any fees and in total confidentiality, without fanfare or extensive publicity, the latter primarily for lack of funds. The CICJ has offered guidance and help to hundreds of men and women every month.

Over 50 percent of the cases that come to the attention of the CICJ involve intermarriage or problems connected with it. Given sympathy and insight, the counselor can do much to guide young people toward an understanding of the liabilities which intermarriage imposes upon the principals, as well as the families and the communities that are involved, aside from generations yet unborn. Such counseling service should be extended to every sizable Jewish community on the continent, for the problem is universal.

It is clear, however, that no matter how successful we are in raising the cultural level of Jewish life and elevating its moral standards, intermarriage will persist as a phenomenon of a free and open society. Minimizing the number would, of course, be an incalculable gain, for as the Mishnah reminds us, "He who saves a single person in Israel is as though he saved an entire world."[29]

The general steps outlined above are essential, but they must be supplemented by procedures for dealing with specific cases where an intermarriage is in prospect. On the basis of the considerations already advanced, I believe that when it is clear that the couple are determined to marry, every effort should be undertaken by rabbis or influential laymen to urge the non-Jewish partner not to convert, because the Jewish tradition is highly skeptical about instant conversions, but to undertake a course of reading, discussion, and organized study of Judaism. Provision must be made for such instruction and guidance under competent instructors, either on an individual basis or through classes, as is already widely the case in many cities.

A substantial measure of success may be anticipated from efforts to persuade the non-Jewish partner to begin a serious program of study, if it is carried out in private with sympathy and tact. This conclusion is supported by the results of a survey conducted under the auspices of the Council of Jewish Federations and Welfare Funds. A study of intermarried families showed that 98.4 percent of children of intermarried couples are raised as Jews when the mother is Jewish and 63.3 percent when the father is Jewish.[30] Obviously the concept of being raised Jewish is very nebulous and lacking in content in many of these instances. Nevertheless, the figures demonstrate that there is a substantial measure of sympathy for Jewish self-identification in such families and that the prospect of establishing religious unity in such homes would have a strong appeal for many.

When such instruction takes place, it is important that the Jewish partner take the same course as the non-Jew. Not only will this establish a greater community of interest between the couple, it will also augment the usually slender stock of Jewish knowledge and dedication that the Jewish partner possesses.

When the non-Jewish partner is made to feel at home, he can become truly integrated into the Jewish community, and the children born of the union can be saved for Judaism and the Jewish people. When the conversion fails, the fault, in most cases, lies not with the proselyte but with the Jewish partner, his family and associates.

No single technique can be prescribed here, in view of the infinite variety of human nature. Some proselytes may prefer to have their entrance into Judaism remain a private affair, without any public recognition. On the other hand, in other cases and perhaps in most, a public ceremony, including a welcome at some special occasion, such as a Sabbath or festival service, is preferable. The Hanukkah season, which stresses dedication to Jewish religious and cultural values, would seem a particularly appropriate occasion for such a ritual of welcome. It is noteworthy that the Jewish tradition, with its innate wisdom, makes the presence of a court of three essential for the *tevilah* ceremony, thus preserving its private character on the one hand, while underscoring its public implications on the other.

The principal responsibility for the successful integration of the proselyte falls upon the Jewish family into which he or she has entered. We have already noted the importance of having the Jewish partner participate in the course of study undertaken by the proselyte, both for personal as well as for intellectual reasons. All too often, the entire family might well have profited from such a course. Frequently, it happens that most of their positive commitment to Judaism has evaporated long ago and all that remains is prejudice against the convert, whom they continue to treat as outside the pale. This suggests the advisability of at least one extended meeting by the rabbi with the family of the Jewish partner before the marriage ceremony, underscoring the religious and ethical obligation to extend to the neophyte a warm and heartfelt welcome and to make an ongoing effort to involve him or her in all aspects of positive Jewish experience.

During the past two decades, a great deal of statistical data regarding the incidence of intermarriage has been assembled. There is no gainsaying the importance of accurate information on the present extent and the future trend of the phenomenon. I do not endorse the cynical definition of sociology as "statistical data quantifying the obvious." I would suggest, however, that there is far more significant data that we re-

1111

quire if we are to meet the problem of intermarriage adequately. We need to know the relative stability of marriages where conversion takes place as against mixed marriages where that is not the case. What is the comparative divorce rate in both groups, as well as viewed against society as a whole? What percentage of children born in these two types of union are raised within the Jewish community? What forms of Jewish observance and commitment are to be found in both categories of intermarriage? What are the principal problems that converts encounter and what are their suggestions for meeting the difficulties inherent in their situation? What steps are taken by the Jewish families involved, and what problems do they feel remain unresolved? Studies along lines such as these would be of immeasurable practical value in planning the strategy of the Jewish community in the years and decades ahead.

Perhaps the most hopeful sign of all is the widespread concern of the American Jewish community in dealing with this problem. In the past, Jewish religious and communal leadership in Europe generally stood by helplessly without taking counsel together or adopting any concrete program of action.

In a free and open society, it is neither possible nor desirable to prevent Jews and non-Jews from establishing contacts in an atmosphere of friendship and mutual esteem. There will inevitably be cases of mutual attraction growing into love that will not easily be set aside. Many other psychological factors will, in some cases, make it impossible to win the non-Jewish partner for Judaism. Nonetheless, it should be possible to win sizable accessions to Jewish ranks from the larger community.

Ours is the first time in many decades when a serious quest for religious commitment is socially and intellectually respectable once again. The widespread proliferation of cults of all kinds, Oriental and Occidental, genuine and counterfeit, represents only the lower end of the spectrum in the far-flung quest by men, women, and young people in our day for a spiritual home for themselves.

One of the persistent weaknesses in the Jewish community

has been its tendency to underestimate the power of Judaism to evoke the interest and loyalty of sensitive and intelligent non-Jews. There are many among our fellow men who are attracted by its outstanding attributes, its capacity to warm the heart without stifling the mind, its blending of idealistic aspiration and realistic understanding, its deep faith in God and wise understanding of man, its colorful way of life, and its noble yet workable ethic. As was true two millennia ago, Judaism has the capacity to win the adherence of men and women, even when the catalyst of a prospective marriage to a non-Jew does not exist. Where this factor is added, the prospects for success in winning a genuine adherent for the Jewish religion is correspondingly enhanced.

The peril that intermarriage poses to the Jewish future cannot be denied, but it is not without elements of compensation. Welcoming non-Jews into full membership in Judaism offers one channel among many by which we may demonstrate to the world that being a Jew is the least difficult way of being truly human.

Looking to the Future

15

TECHNIQUES AND GOALS

The Role of Education

At this point, it is desirable to cast a glance backward over the road we have traveled. After sketching the worldwide dimensions of the sexual revolution, we contrasted its major features with the fundamental elements of the traditional code by which Judeo-Christian society has been governed for centuries. We then turned to a presentation of the factors that led to the emergence of the new morality—first, its cultural antecedents in the history of the last four centuries; second, the far-reaching socio-economic changes in society in general and in the position of women in particular; and third, the largely unsuspected but crucial role of traditional Christianity in this process.

We then sought to evaluate the consequences of the sexual revolution in terms of human welfare, the degree to which it has delivered on its promise to enhance the happiness of people. Undoubtedly, it has to its credit the broadening of the horizons of freedom and experience and the reduction of incidents of oppression in the relationships of men and women. The debit side of the ledger, however, contains evidence of vast areas of human misery, revealed in a variety of overt social and physical problems that are constantly growing in depth and extent. There is also the covert unhappiness of modern men and women, the loneliness and the quiet—and the not so quiet—desperation lurking behind a façade of artificial gaiety and sophistication. Then there are the major social ills of our time that cannot be attributed exclusively to sexual dislocations. Yet it is undeniable that sexual difficulties play a significant role in the growth of violence, the spread of the drug culture, and the rise in alcoholism. One can only conclude that the new morality has not been able to provide an adequate solution for the major problems in the sexual domain, as had been confidently predicted by its advocates.

In the current quest for light and guidance, the Jewish tradition as a whole, though it arose under radically different conditions, possesses valuable resources for approaching the complex area of love, sex, and marriage. Of particular relevance to our concern is the Jewish concept of sex. Its content transcends the Jewish community and can prove a boon to all men and women in at least six frontier areas—one is tempted to say six disaster areas—in contemporary society. These comprise the phenomena of modern divorce, birth control and abortion, homosexuality, sexual relations outside of marriage, and illegitimacy.

We would be less than candid if we did not recognize that, far from having all the answers, Judaism has problems all its own. These are the products of a long and unique history that extends from ancient times through the Middle Ages to our own day. A survey and an analysis of the role of women in Jewish life and law is no mere exercise in historical research, nor is its significance limited to the Jewish community. An understanding of the process of growth and development in women's rights in Judaism in the past can indicate the direction that should be followed in the future. It may also serve as a paradigm for other traditions that are wrestling with these problems.

In addition to women's rights, there is one other major issue confronting the Jewish people in this area—the phenomenon of intermarriage. It has engaged our attention because no other aspect of contemporary marriage is freighted with deeper ethical concern or personal agony for modern Jews. From this wide-ranging discussion, several major conclusions have emerged. First, neither the old code in its entirety nor the new pattern as currently practiced can adequately serve men and women in the twentieth century and beyond. What is needed is a system of values and a code of behavior that will draw upon the best elements in both.

Second, we cannot stress too strongly the importance of recognizing the limitations that the civil law encounters in attempting to deal with the intimate area of love and sex. Civil or secular law can enact the formal requirements and the technical procedures needed for marriage, divorce, the division of property, financial support, and similar matters. But we have seen how self-contradictory and helpless secular law finds itself on such questions as abortion, homosexuality, pornography, and prostitution. Most important of all, it cannot legislate inner attitudes or foster the virtues of fidelity, compassion, forbearance, love, and concern. It is the basic virtue of a religious ethic such as the Halakah that it can transcend the limitations of secular law and penetrate into those areas which, in the fine talmudic phrase, are "matters handed over to the heart."

If men and women are to achieve a substantial measure of happiness in this area, it will depend upon the education of their minds, their hearts, and their wills, the inculcation of sound ideals, and the strengthening of the resolution to live by them.

It is, therefore, clear that the teacher and not the policeman must point the way. We must turn to education in its broadest sense, the drawing out of the finest capacities of men and women, by inculcating standards of conduct that will do justice both to human nature and human idealism.

The program must operate on two levels, *the teaching of the group and the counseling of the individual.* For too long, the entire subject of sexual ethics has been taboo in our educational system, with the predictable result that the transmission of information and the establishment of behavior patterns have been left to the gutter and the back alley, the smoker and the brothel. The time is long overdue for a broadly based program of education which will encompass every age group in the population.

A thorny problem arises at this point. Under whose auspices should this program for elementary- and high-school students be conducted? At one time, I was tempted to answer that it belongs to the public school, since it is the most broadly based system of training we possess and is the major instrument for the education of the young. Unfortunately, this answer is too simple. Two or three generations ago it might well have been an adequate response. There was a substantial consensus of outlook on the fundamentals of sex ethics in American society. It derived from the Judeo-Christian tradition as it was commonly understood. Today, however, no such consensus exists. Indeed, some observers of the contemporary scene speak of our age as post-Christian. What is clear is that wide sections of the population today, including many elements of the teaching fraternity, do not accept the theory, or even the practice, of the traditional sex code. It is not to be expected that they could transmit its content and values to their charges with any degree of conviction or success.

Moreover, the code of sexual morality to which believing Jews and Christians give their allegiance is rooted in their religious world-view. It cannot, therefore, be taught without reference to fundamentals of religious faith. Man's place in the cosmos, his role as a creature of a Power greater than himself, the character of human nature, the duty to show love, concern, and responsibility for others—all these must undergird and affect the treatment of sex, love, marriage, divorce, and all the other issues that have been dealt with here. This raises the problem of church-state relationships. To present the religious background of sexual ethics in the public school would be a flagrant violation of the basic American doctrine of separation of church and state. To omit this religious underpinning would mean to stultify the entire undertaking.

Finally, there are highly significant differences, as has been highlighted in this volume, between Judaism and Christianity, precisely in this area, that cannot be ignored or glossed over. What is more, while fundamentalists and liberals in Christianity have a great deal in common, there are significant differences between them as well. So, too, a modern Jewish thinker and a Hasidic rabbi share the same tradition and will thus have a basis for agreement on many aspects of sexual ethics, but there will also be important divergences between them.

One is therefore compelled to conclude that sexual ethics cannot be taught effectively and meaningfully in a secular school system today. The public school can present lectures on the physical endowments of men and women and the reproductive process, all of which is properly part of a course in biology. Such topics are undoubtedly necessary as a basis upon which a sexual ethic can be built. The structure, however, can be reared only by each religious group for its own adherents and for those who are sympathetic to its viewpoint.

Ways and means must therefore be found for setting up independent courses on love, sex, and marriage for boys and girls beginning with the middle grades of the elementary school and continuing to higher levels. Such a broadly based program will necessarily require the preparation of texts and audio-visual aids and, above all, the adequate training of teaching personnel. These classes might be offered as a supplement after the public-school day, with or without a direct relationship to existing religious schools. I believe, however, that religious schools, both in their elementary- and high-school departments, are likely to be more successful in giving instruction on personal morality and contemporary issues.

These observations would seem to be valid for Christians as well as for Jews. Speaking in Jewish terms, the growing number of Jewish summer camps offer an especially promising field for the education of teenagers, who are perhaps the most important age group in this connection. College students must be made aware of the insights of the Jewish tradition through credit courses in Judaic studies conducted by the universities, as well as by discussion groups and classes sponsored by Hillel foundations.

Adult education in synagogues and Jewish centers also requires the preparation of appropriate material for teaching and discussion. The frankness and honesty of the biblical and rabbinic approach to love and sex should serve as a model for rabbis in their preaching and teaching, both in the pulpit and in the classroom. Continuing education in the broadest sense and at every level of life is indispensable.

Personal Counseling—Secular and Religious

The rich insights of the Jewish tradition need, however, to be sharpened and applied through personal counseling. It is necessary to make psychological and psychiatric aid more available through social-service agencies. Such technical assistance is a necessary condition for any program of counseling, but it is not a sufficient condition. As the practitioners of these disciplines constantly point out, their approach is non-judgmental. Generally, psychological counselors insist upon adopting a neutral stand, offering their clients the opportunity of speaking and thinking about their problems but refraining from extending any counsel and direction. Thus, the Jewish Family Service of Philadelphia informs us: "Through the guidance of the group leader, single mothers are helped to make free choices [with regard to their sex patterns] by exploring all the options. *As an agency, we reject stereotyped models as the only solutions and help them find answers within the context of their individual situations* [italics ours]. Most of the mothers hope to marry and join the 'couples' world, but they are helped to understand that for some this might never happen and they are encouraged to make meaningful lives for themselves as singles."[1]

Undoubtedly there is substantial realism involved in such an approach, but exploring all the options is not as non-judgmental as it seems. Built into this technique is an implicit approval of the new life styles, including those that we have weighed and found wanting. Actually, most people today do not turn to social-service agencies in order to learn that extramarital relations are, in theory at least, a live option for them. Many, if not most, of the men and women, primarily the latter, come seeking guidance and direction. They want standards, something that the non-judgmental counselors are unwilling, or perhaps unable, to offer.

To meet this crying need in the areas of love, sex, and marriage, as well as in all other fields of human and Jewish concern, the author has long advocated the establishment in each substantial Jewish community of a consultation and information center on Judaism. His efforts in this direction have been crowned with success in the New York area. The New York Board of Rabbis is now conducting such a project at its headquarters through a panel of volunteer rabbis. The calls that have been made to the Consultation and Information Center have reached over a thousand within two years.

There is, therefore, a great need for sex and marriage counselors who are religiously motivated and dedicated to a specific ethical point of view. Rabbis—some rabbis—naturally come to mind in this connection, but the function should not be restricted to them. Personal qualities are far more significant than a diploma on the wall. The counselors needed here, as in all human relationships, must possess sense and sympathy, understanding and patience. Obviously, the dangers of dogmatism and unbending rigor must be guarded against. At the same time, the counselors must be able to present norms and interpret standards for a generation that is desperately in need of guidance and, whether it is always conscious of it or not, genuinely yearns for direction. Counselors, whether rabbinic or lay, must be endowed with a genuine human sympathy coupled with an insight into human nature which only the untranslatable Hebrew term *sekhel* can convey.

Finally, they should be men and women who are not indifferent to Jewish life, but believe in Judaism and want it to survive. Today there are many rabbis who are equipped with the technical expertise traditionally associated with the social worker, and conversely there are many social workers who have a sense of commitment to Jewish life. Whether they are laymen or rabbis, the counselors would place in the center of their concern the well-being of the individual and his family, while remaining aware of the needs and goals of the community.

There is another reason for setting up consultation centers with a religious orientation. Several years ago, a Jewish refugee from Nazi Germany, who was later converted to Catholicism, published his autobiography. In his book the author claimed that when he was wrestling with agonizing spiritual problems he could not find a rabbi in Germany to whom he could talk. Whatever the truth of his contention, I believe that in America such a feeling is widespread among the laity. Here, where rabbis are much more harried than they were in Germany, it is widely thought that there are no rabbis to talk to, no place for people to go with their problems. Often, too, people may be loath to go to their own family rabbi for counseling, whatever the reason may be.

The establishment and maintenance of such family counseling centers in every Jewish community should be given an extremely high priority in the funding of communal projects if headway is to be made in solving the problems of personal relations, which are constantly growing in numbers and intensity. The mere existence of such competently staffed consultation centers would serve to demonstrate to the young that the Jewish community is concerned about them and has a genuine interest in their well-being, because they are important in and of themselves, for the Jewish people, and for the heritage which only they can preserve and transmit to the world.

A Sex Code for Our Age

The fundamental thesis of this volume, which we have sought to buttress by an honest examination of the historical record on the one hand and the realities of the present situation on the other, is that a rational and viable sex code for the future will not be identical either with the traditional morality of the past or the various manifestoes of the sexual revolution in the present. On the contrary, as in all true progress, it will draw on the best insights and ideals of both.

We may, however tentatively, set forth twelve principles. There is no magic in the number and no claim to the ultimate truth in the formulation. But it is noteworthy that five of the goals proclaimed as the gospel of the new morality have always been implicit or explicit in Jewish tradition.

1. Personal happiness is a legitimate goal for human beings in general. Sexual experience is a major source of pleasure and well-being for men and women, and its successful functioning is a proper objective in marriage.

2. Marriage is intended, not merely for the procreation of the race, but also for companionship and love.

3. The equality of men and women, which has been a basic thrust of the Jewish tradition, particularly during its most creative periods, has not yet been fully achieved in any society. It must be carried forward until its legitimate goals are achieved.

4. Mutuality in love and respect are the foundations of marriage. Domination of either partner by the other violates the equality which is the heart of the marriage relationship. But the partners are not discrete individuals, each concerned basically with maintaining his own independence and, therefore, jealously minimizing the points of contact with the other. On the contrary, the relationship of the two partners in a marriage is best conceived of as two circles intersecting with each other, constantly striving to come closer, so that they may possess a larger area in common.

5. Sex is not a sin, marriage is not a prison, and divorce is not a crime.

With regard to the seven other principles, however, Jewish tradition parts company, either in substance or in emphasis, with the views being promulgated today in the name of the new morality. While they may be out of fashion today, these attitudes of Jewish tradition are indispensable for a viable code of sexual morality in our age. They must, therefore, be presented and emphasized again and again with all the persistence and skill at our command, until they are accepted into the value system of modern men and women.

6. Each human being is an arena in which body, mind, and spirit are interwoven and inseparable. Hence, love and sex are indivisible in a complete, satisfying man-woman relationship, for only then is the total human personality involved. To sanctify love and denigrate sex, or, conversely, to cultivate sex and scorn love, is to invite schizophrenia in the human personality and must lead to the impoverishment and degradation of human life.

7. The loud chorus to the contrary notwithstanding, marriage is not merely one of many life styles of equal legitimacy. The union of one man and one woman in marriage and in marriage alone is *kiddushin*, "an act of holiness." Marriage cannot fulfill its true function without a religious attitude (using the term in its broadest sense). The popular etymology of "religion" associates it with the Latin verb *religare*, "binding up." Through marriage, the finite lives of a man and a woman are bound up with infinity, the limitless expanse of time we call the future and the vast extent of space we call the universe. By their love, they have it within their power to enhance the glory of the world and to sanctify its Creator.

8. We must recapture the conviction that marriage is a union involving not two but three partners—a man, a woman, and God. Only in this way can we hope to re-create a sense of the seriousness of the obligation undertaken by young people entering into marriage. Our generation needs to learn anew

the old truth that marriage is a compact in which husband and wife are bound to each other by a sacred duty that goes far beyond the drive of physical infatuation or the economic and social advantages of living together.

9. We must reject the dangerous and often insincere doctrine that "love," the physical attraction of two persons, is an all-sufficient condition for marriage and that the absence of compatibility in religious background, education, interests, ideals, or temperament is an irrelevant consideration.

It is this attitude which leads directly to the idea that any new affair into which either partner may permit himself to be drawn may be justified on the ground of love, and that the oath of mutual loyalty, which is the heart of the marriage ceremony, may then be abrogated without compunction.

10. Because the love-sex relationship has long-range consequences, both for the principals and for generations yet unborn, it requires the sense of stability and permanence that only the marriage institution can offer. This has always been recognized, however dimly and imperfectly; in spite of all onslaughts against it, the marriage institution remains unique and irreplaceable.

11. Since procreation is not the only goal of marriage, it may be set aside under special circumstances. Nevertheless, the birth and nurture of children remains the basic objective of the family structure. Children require the security and sense of direction possible only in a home with two parents, both of whom are needed, so that the children may be properly cared for, reared, and prepared for mature and independent living.

12. The family is the bridge linking the individual and society, each influencing and benefiting the other. The home, in which sexual activity attains to its highest potential as love, is the single greatest instrument for teaching the truth that human happiness must be sought and can be found only in adhering to both elements in Hillel's great injunction, "If I am not for myself, who will be for me? But if I am only for myself, of what good am I?"

Principles such as these, however formulated, must serve as the basis for a system of education on the ethics of love, sex, and marriage geared to every age group and culture level in the population. These canons must inform the work of personal counselors if their efforts are to be truly successful.

In our day, it may appear quixotic and downright futile to propose a code of sexual ethics of this kind when the tide seems to be running strongly in the opposite direction. Obviously it may persuade only a minority of men, women, and young people today, who will give their loyalty to its principles and strive to embody them in their conduct. The majority may well remain unmoved and unconcerned by the entire enterprise.

But one of the most fundamental insights of the Hebrew Prophets is that of the Saving Remnant as the secret of Jewish survival—the vision of a dedicated minority holding fast to the truth as it sees it in the face of an indifferent and even hostile majority. In the inscrutable processes of history, the Jewish people today is the remnant of a remnant of a remnant, but it is these survivors of the millennial struggle for existence who have been the bearers of the body of Judaic values and ideals. It is the Saving Remnant that has helped men and women to inch forward and strive to become truly human.

Besides, Jewish history is replete with instances of communities far removed from the Jewish way of life and indifferent to their tradition who underwent a revolutionary transformation, generally through the instrumentality of dedicated and courageous leaders. A century after the return from the Babylonian exile, Ezra and Nehemiah found a weak and demoralized Jewish settlement in Jerusalem and its environs. They succeeded in reconstituting the community and endowing it with a sense of purpose, thus laying the foundations of the Second Commonwealth. Some six centuries later, two scholars, Rab and Samuel, after completing their studies in Palestine, returned to their native Babylonia. They "found an open valley and fenced it in,"[2] and laid the groundwork for the second massive achievement of the Jewish genius, the Babylonian Talmud. Centuries later, according to tradition, a Babylonian scholar, Moses ben Enoch, redeemed from captivity, came to Spain and visited a school. He found the instructor teaching a rabbinic text and expounding it incorrectly. Rabbi Moses determined to devote himself to the establishment of a center for Jewish learning in Spain, which ultimately flowered in the "Golden Age" of Spanish Jewry. In the nineteenth century, Rabbi Hayyim of Volozhin, calling for the creation of a new Yeshiva, lamented the widespread Jewish ignorance in Lithuania, which was to become synonymous with Jewish intellectual excellence in the decades ahead.

The Jewish ethos has survived because in every age there have always been "seven thousand, all the knees that did not bow down to Baal." (I Kings 19:18) Through the centuries, the Saving Remnant has been the living nucleus within the protoplasm of the Jewish people, maintaining the tradition, giving it new life, and inspiring the masses of the people with new loyalty to the Torah of righteousness and truth.

The patience and courage needed to preserve and propagate the viable ideals of the Jewish tradition in our day can be strengthened by one observation. Modern men and women and, above all, young people today often fail to respond affirmatively to the idea of the holiness of marriage as taught by religion, because they have generally seen it linked to an irrational and unrealistic concept of human nature. Rejecting the latter, they refuse to accept the former. Yet there is no necessary connection between the two. Judaism proves that a rational yet idealistic attitude toward life is entirely possible. To accept the natural and to sanctify it is the heart and essence of the Jewish tradition.

These goals can never be achieved universally and to perfection. In an age of chaos and dissolving standards, they become even more difficult to accomplish. Hence, men and women who falter and stumble should be met with sympathy and insight and helped to find the path of integrity which is the only sure road to enduring happiness.

There are three basic, interdependent Jewish concepts—

the sanctity of the total human personality, the union of sex and love, and the holiness of marriage. They offer men and women the greatest measure of hope as they seek the elusive but eternally beckoning goal of nobler, wiser, and happier living.

Notes
Bibliography
Indices

Notes

CHAPTER 1

1. The passages are Mic. 7:5, 6; Hos. 4:13, 14.
2. See Robert Briffault, *The Mothers* (New York, 1959).
3. Mishnah Ketubbot 4:4; Babli Ketubbot 47b.
4. B. Kiddushin 29a.
5. B. Yebamot 115a; Avodah Zarah 25b.
6. B. Keritot 28a and Rashi and Ibn Ezra on the biblical passage.
7. Hos. chaps. 1–3, esp. 2:21, 22; Isa. 8:3; Ezek. 24:16.
8. B. Shabbat 33b.
9. Abot 1:5.
10. B. Erubin 53b.
11. U.S. Bureau of the Census, *Statistical Abstract of the U.S.* (Washington, D.C., 1975) p. 40, table No. 52. Cited hereafter as *SA*.
12. *Time*, January 24, 1964.

CHAPTER 2

1. See, for example, Lev. 26:3–45; Deut. 27:11–26; 28:1–68; 32:1–43; Jud. 2:11 ff.; Hos. 8:7; Isa. 3:10, 11; Prov. *passim*, etc.
2. See the reflection of the biblical sage Koheleth in Eccles. 3:16–4:3; 7:15; 8:10–9:3.
3. The author's treatment of the problem may be found in the chapter "Evil in God's World," in Gordis, *A Faith for Moderns* (New York, 1960, augmented edition, 1971). The biblical doctrine and its important consequences are treated in *The Book of God and Man; A Study of Job* (Chicago, 1965), chap. XI, "Job and the Mystery of Suffering." It is, of course, also treated in virtually every book on religion and theology.
4. *SA*, p. 334.
5. B. Kiddushin 7a.

CHAPTER 3

1. Cf. my study *Politics and Ethics* (Santa Barbara, Cal., 1961), pp. 9–16, and *The Root and the Branch: Judaism and the Free Society* (Chicago, 1962), chap. 10.
2. Mat. 19:21; Mark 10:21; 12:72; Luke 18:22.
3. Mark 10:10–12; see also Mat. 5:31–32.
4. *I Cor.* 7:1–3, 5–11, 26–28, 36–40.
5. The creation of Adam serves the rabbis as the foundation for their concept of man's God-given and, hence, inalienable right to dignity, freedom, equality, and justice. See "What Is Man" in Gordis, *A Faith for Moderns,* chap. XI.
6. See "The Knowledge of Good and Evil" in Gordis, *Poets, Prophets and Sages* (Bloomington, Ind., 1971), chap. 7.
7. For the documentation, see Gordis, *Judaism for the Modern Age* (New York, 1955), pp. 227–31 and notes.
8. See *The New York Times,* September 21, 1952.
9. See *The New York Times,* December 3, 1966, for a summary of the results of the survey presented to the Fifth Annual Notre Dame Conference on Population, by Professor Charles W. Westoff of Princeton University and Professor Norman B. Ryder of the University of Wisconsin.
10. *The New York Times,* October 29, 1966.
11. For several aspects of the subject, see the illuminating studies of Monford Harris: "The Concept of Love in *Sefer Hasidim,*" *Jewish Quarterly Review,* July 1959, pp. 15–44; "The Way of a Man with a Maid—Romantic or Real Love," *Conservative Judaism,* Winter 1960, pp. 29–39; "Reflections on the Sexual Revolution," *Conservative Judaism,* Spring 1966, pp. 1–17.
12. See A. O. J. Cockshut, *The Unbelievers* (New York, 1966); and Gertrude Himmelfarb's perspicacious analysis in *The New York Review of Books,* November 1, 1966.

CHAPTER 4

1. The passages are *Eccles.* 2:24; 5:17–19; 8:15; 9:7–10; 11:7–9. The translation is taken from Gordis, *Koheleth: The Man and His World* (New York, 3rd augmented ed., 1968).
2. Ben Sira 14:11; see also 14:15–19; 30:21–23.
3. "The Manual of Discipline" in Theodore H. Gaster, *The Dead Sea Scriptures,* 3rd edition (New York, 1976), p. 49.

4. B. Erubin 54a.
5. J. Kiddushin, end.
6. Perek Kinyan Torah, par. 8.
7. Perek Kinyan Torah, par. 9.
8. Mishnah Abot 4:1.
9. See his Introduction to the Mishnah Abot, Shemoneh Perakim, now conveniently accessible in English in Isadore Twersky, *A Maimonides Reader* (New York, 1972), pp. 361–86.
10. U.S. Bureau of the Census, Current Population Reports, series P-20, No. 271, reproduced in *SA*. See also *The New York Times,* March 20, 1977.
11. Cleveland Amory, *The Last Resorts* (New York, 1952).
12. See "Report on Teen-Age Sexuality," by Melvin Zelnik and John F. Kantner, in *Family Planning Perspectives,* April–May 1977, and *The New York Times,* April 8, 1977.
13. "The Increasing Single Parent Families," *The New York Times,* December 3, 1974.
14. Ruth T. Pierce, *Pregnant and Single* (Boston, 1975).
15. See Judy Klemesrud, "Women Bachelors: The City Is Not Eden," in *The New York Times,* October 7, 1974. For some full-length studies that offer a spirited defense of singleness as a *modus vivendi* for women, see Margaret Adams, *Single Blessedness: Observations on the Single Status in Married Society* (New York, 1976), and Katherine Breslin, *Promiscuous Condition* (New York, 1976). After 200 interviews, Breslin concludes that "freedom is a lot of interesting things, but nobody ever said it was easy."
16. George Gilder, *Naked Nomads* (New York, 1974). See also his paper, "In Defense of Monogamy," *Commentary,* November 1974.
17. See, for example, Phillip Sarrel, *Student Guide to Sex on Campus* (New Haven, n.d.).
18. See U.S. National Center for Health Statistics, *Vital Statistics of the U.S. Annual,* cited in *SA,* p. 57.
19. *SA,* p. 40, table 52; *The New York Times,* June 28, 1974.
20. See "All the Lonely People" by Auberon Waugh, in *Books and Bookmen* (London), vol. 22, no. 1, October 1976, p. 6.
21. Edmund L. Van Deusen, *Contract Cohabitation: An Alternative to Marriage* (New York, 1974).
22. *SA,* p. 87, table 140.
23. Midrash Bereshit Rabba, chap. 9; Midrash Koheleth Rabba 3:11; Midrash Tehillim on Psalm 9; and elsewhere.

CHAPTER 5

1. See "The Reality of the Judeo-Christian Tradition" in Gordis, *Judaism in a Christian World* (New York, 1966).
2. B. Yebamot 63b.
3. On these new trends, see David Schimmel, "Free-Will, Guilt and Self-Control in Rabbinic Thought and Contemporary Psychology," in *Judaism*, Fall 1978.
4. *Patur abhal asur.*
5. *Patur b^edinei adam v^ehayyabh b^edinei shamayim.*
6. *D^ebharim ham^esurim lallebh.*
7. *Ein goz^erin g^ezerah al hassibur'ela im ken hassibbur yekholin la 'amod bo.*
8. *Mutabh shey^ehu shogegin ve'al yehu m^ezidin.*
9. *Asur l^ekhat^ehilah uphatur b^edi^abhad.*
10. *B^ehephsed m^erubbeh.*
11. *Mip^enei darkhei shalom.*
12. *Mipnei tikkun ha' olam.*
13. *Halakhah v^e' ein morim ken.*
14. *Lifnim mishurat hadin.*

CHAPTER 6

1. Tosefta Yebamot 8:4; B. Yebamot 63b.
2. B. Yebamot 62b.
3. Mishnah Yebamot 6:6; Shulhan Arukh, Yoreh Deah 1:5.
4. Even Ha-ezer 23:5, and Rabbi Moses Isserles 1:3.
5. Harry Elmer Barnes, "Sex in Education," in V. F. Calverton and S. D. Schmalhausen (eds.), *Sex in Civilization* (New York, 1929), p. 385.
6. For a comprehensive survey of the ideal of *tzeniyut* as applied to modesty in dress and to the segregation of the sexes in talmudic and post-talmudic Judaism, see Louis M. Epstein, *Sex Laws and Customs in Judaism* (New York, 1948), pp. 25–103.
7. This is an indication, among others, that the literal interpretation of this biblical book alongside the allegorical, more recondite, interpretations was known to the rabbis.
8. Ex. 21:10; Mishnah Ketubot 5:6; B. Ketubot 61b–62b; Shulhan Arukh, Even Ha-ezer, sec. 76.

9. See Rashi on B. Ketubot 62b, *s.v. May'erev Shabbat: Shehu layl ta'anug ushevitah vehana'at ha-guf;* Nahmanides, *Iggeret Hakodesh,* sec. 2.

10. B. Yebamot 34b and Tosafot *ad locum;* B. Nedarim 20b, and see Isserles Even Ha-ezer 25:2. The classical passage on family limitation occurs in Tosefta Niddah 2:6, with a significant addition, the implications of which are overlooked by Luria and by Lauterbach, whose important paper is cited below. This addition gives considerably greater latitude to irregular forms of sexual play. *Cf.* Mitzpeh Shemuel *ad locum,* and see also Yam Shel Shelomoh, Yebamot 1:8.

11. For this interpretation of the Paradise tale, see "The Knowledge of Good and Evil in the Old Testament and the Dead Sea Scrolls," in Gordis, *Poets, Prophets and Sages,* pp. 198–216.

12. Ex. 21:10. While the word *'onathah* has been given various other interpretations, such as "dwelling place," the traditional rendering is "conjugal rights," perhaps as "living together."

13. B. Erubin 100b.

14. These biblical passages are to be found in Deut. 6:5, Lev. 19:18, and the Song of Songs 7:7, respectively.

15. See Gordis, *The Song of Songs* (New York, 1974), *passim.*

16. Tosefta Sanhedrin 12:10.

17. See Mishnah Eduyot 5:3, Tosefta Yadayim 2:14, and the final decision in favor of its canonicity in Mishnah Yadayim 3:5.

18. Midrash Shir Ha-shirim Rabbah 1:1.

19. Habbukuk 1:13.

20. The text of the *Letter* is to be found in the excellent edition of Nahmanides's writings by Charles B. Chavel, *Kitbei Rabbenu Moshe ben Nahman* (Jerusalem, 5724–1964), vol. 2, pp. 315–337. The passage we have translated above is in chapter 2 (p. 323). Chavel, who challenges the traditional attribution of the treatise to Nahmanides, was anticipated by Gershom G. Scholem in *Kiryat Sepher,* vol. 25, 1944–45, pp. 179–186. However, as Chavel recognizes, the intrinsic interest of the *Iggeret* is not impugned by the possibility of another author. An English translation is to be found in S. J. Cohen, *The Holy Letter* (New York, 1976).

    Nor does Monford Harris's interpretation of the *Iggeret* as possessing an esoteric, kabbalistic meaning (see his paper, "Marriage as Metaphysics—A Study of *Iggeret Hakodesh,*" *Hebrew Union College Annual,* vol. XXXIII, 1962, pp. 197–220) deny its exoteric content as a treatise on love and sex in marriage. It is significant, as Harris points out, that the author uses the marriage relationship as a vehicle for metaphysical and mystical truth. He thus remains true to Judaism by rejecting the two extremes of libertinism and asceticism, both of which constitute genuine temptations for the devotees of gnosticism, as history demonstrates (*op. cit.*, p. 218 ff.).

21. B. Berakhot 62a.
22. *Cf.* Bereshit Rabbah, chap. 9; Kohelet Rabbah on Ecclesiastes 3:11; Midrash Tehillim on Psalm 9.
23. *Cf.* B. Berakhot 17a; "Rabbi Alexander, after he prayed, would add, 'O Master of the World, it is revealed and known unto Thee that it is our duty to do Thy will, but what prevents us? The leaven in the dough [*i.e.*, the evil impulse] and the subjection to foreign powers.' "
24. B. Yoma 69b.
25. B. Berakhot 54a.
26. On the theological doctrine of the Fall of Man, which is fundamental to Christian theology, and on the Jewish view of human nature, see Gordis, *A Faith for Moderns,* chaps. XI and XII.
27. See Gen. 1–31 and Bereshit Rabbah, chap. 8.
28. *Cf.* Shir Ha-shirim Rabbah, chap. 7.
29. See Job 5:24 and B. Yebamot 62b.; B. Sanhedrin 76b.

CHAPTER 7

1. Mark 10:11, 12; see also Luke 16:18.
2. M. Gittin 9:10.
3. On the background, the actions taken, and the prospects of the "Call to Action" conference, see Thomas C. Fox, "Made in Detroit," *Commonweal*, November 19, 1976, pp. 746–48.
4. Mishnah Gittin 9:10.
5. Deut. 24:3. Mishnah Kethubbot 7:9, 10; Rambam, Mishneh Torah, Hilkhot Ishut 25:11–12: ". . . if the husband developed a mouth odor or a nasal odor or he returned to the occupation of collecting dogs' dung or coppermining from the ore or that of a tanner, the rabbinical court compels him to divorce her and pay her *ketubbah*. But if she wishes to remain with him, she may do so. If he develops chronic boils, we compel him to divorce her and pay her *ketubbah*. We compel him to divorce because intercourse would enervate him."
6. Mishnah Gittin 9:10.

7. A reasoned plea for recognizing that divorce may be the preferable alternative to an unhappy marriage is made in Morton M. Hunt's book, *The World of the Formerly Married* (New York, 1966). His views are summarized in his article, "Help Wanted: Divorce Counsellor" in *The New York Times Magazine*, January 1, 1967, pp. 14–17. He maintains that this approach is making relatively slow progress because "one does not argue about such things; what is right is right and what is wrong is wrong, because it has always been so and because everyone knows it to be so." The true reason inheres in the New Testament teaching forbidding divorce, which has survived in theory even when it has been abandoned in practice.

8. Sociologist F. Nye found more delinquent behavior, poorer adjustment to parents, and more psychosomatic ailments among a large group of adolescents from intact, unhappy homes than among the offspring of broken homes. Dr. Lee Burchinall found no significant differences in the emotional health of grade-school students from intact homes (happy or unhappy) and that of children whose parents had been divorced. Also see the article by Morton M. Hunt cited in note 7. His last conclusion, suggesting that conditions do not affect mental health, is questionable. It may be based on limited data.

9. See chapter 13.

10. *Cf.* B. Gittin 90b.

11. *Cf.* Moses Mielziner, *Jewish Law of Marriage and Divorce*, 2nd ed. (New York, 1901); Louis M. Epstein, *The Jewish Marriage Contract* (New York, 1927); and *Marriage Laws in the Bible and Talmud* (Cambridge, 1942); Boaz Cohen, *Law and Tradition in Judaism* (New York, 1959), chap. V, "Concerning the Jewish Law of Domestic Relations," pp. 100–118. For a recent consideration of this mounting problem, see *Proceedings of Conference on Divorce in the Jewish Community*, October 19–20, 1966, published by the Federation of Jewish Philanthropies of New York.

12. B. Kiddushin 29b.

CHAPTER 8

1. B. Nedarim 64b; B. Abodah Zarah 5b.

2. B. Yebamot 65b.

3. The institution of the levirate, with many variations and exten-

sions beyond the biblical institution, was literally worldwide. See E. Westermarck, *The History of Human Marriage* (New York, 1922), vol. 2, pp. 207–20, 261–3. For a conspectus on the history of the levirate in Judaism, see *Encyclopedia Judaica* s.v. and my study, "Love, Marriage and Business in the Book of Ruth," reprinted in *The Word and the Book: Studies in Biblical Language and Literature* (New York, 1976), pp. 84–107, especially pp. 89–106.

4. *Cf.* Even Ha'ezer 23:5 and Rabbi Moses Isserles 1:3.

5. Tosefta Yebamot 8:4.

6. Solomon Luria, *Yam Shel Shelomoh, Yebamot* 4:44.

7. The entire subject has been admirably surveyed in the comprehensive work of David M. Feldman, *Birth Control in Jewish Law* (New York, 1968). He deals in great detail with the different interpretations advanced by medieval and modern codes and decisions on various aspects of the subject. I am indebted to him for many of the sources cited in this chapter and the next. It is only fair to add that I do not accept Rabbi Feldman's view that the Baraita is concerned with the question of hazard rather than with birth limitation. On another highly important difference, see note 12 below.

   An earlier and briefer treatment of the subject may be found in the lucid essay of Jacob Z. Lauterbach, "The Talmudic-Rabbinic View on Birth Control," in the *Central Conference of American Rabbis Year Book*, vol. 37, 1927, pp. 367–84.

8. B. Yebamot 12b, 100b; B. Ketubot 39a; B. Nedarim 35a, 45b; B. Niddah 45a; Tosefta Niddah 2:6.

9. The Hebrew participle *"meshammeshot"* simply means "practice, use." It is given permissive force, "may use," by Rashi (on B. Yebamot 100b), and compulsive force, "must use," by Rabbenu Jacob Tam (Tosafot on B. Ketubot 39a), Asheri, and Rabbenu Nissim (on B. Nedarim 35b). Both interpretations are grammatically sound.

10. Later authorities differ on other phases of the question. Thus Rashi and Rabbi Jacob Tam permit the use of the absorbent only after intercourse; other medieval and modern decisors permit its use even during the act.

    The detailed differences of opinion are presented systematically and analytically by Feldman, *op. cit.* pp. 169–248.

11. *Cf.* Lev. 18:5 and the interpretation in B. Yoma 85b.

12. It seems highly plausible to suggest that the desire to further larger families led many rabbinic authorities to interpret the

Baraita as being basically *da'at yahid,* "an individual opinion," of Rabbi Meir, with his colleagues disagreeing with him with regard to all three categories—the minor, the pregnant woman, and the nursing mother. However, this cannot be the meaning of the text. Were it the intent of the Baraita to refer to all three categories, the language would have been *kullan meshammeshot kedarkan,* "all have marital intercourse in the normal manner." The phrase *ahat zo veahat zo,* "both the one and the other," can refer only to *two* classes just specified, not three: Rabbi Meir permits a minor (between the ages of eleven years and a day until twelve years and a day) to use a contraceptive, but rules that those outside this age bracket carry on sexual relations in the normal manner since they are not in danger, because the one younger than eleven is not likely to conceive, while the one older than twelve will not suffer in health by pregnancy. Rabbi Meir's colleagues differ with him and maintain that both those within the eleven-to-twelve-year bracket on the one hand and those outside the age bracket on the other carry on normal intercourse. With regard to the two other basic categories, the pregnant woman and the nursing mother, Rabbi Meir's colleagues express no opinion against his, *thus agreeing with his decision.*

Moreover, the biblical verse cited which refers to *pethaim,* "fools, simpletons," is applicable to a minor but not to a pregnant woman or nursing mother. Note the common talmudic phrase *heresh shoteh vekatan,* "a deaf-mute, a simpleton, and a minor." It may be added that in biblical Hebrew *pethi,* "fool," means inexperienced through youth; *cf.* the parallelism with *na'ar* in Prov. 1:4 and the Arabic cognate *fathay,* "youth, young man."

13.   It is also lacking in the *Sefer Mitzvot Gadol, Tur, Bet Yoseph,* and several lesser codes. Feldman's suggestion that "it is possible that Maimonides saw no practical ruling at all emerging from the Baraita" (p. 204) is unconvincing. The practical implications of the Baraita are obvious and, besides, Maimonides's code contains many laws no longer operative in his time or in ours.

14.   Rabbi Immanuel Jakobovitz, *Jewish Medical Ethics* (New York, 1959), p. 169, italics ours.

15.   The talmudic opposition to the medieval sanction of child marriage is discussed by Feldman, *op. cit.,* pp. 176–80.

16.   The literature on the subject is enormous and continually grow-

ing. For a brief, balanced statement, see Philip M. Hausner, ed., *The Population Dilemma*, The American Assembly (New York, 1963).

17. For a brief summary of the present situation, see "Shape of the Future," in *The Wall Street Journal*, December 6, 1966.
18. *Ibid.*
19. *American Jewish Year Book* (Philadelphia and New York, 1976).

CHAPTER 9

1. The history of the question in Catholicism is conveniently summarized in Feldman, *op. cit.*, p. 269. He presents a detailed summary of the rabbinic sources in "Abortion," part 5 of his excellent volume, pp. 251–94. Our approach to the issue and the conclusions we have drawn from the vast amount of often contradictory data that he has assembled are our own and diverge at times from the views he apparently holds.
2. The Hebrew words for "form, shape," *ṣelem d*^{e}*mut, ṣurah*, are all totally unlike the Hebrew *ason* in appearance or in sound.
3. The Septuagint interpretation is followed by Philo, as well as by the Samaritans and the Karaites. This interpretation Aptowitzer regards as a compromise between Plato, who held the foetus to be dependent upon its mother, and the Stoics, who held it to be an independent living human being. See *JQR*, vol. 15 (1924), p. 114, and Feldman, *op. cit.*, p. 259. Actually, the Septuagint seems to be an approximation of the Stoic position rather than a compromise.
4. Mishnah Oholot 7, 6.
5. *'Ubar yerekh 'immo* (B. Hullin 58a; see also B. Gittin 23b). The phrase, as Feldman points out, is the equivalent of the Latin *pars viscerum matris* or *spes animati*.
6. See Rashi and Meiri on B. Sanhedrin 72b, "The foetus in the womb is not a living being, *lav nefesh hu.*"
7. Yad, Hilkhot Rotzeah Ushemirat Nefesh 1, 9.
8. Feldman, *op. cit.*, p. 277.
9. In Feldman, *op. cit.*, pp. 284–94, a large number of varied Responsa are collected and summarized.
10. *Ta'am kalush*, Feldman, *op. cit.*, p. 291.
11. Noam, IX, 1966, pp. 193–215.
12. See Responsa cited on the subject by Feldman, *op. cit.*, pp. 285–6.

13. See Leo Pfeffer, "Abortion and Religious Freedom," in *Congress Monthly*, June 1976, pp. 9–12.

14. A strongly negative approach to abortion is espoused by Rabbi Immanuel Jakobovitz in "Jewish Views on Abortion," in David T. Smith, *Abortion and the Law* (Cleveland, 1967), chap. 6. The impulse to be more Catholic than the Pope apparently continues to prove irresistible. His view is energetically rebutted by Feldman, *op. cit.*, p. 294, n. 144.

15. On this growing problem, see *The New York Times*, February 1, 1977.

16. According to a report by the International Planned Parenthood Federation, published in *The New York Times*, February 6, 1977.

17. *Mema'atim 'et had^e mut* (B. Yebamot 63b). The phrase is applied to those who avoid procreation (without reference to abortion).

CHAPTER 10

1. *Cf.* Epstein, *Sex Laws and Customs in Judaism*, pp. 135–8.

2. B. Kiddushin 82a.

3. See I Ki. 14:24; 15:12; 22:47; II Ki. 23:7. Sacred prostitution, both male and female, was prohibited by the Torah on religious as well as on sexual grounds (Deut. 23:18.).

4. A moving account of the tribulations of a secret homosexual, followed by his public avowal of homosexuality, may be found in Howard Brown, *Familiar Faces—Hidden Foes: The Story of Homosexual Men in America Today* (New York, 1976).

5. See Peter Fisher, *The Gay Mystique: The Myths and Reality of the Male Homosexual* (New York, 1972), p. 128.

6. For the important implications of the evolutionary process for religious faith, see Gordis, *A Faith for Moderns*, chap. 6.

7. I am indebted to my son, Dr. Enoch J. Gordis, director of the Alcoholism Center at Elmhurst General Hospital in New York and a recognized authority in the field of alcoholism research, for this information.

8. *Patur 'abhal 'asur.*

9. For a trenchant analysis of the public activities of homosexuals and the utilization by the gay-liberation movement of the widespread disillusion with marriage in order to further its objectives, see "Homosexuality and the Family," *The New York*

Times, August 22, 1975, by Herbert Hendin, Director of Psychosocial Studies at the Center for Policy Research and a member of the Psychiatry Department of Columbia University.

10. John J. McNeill, S.J., *The Church and the Homosexual* (New York, 1976). As instances of "Old Testament legalism," he maintains that the prohibitions of homosexuality in Leviticus are not binding on the Christian conscience. As for the incidents in Genesis and Judges, he declares that the sin of the Sodomites and the Benjaminites was the violation of hospitality rather than homosexuality. This may be inferred from Ez. 16:49–50 and Ben Sira 16:8, which describe the sin of Sodom as basically that of the arrogance of wealth and inhospitality. Father McNeill's conclusion as to the offense committed may well be correct, but it is difficult to see how the clear indication in both Genesis and Judges that homosexuality is worse than rape can be ignored.

11. Theodore W. Jennings, "Homosexuality and Christian Faith: A Theological Reflection," in *Christian Century,* February 16, 1977, pp. 137–42.

17. For a balanced presentation of the problem from the standpoint of Jewish law and ethics, see Herschel J. Matt, "Sin, Crime, Sickness, or Alternative Life-Style," scheduled for publication in *Judaism,* Winter, 1978.

CHAPTER 11

1. U.S. National Center for Health Statistics, "Vital Statistics of the United States," cited in *SA,* Table 271.

2. M. Kiddushin 4:1, 2; B. Yebamot 100b.

3. Mishneh Torah, Hilkhot Ishut 10:1; Tur, Even Ha-ezer 55:1.

4. Thus they interpret *benay tabaot* in Neh. 7:46 as the offspring of such prenuptial unions; cf. Otzar Ha-geonim, Kiddushin, sec. 23, p. 187.

5. Mishnah Ketubot 1:5; Tosefta Ketubot 1:4; B. Ketubot 12a.

6. See *Enzyklopedia Talmudit* (Jerusalem, 1949), vol. 2, p. 182b, and Epstein, *Sex Laws in the Bible and the Talmud,* p. 126.

7. See the *Rabbi's Manual,* published by the Rabbinical Assembly, and other handbooks for officiants.

8. J. Pesahim 10:1, p. 37b; Rambam, Mishneh Torah, Hilkhot Hametz Umatzah 6:12.

9. Sifra, Emor, chap. 1; B. Yebamot 61b.

10. He cites Nahmanides's view in his Responsa, No. 6, 398.

11. The Hebrew phrase is *pelonit penuyah muteret.*
12. Responsum 425; see also no. 6 and no. 395 on concubinage. See A. M. Hershman, *Rabbi Isaac bar Sheshet Perfet and His Times* (New York, 1942), esp. pp. 143–5, and Yitzhak Baer, *A History of the Jews in Christian Spain* (Philadelphia, 1966), vol. II, pp. 465–6.
13. Raphael Patai and Jennifer P. Wing, *The Myth of the Jewish Race* (New York, 1976), p. 131.
14. Genesis 25:6; 35:22; I Chr. 1:32; 7:14.
15. Jud. 8:31; 19:1 f.; 20:4 f*f*; I Chr. 2:46, 48.
16. II Sam. 3:7; 5:13; 15:16; 16:21 f.; 19:6; 20:3; 21:11; I Ki. 11:3; Song of Songs 6:9; Est. 2:14.
17. See Benjamin B. Lindsey and Wainright Evans, *The Companionate Marriage* (1927; New York, 1972).
18. Mishnah Abot 3:16.
19. Amy Gross, "Marriage Counseling for Unwed Couples," in *The New York Times Magazine,* April 24, 1977, p. 52.
20. Sanford N. Sherman, Executive Director of Jewish Family Service, cited by Gross, *ibid.,* p. 56.
21. The passage occurs in a memoir entitled "A Sketch of the Past," which appears in *Virginia Woolf: Moments of Being,* ed. by Jeanne Schulkind (New York, 1977).

CHAPTER 12

1. Ex. 20:14; Deut. 5:17; 22:23–29.
2. For example, Hosea 4:2, 3, 14, and the entire incident narrated in chaps 1–3. On the nature and significance of the experience, see "Hosea's Marriage and Message," in Gordis, *Poets, Prophets and Sages,* pp. 230–54; originally published in *Hebrew Union College Annual,* vol. 29, 1954, pp. 9–31.
3. Prov., chaps. 7, 9, and individual passages throughout the book.
4. Mishnah, Sotah 5:1.
5. See our study, "Love, Marriage and Business in the Book of Ruth—a Chapter in Jewish Customary Law," in Howard N. Bream, Ralph D. Heim, and Carey A. Moore, eds., *Jacob M. Myers Festschrift: A Light to My Path* (Philadelphia, 1974), pp. 241–63, reprinted in Gordis, *The Word and the Book,* pp. 84–107. My discussion of the available evidence on customary law is to be found on pages 99–103 and in notes 60–70. See also chapter 13 of this work.
6. Notably in the research on Genizah material by Mordechai A.

Friedman. His various papers dealing with these documents will be incorporated in his forthcoming full-length study, *Jewish Marriage Law in the Genizah.* However, he is not responsible for the biblical and talmudic material I have adduced, for my categorization of rabbinic law as "codified" and "customary," for the conclusions I have drawn from the texts he has published, and for the implications I have derived from all the data for charting the direction and spirit of Jewish tradition, which encompasses both codified and customary Halakah.

7. On the nature of the experience and the various views proposed for the understanding of the first three chapters of Hosea, see Gordis, "Hosea's Marriage and Message," originally published in *Hebrew Union College Annual,* vol. 27, 1954, pp. 9–35, reprinted in *Poets, Prophets and Sages,* pp. 230–54.

8. The theory that the entire experience is only a dream or an allegory has found few defenders among modern scholars. See my paper, p. 231 and note 5.

9. The Hebrew text reads *vatizneh 'alav pillagesho.* Several manuscripts of the Septuagint, the Greek translation, followed by the Old Latin Version, render the clause "She became angry with him." This rendering was adopted by these ancient translators and followed by many modern interpreters, because the Hebrew Masoretic text was in obvious contradiction to the codified law on adultery. However, the reading which has been proposed as the original Hebrew *(vatizaph)* is totally dissimilar from the extant text. The Masoretic text is unquestionably to be preferred, precisely because it is the more difficult reading. The preposition *'al* in the text is the idiomatic, pathetic use. This usage is excellently described by Brown-Driver-Briggs, *Lexicon of the Old Testament* (Boston, 1907), p. 753b: "It gives pathos to the expression of an emotion by emphasizing the person who is its subject and who, as it were, feels it acting *upon* him." For some instances of this use, see Jonah 2:8; Ps. 42:5; 142:4; 143:4; Job 10:1; 30:16; Dan. 2:1; I Sam. 17:32; 25:36; Jer. 8:18; 49:20.

10. The Responsa are summarized in Louis Jacobs, *Theology in the Responsa* (London, 1975), pp. 175, 237, 264.

11. The principle *'ein 'adam meisim 'atzmo rasha'* is frequently invoked in the Talmud, as for example in B. Yebamot 25b; B. Sanhedrin 9b. Thus Rambam summarizes the rabbinic law, "If a man says that he has eaten the flesh of an animal that had died a natural death and is therefore forbidden, or taken part in forbidden sexual intercourse, he is not ruled invalid as a witness

until there are two witnesses who saw him perform the act in question. For no one makes himself out to be a sinner," Yad Hahazakah, Hilkhot Edut, 12, 2; Tur, Shulhan Arukh, Hoshen Mishpat 34, 25. "Just as he cannot become invalidated as a witness through his own testimony, so he is not punished with flagellation or fines" (Rashi on Yebamot 28b, s.v. *v'ein*). The same principle also applies to a woman. On this important principle see *Enzyklopedia Talmudit*, vol I, pp. 255–6.

12.   While the preceding verses in Deuteronomy speak of incest with one's father's wife and one whose sexual organs have been damaged, the verses following (2, 4, 8, 9) are concerned with neighboring nations, the Ammonites, the Moabites, the Edomites, and the Egyptians. In Zechariah 9:6, the term *mamzer* occurs in parallelism with the Philistines.

13.   Leviticus Rabbah 32:8.

CHAPTER 13

1.   I Kings 16:29–34; chaps. 18 and 19; 21:17–29.
2.   Prov. 31:10–31.
3.   Prov. 5:1–14; 7:1–27. Also Prov. 2:16–19.
4.   Prov. 7:10; 23:27; 29:3.
5.   Ex. 20:12; Deut. 5:16; Lev. 19:3; Prov. 1:8; 6:20; 10:1; 15:20; 20:20; 23:25; 28:24; 29:15; 30:11; 31:1.
6.   Num. 27:1–11; 36:1–13.
7.   Deut. 24:1. Actually, the verbs $v^e khatabh$, $v^e nathan$, and v^e-*shillehah* are not the apodosis, the conclusion of the condition ("Then he shall write . . . and he shall put . . . and he shall send her away"), but part of the protasis ("If he writes . . . puts . . . sends her away"). The apodosis or conclusion does not appear until verse 4 ("Then her former husband may not take her again as his wife"). See the Revised Standard Version, or any other Bible translation.
8.   Mishnah, Rosh Hashana 1, 8.
9.   Tobhit 9:13.
10.   Ruth 4:5. I have sought to demonstrate that it is not actual property in her possession that was at stake, for Naomi is destitute, but the transference of an "obligation—right" to a near kinsman to redeem the property that her husband and sons had sold during their lifetime to outsiders. On the nature of the transaction recorded in Ruth, see my study, "Love, Marriage

and Business in the Book of Ruth," in *The Word and the Book*, pp. 84–107.

11. The material is assembled in B. Porten, *Archives from Elephantine* (Berkeley and Los Angeles, 1960), pp. 235–63.

12. For *Muraba'at* see the as yet unpublished document in P. Benoit, J. T. Milik, R. de Vaux, *Discoveries in the Judean Desert II* (Oxford, 1961), p. 108. For the talmudic period, see J. Ketubot 30b, V, 8; 31c, VII, 6; and Epstein, *The Jewish Marriage Contract*, pp. 197 ff. For the practice in vogue in the tenth or eleventh centuries, see the forthcoming work by Friedman, cited on p. 272.

13. These procedures included either a special prenuptial arrangement, or the court's compelling the husband to issue the divorce, or the rabbis' annulling the marriage retroactively by invoking their fundamental authority in domestic law.

14. M. Kiddushin 1:1.

15. Deut. 25:5–9. The next stages in the development of the institution are subject to varying interpretations. See my study in *The Word and the Book* already cited in note 10 (pp. 93–95). For the methods employed by the rabbis to meet the problems, see *ibid.*, p. 94 and notes.

16. B. Yebamot 39b. One Sage, Abba Saul, regards *yibbum* under such circumstances as tantamount to incest.

17. Gordis, *op. cit.*, p. 94.

18. *Ibid.*, n. 50.

19. M. Ketubbot 4:7–5:1; 5:6; 7:1–5, 10; Yebamot 14:1. Archaeological discoveries and modern research have revealed earlier and varied stages in the character and form of this legal instrument.

20. Sifra, Vayikra; B. Kiddushin 50a; B. Baba Batra 48a; B. Arakhin 21a.

21. This procedure had been proposed originally by Rabbi David Aronson in 1951.

22. *Kol hammekaddesh ada'ata derabbanan mekaddesh* (Babylonian Talmud, Kethubbot 3a).

23. *Afk͏ᵉ'inho rabbanan lekiddushei minneh (ibid.).*

24. Orah Hayyim, sec. 282, par. 3, and the comment of Rabbi Moses Isserles.

    The talmudic source for this statement, repeated verbatim in the Codes, is B. Meg. 23e. For the entire issue, see A. H. Blumenthal, "An Aliyah for Women" in Seymour Siegel (ed.), *Con-*

servative Judaism and Jewish Law (New York, 1977), pp. 265–80.

25.   *Mitzvot 'aseh shehazman garma.*

CHAPTER 14

1.   Num. 25:1–5; 31:16.
2.   The biblical prohibitions are set forth in Deut. 23:4–9. The rabbis extend them in time so that they become permanent by interpreting "the tenth generation" to mean "forever" *(Sifre ad loc.)* and limit the prohibition in the case of Ammon and Moab only to males (J. Yebamot 8, 3).
3.   *She'ar'umot* (B. Kiddushin 86b; Avodah Zarah 36b).
4.   This is argued most energetically by David Max Eichhorn, *Jewish Intermarriage; Fact and Fiction* (Satellite Beach, Fla., 1974). In spite of the strident tone of the book and errors in interpretation both of texts and of views not to the author's liking, the book deserves more attention than it has received.
5.   Gen., chap. 24, esp. 2–8.
6.   For the struggle against mixed marriages, see Neh. 10:31; 13:1–9, 23–30. For the rationale, see Neh. 13:23–24.
7.   *Cf.* Num. 12:1–15 and see Gordis, "Race and the Religious Tradition," in *The Root and the Branch*, pp. 115–36.
8.   *Cf.* Jud. 1:19, 21, 27–36, and also Jos. 11:21–23.
9.   B. Berakhot 28a.
10.   Shemaiah and Abtalion are described as being the descendants of Sennacherib (B. Gittin 57b). The Rambam, in the introduction to Mishneh Torah, cites a tradition that Akiba's father, Joseph, was a convert. See Dikdukei Sopherim on B. Sanhedrin 96b.
11.   Rabbi Meir is described as a descendant of the Emperor Nero (Gittin 56a).
12.   Midrash Leviticus Rabbah 2:9.
13.   B. Pesahim 87b.
14.   B. Yebamot 47b. The biblical verse is Isa. 14:1.
15.   B. Yebamot 46a.
16.   Arthur Koestler, *The Thirteenth Tribe* (New York, 1976).
17.   Ahad Ha'am *Al Parashat Derakhim*, 3rd ed. (Berlin, 1921), Vol. I., pp. 121–32.
18.   *Universal Jewish Encyclopedia*, s.v. Intermarriage.
19.   The available data was summarized and analyzed in 1964 by

Professor Nathan Goldberg of Brooklyn College in his valuable study "Intermarriage from a Sociological Perspective," in *Intermarriage and the Jewish Future* (New York, 1964), pp. 27–58. Erich Rosenthal's epoch-making study appeared in the *American Jewish Yearbook*, Volume 64, 1964, pp. 3–53. He chose the two communities involved because the study in Washington was sponsored by the Jewish Community Council in Washington and the state of Iowa requires religious data on the marriage license, so that the statistical data was more readily available. There were several other interesting conclusions to be drawn from his data:

1. Intermarriage tended to increase for smaller Jewish communities, where the number of available partners was restricted.

2. There was a higher incidence of intermarriage where the bride was younger than the mean age.

3. In Iowa, there was a higher percentage of intermarriage when remarriages took place.

Some data in Rosenthal's study are difficult to explain, because they reveal no consistent pattern. Thus, the intermarriage rate in the Washington area for males of the first (immigrant) generation with a college education was 1 percent. It rose to 4 percent for those possessing a graduate degree, a fourfold increase. On the other hand, in the second (first native-born) generation, the intermarriage rate for males with a college degree rose to 15.6 percent, but it fell to 11.4 percent for those with a postgraduate education. In the third (second native-born) generation, the intermarriage rate for male college graduates was 37 percent, but it fell to 14.9 percent for those with postgraduate education (pages 19, 22).

One might hazard the guess that postgraduate students, being older than undergraduates, would be less prone to be carried away by sexual infatuation and more likely to reckon with the hazards of intermarriage. However, the radical decline in the figures for the third generation as against the slight reduction for the second generation makes all theorizing precarious. It may be that the number of instances available was too slight to be statistically significant.

20. Fred Masarik, *Intermarriage: Facts for Planning* (New York, 1974).

21. At least one rabbi is so impressed by this consideration that he insists on calling intermarriages between a Jew and a proselyte

mitzvah marriages, a lofty designation that the tradition does not apply even to completely Jewish nuptials! For his defense of the term, see, for example, Allen S. Maller, "Intermarriage and Jewish Continuity," *Congress Monthly,* 1976, vol. 43, no. 8, pp. 14ff.

22. Eichhorn, *op. cit., passim.*
23. *Ibid.,* p. 4.
24. This position is maintained by Rabbi J. David Bleich, "Where it is evident that the candidate will be non-observant, the conversion is null and void, despite the candidate's oral declaration of acceptance of the yoke of *mitzvot*" (*Tradition,* 1971, vol. 2, no. 4, pp. 16–42). Rabbi Shlomo Goren, Ashkenazic Chief Rabbi of Israel, whose practices in this area have often been bitterly attacked as too lenient, issued a decision declaring that "a convert who *does not live in accordance with Jewish law and reverts to his former practices*" has nullified his conversion (*Pesak Hadin,* Jerusalem, 5733, pp. 137 ff.). However, he does not define the precise meaning of the words we have italicized. On the other hand, the former Sephardic Chief Rabbi Uziel is quoted as ruling, "There is no requirement to ask the non-Jew actually to observe the *mitzvot.* We do not require his assurance that he will be an observant Jew" (reported by Rabbi Marc D. Angel, "Another Halachic Approach to Conversion," in *Tradition,* 1972, vol. 12, no. 3–4, pp. 107–113). See also note 28 below for a further discussion of the questions involved.
25. *Tzarat rabbim hatzi neḥamah.* The statement occurs in *Melekhet Mahshevet, Parshah Ki Tabo,* by Rabbi Moshe Hefetz, but may have older Midrashic antecedents.
26. *Kewan she'adam 'oseh 'abherah veshanah bah na' aset lo keheter,* B. Yoma 87a.
27. B. Yebamot 47a.
28. The Rambam is characteristically clear and explicit on the subject. "A proselyte, whom the *Bet Din* did not investigate or to whom they did not inform the particulars of the commandments and their punishments, but who was circumcised and ritually immersed before three common judges, is considered a convert. And even if they discover that it was for some ulterior motive that he converted, since he was circumcised and ritually immersed, he has left the category of Gentile. . . . And even if he returns [to his former ways] and serves idols he is considered an apostate Jew, whose marriage is a marriage" (Mishneh Torah, Hilkhot Issurei Bi'ah 13:17). This position as to

the validity of the conversion is all the more noteworthy in view of the fact that the Rambam believes that "most converts accept Judaism for some ulterior motive and thus lead Jews astray" *(Rubban hozrin bishevil davar umat'in 'et yisrael), ibid.* 13:18. This negative judgment on the motivation of converts to Judaism does not hold true of the vast majority of converts today. Their good faith cannot legitimately be questioned in an age when intermarriage (without conversion) is an everyday occurrence. The halakic decision of the Rambam is, of course, independent of the alleged motives of proselytes.

Rabbi Steven Riskin discusses the subject ("Conversion in Jewish Law," in *Tradition,* vol. 14, no. 2, 1973, pp. 29–42) and argues that "acceptance of the commandments" is a necessary element in a valid conversion, a position which is reasonable. But he then proceeds to declare, "I cannot accept an essential distinction between the acceptance of commandments and the observance of commandments." This conclusion is unwarranted, either on the basis of the language employed or on logical grounds. The linguistic consideration is set forth in the text above. Logically, a naturalized citizen may be remiss in obeying all the laws governing the society, but he does not on that account forfeit the right of citizenship. Rabbi Riskin also ignores the position of Hillel and Rabbi Hiyya, who maintain that even ulterior motives do not invalidate a conversion, as Rambam clearly affirms. The effort is made to support the negative position by an involved deduction from a phrase used in connection with a different regulation affecting the conversion of a minor (Riskin, *op. cit.,* pp. 35–6).

29. M. Sanhedrin, 4:5.
30. Reported in *U.S. News and World Reports,* April 11, 1977, p. 68.

CHAPTER 15

1. Ben Gallob, "Single Mothers," in *Israel Today,* July 15–28, 1974, p. 13, from Elizabeth Geggel and Ruth I. Schwartz in *Journal of Jewish Communal Service,* 1974.
2. B. Hullin 110a.

Bibliography

CLASSICAL SOURCES

The Bible
The Mishnah
The Tosefta
The Babylonian Talmud
The Palestinian Talmud
The Midrashim
Rabbi Moses ben Maimon, *Yad Haḥazakah, Hilkhot Ishut*
Rabbi Joseph Karo, *Shulhan Arukh, Even Ha-ezer*

MODERN WORKS

Adams, Margaret, *Single Blessedness: Observations on the Single Status in Married Society* (New York, 1976).
American Jewish Yearbook (published annually).
Amory, Cleveland, *The Last Resorts* (New York, 1952).
Baer, Yitzhak, *A History of the Jews in Christian Spain*, 2 volumes (Philadelphia, 1966).
Bailey, D. S., *Sexual Relation and Christian Thought* (New York, 1959).
Baum, Charlotte, Paula Hyman, and Sonya Michael, *The Jewish Woman in America* (New York, 1976).
Benoit, P.; J. T. Milik; R. de Vaux, *Discoveries in the Judean Desert II* (Oxford, 1961).
Bohannan, Paul, ed., *Divorce and After* (New York, 1971).
Bream, H.N.; R. D. Heim; C.A. Moore, *Jacob M. Myers Festschrift, a Light to My Path* (Philadelphia, 1974).
Breslin, Katherine, *Promiscuous Condition* (New York, 1976).
Briffault, Robert, *The Mothers* (London, 1927; abridged ed., New York, 1959).
Brown, Francis, S. R. Driver, and C. A. Briggs, *Lexicon of the Old Testament* (Boston-New York, 1907).
Brown, Howard, *Familiar Faces—Hidden Foes: The Story of Homosexual Men in America Today* (New York, 1976).

Calverton, V. F. and S. D. Schmalhausen, eds., *Sex in Civilization* (New York, 1929).
Central Conference of American Rabbis Year Book (published annually).
Chavel, Charles B., *Kitbei Rabbenu Moshe ben Nahman* (Jerusalem, 5724–1964).
Cockshut, A. O. J., *The Unbelievers* (New York, 1966).
Cohen, Boaz, *Law and Tradition in Judaism* (New York, 1959).
Cohen, Seymour J., ed., *The Holy Letter: A Study in Medieval Jewish Morality* (New York, 1976).
Doniger, S., ed., *Sex and Religion* (New York, 1953).
Eichhorn, David Max, *Jewish Intermarriage: Fact and Fiction* (Satellite Beach, Florida, 1974).
Elman, Peter, *Jewish Marriage* (London, 1967).
Encyclopedia Judaica
Enzyklopedia Talmudit
Epstein, Louis M., *Sex Laws and Customs in Judaism* (New York, 1948).
——*The Jewish Marriage Contract* (New York, 1927).
——*Marriage Laws in the Bible and Talmud* (Cambridge, 1942).
——*Lishe'elat Ha'agunah* (New York, 5700–1940).
Feldman, David M., *Birth Control in Jewish Law* (New York, 1968).
Fisher, Peter, *The Gay Mystique: The Myths and Reality of the Male Homosexual* (Briarcliff Manor, N.Y., 1972).
Freimann, A. J., *Seder Kiddushin Unesu' in* (Jerusalem, 5702–1945).
Friedman, Mordechai, *Jewish Marriage in Palestine: A Genizah Study* (not yet published).
Gaster, Theodore, *The Dead Sea Scriptures,* 3rd edition (New York, 1976).
Gilder, George, *Naked Nomads* (New York, 1974).
Gittelsohn, Roland, *Consecrated unto Me* (New York, 1965).
Goldberg, B. Z., *The Sacred Fire* (New York, 1930).
Goldberg, Nathan, *Intermarriage and the Jewish Future* (New York, 1964).
Goldstein, Sidney E., *The Meaning of Marriage and Foundations of the Family* (New York, 1940).
Gordis, Robert, *A Faith for Moderns* (New York, 1960, augmented ed., 1971).
——*The Book of God and Man: A Study of Job* (Chicago, 1965).
——*Poets, Prophets and Sages* (Bloomington, Ind., 1971).
——*Judaism for the Modern Age* (New York, 1955).
——*The Root and the Branch: Judaism and the Free Society* (Chicago, 1962).

——*Koheleth: The Man and His World* (New York, 3rd augmented ed., 1968).

——*Judaism in a Christian World* (New York, 1966).

——*The Song of Songs and Lamentations* (New York, 1961, 1974).

——*The Word and the Book: Studies in Biblical Language and Literature* (New York, 1976).

——*Politics and Ethics* (Santa Barbara, Cal., 1961).

Hardin, Garrett, ed., *Population, Evolution, Birth Control* (San Francisco, London, 1964).

Hausner, Philip M., ed., *The Population Dilemma,* (New York, 1963).

Hershman, A. M., *Rabbi Isaac bar Sheshet Perfet and His Times* (New York, 1942).

Hunt, Morton M., *The World of the Formerly Married* (New York, 1966).

Jacobs, Louis, *Theology in the Responsa* (London, 1975).

Jakobovitz, Immanuel, *Jewish Medical Ethics* (New York, 1959).

Kahana, I. Z., *Sefer Ha-agunot* (Jerusalem, 5714–1954).

Kahana, K., *The Theory of Marriage in Jewish Law* (Leiden, 1966).

Lindsey, Benjamin B., and Wainright Evans, *The Companionate Marriage* (1927; New York, 1972).

McNeill, John J., S.J., *The Church and the Homosexual* (New York, 1976).

Masarik, Fred, *Intermarriage: Facts for Planning* (New York, 1974).

Mielziner, Moses, *Jewish Law of Marriage and Divorce,* 2nd ed. (New York, 1901).

Ottwell, John H., *And Sarah Laughed: The Status of Woman in the Old Testament* (Philadelphia, 1977).

Patai, Raphael, and Jennifer P. Wing, *The Myth of the Jewish Race* (New York, 1976).

Pierce, Ruth T., *Pregnant and Single* (Boston, 1975).

Porten, B., *Archives from Elephantine* (Berkeley and Los Angeles, 1960).

Proceedings of Conference on Divorce in the Jewish Community (October 19–20, 1966, published by the Federation of Jewish Philanthropies of New York).

Proceedings of Conference on Intermarriage and the Future of the American Jew (December 1964, sponsored by Commission on Synagogue Relations, Federation of Jewish Philanthropies of New York).

Rabbinical Assembly, *Proceedings* (issued annually).

Rabinowitz, Stanley, *A Jewish View of Love and Marriage* (Washington, D.C., 1961).

Rosenberg, Charles E., *The Family in History* (Philadelphia, 1975).

Rosenthal, Gilbert S., ed., *New Directions in the Jewish Family and Community* (New York, 1974).

Sarrel, Phillip, *Student Guide to Sex on Campus* (New Haven, n.d.).

Schlesinger, Benjamin, *The Jewish Family: A Survey and Annotated Bibliography* (Toronto, 1971).

Schulkind, Jeanne, ed., *Virginia Woolf: Moments of Being* (New York, 1977).

Sex and the College Student, Group for the Advancement of Psychiatry, Report #60 (New York, 1965).

Smith, David T., *Abortion and the Law* (Cleveland, 1967).

Sussman, Marvin B., ed., *Sourcebook on Marriage and the Family*, 2nd ed. (Boston, 1963).

Twersky, Isadore, *A Maimonides Reader* (New York, 1972).

U.S. Bureau of the Census, *Statistical Abstract of the U.S.*, (Washington, D.C., 1975).

Universal Jewish Encyclopedia

Westermarck, E., *The History of Human Marriage*, 3 vols. (New York, 1922).

Zelnik, Melvin, and John F. Kantner, *Family Planning Perspectives* (April–May, 1977).

Index

Abélard, Pierre, 49
Abimelech, 193
abortion, vi, 21, 39, 74, 137–48,
  244, 268
Abraham, 9, 11, 12, 125, 168, 192,
  211, 212
Abraham the proselyte, 216
Absalom, 193
Abtalion, 214
Adam, 49, 100, 107
Adam and Eve, 3, 11, 12, 47, 48,
  100, 101, 102
adultery, see extramarital sex
agape, 53, 103
agencies, social service, 248
agunah, 201–4
Ahab, 193
Ahad Ha'am, 219
Akiba, 104, 119–20, 169, 214
Alcoholics Anonymous, 156
alcoholism, 76, 156, 244
Ammon, 211, 212
Ammonites, 211, 212
annulment, 115, 204
anti-Semitism, 219
Apocrypha, 214
Aquinas, Thomas, 49
Areopagitica, 175
American Psychological
  Association, 159
Aquila, 216
Asa, 150
asceticism, 44, 45, 62–63, 86
assimilation, 220, 222, 224–30
Augustine, 48
Ausubel, David, 92

Babylonia, 16, 254, 255
Babylonians, 178
Bacon, Francis, 63
Balaam, 210
Barak, 192
Baron, Salo, 215

bastard, see mamzer; illegitimate
  births
Bebai, 128
ben Azzai, Simeon, 98
Ben Sira, 61
Bergman, Ingmar, 67
Beruriah, 16
Bilhah, 11
birth control, vi, 38, 50, 51,
  125–36, 164, 169, 244, 266–67
blacks, 213
Bodo, 216
Book of the Dead, Egyptian, 177
Borough Park, 219
Buber, Martin, 91
Buddhism, 62
Bunam of Pshysha, 154

Calvin, John, 49
camps, summer, 234, 247
Canaanites, 150, 210, 211, 213
Carter, Jimmy, 220
Catholicism, viii, 49–52, 115, 116,
  117, 125, 129, 139, 172, 178,
  206, 268
celibacy, 46, 49, 50, 52, 54, 63, 98,
  124
children: after divorce, 70, 71,
  119; value of, 99, 125–31, 253
Christianity, 7, 13, 29, 39, 40,
  41–58, 82, 85, 86, 211, 216, 243,
  247
Chronicles, 213
coitus interruptus, 127
concubinage, 168
concubine, 9, 11, 183
Constantine, 216
Constantinople, 26
Consultation and Information
  Center on Judaism, 236, 249
contraceptives, see birth control
contract cohabitation, 74, 75

Index of Sources